Frommer's®

Normandy

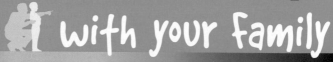 **with your family**

The best of Normandy from charming villages to best beaches

by Rhonda Carrier

1807
WILEY
2007

Wiley Publishing, Inc.

Published by:
Wiley Publishing, Inc.
111 River St.
Hoboken, NJ 07030-5774

ISBN: 978-0-470-31951-2

UK Publisher: Sally Smith
Executive Project Editor: Martin Tribe (Frommer's UK)
Development Editor: Anne O'Rorke
Content Editor: Hannah Clement (Frommer's UK)
Cartographer: Tim Lohnes
Photo Research: Jill Emeny (Frommer's UK)
Typesetting: Wiley Indianapolis Composition Services

For information on our other products and services or to obtain technical support, please contact our Customer Care Department within the U.S. at 800/762-2974, outside the U.S. at 317/572-3993 or fax 317/572-4002. Within the UK Tel. 01243 779777; Fax. 01243 775878.

Wiley also publishes its books in a variety of electronic formats. Some content that appears in print may not be available in electronic formats.

Printed and bound by Markono Print Media Pte Ltd

5 4 3 2 1

CONTENTS

ABOUT THE AUTHOR

Rhonda Carrier studied French language, literature and culture at the universities of Cambridge and the Sorbonne in Paris. After travelling widely, she spent 10 years working in London as a writer and editor for local guides and listings magazines, as well as producing some award winning short fiction. In 2005, after living in France for a year, she rediscovered London with her young sons while researching the first edition of Frommer's *London with Kids*. She currently divides her time between France and Manchester.

Acknowledgements

As ever, unending thanks to to my husband Conrad Williams, who somehow manages to be a brilliant dad by day and write wonderful novels by night.

Immense gratitude goes also to Daniel, Yoyo and Sophie Amaglio, for long-ago summers that sparked my love affair with France and its language, and to Madame Haynes, my teacher at Leicester High School, for nurturing and inspiration.

I'd also like to express fondest thanks to Teresa Hardy and Richard Dale for help with research, to Fiona Dunscombe for the kind of encouragement every writer needs, to my brother David for cat-sitting duties, to Conrad, Hester and Hildelith Leyser and Kate Cooper for a house and for Finistère leads, to Jane Watt for another house in another country and for local knowledge, and to Nick Royle for holiday reading and much, much more.

The following people have also offered greatly appreciated support, input and/or feedback over the years.

Gemma Hirst; Holly, Alan and Jarvis McGrath; Kate, Charlie and Bella Royle; Jan Parker and Chris, Lucy and James Newman; Paula Grainger and Michael and Nate Marshall Smith; Judy and Joe Reynolds; Liz Wyse; Malcolm Swanston; Christi Daugherty, Pete Fiennes and Sarah Guy; Diana Tyler; Heather Brice and family; Dea Birkett; and all the talented Lumineuse writers around France.

Thanks too to our parents David, Mary, Leo and Grenville, and to my stepfather Tim, for support and faith over the years.

Lastly, *sincères remerciements* to all the hardworking professionals in tourist offices all over northern France, for their unfailingly prompt advice and assistance.

Dedication

For Conrad, Ethan and Ripley – the perfect travel companions.

AN ADDITIONAL NOTE

Please be advised that travel information is subject to change at any time and this is especially true of prices. We therefore suggest that you write or call ahead for confirmation when making your travel plans. The authors, editors and publisher cannot be held responsible for experiences of readers while travelling. Your safety is important to us, however, so we encourage you to stay alert and be aware of your surroundings.

Star Ratings, Icons & Abbreviations

Hotels, restaurants and attraction listings in this guide have been ranked for quality, value, service, amenities and special features using a star-rating system. Hotels, restaurants, attractions, shopping and nightlife are rated on a scale of zero stars (recommended) to three (exceptional). In addition to the star rating system, we also use 4 feature icons that point you to the great deals, in-the-know advice and unique experiences. Throughout the book, look for:

FIND	Special finds – those places only insiders know about
MOMENT	Special moments – those experiences that memories are made of
VALUE	Great values – where to get the best deals
OVERRATED	Places or experiences not worth your time or money

The following **abbreviations** are used for credit cards:

AE	American Express
MC	MasterCard
V	Visa

A Note on Prices

Frommer's provides exact prices in each destination's local currency. As this book went to press, the rate of exchange was 1€ = £0.67. Rates of exchange are constantly in flux; for up-to-the minute information, consult a currency-conversion website such as www.oanda.com/convert/classic.

An Invitation to the Reader

In researching this book, we discovered my wonderful places – hotels, restaurants, shops and more. We're sure you'll find others. Please tell us about them, so we can share the information with your fellow travellers in upcoming editions. If you were disappointed with a recommendation, we'd love to know that too. Please write to;

Frommer's Normandy with Your Family, 1st edition
John Wiley & Sons, Ltd
The Atrium
Southern Gate
Chichester
West Sussex, PO19 8SQ

PHOTO CREDITS

1 Family Highlights of Normandy

I lost my heart to France as a teenager, spent part of almost every year in the country over the ensuing two decades and finally succumbed and bought a ramshackle old farmhouse here when pregnant with my first child. Like the 75 million foreign visitors to France every year, who make it the world's most popular holiday destination, I'm drawn here by a number of factors – the sublime cuisine, the gorgeous landscapes and the less hectic pace of life to name just three. For British visitors at least, this is also a place where you can holiday relatively inexpensively, bringing your own car or travelling by low-cost airline and hiring one, enjoying cheaper (as well as better) food and drink than you do back home and staying in accommodation that would be unaffordable on the other side of the Channel.

Normandy, with its classic holiday resorts and wide-open rural spaces, has long been popular among young families, not least because it is so easily accessible from Britain. The coast alternates between the vast toddler-friendly beaches (and elegant family hotels) of the Norman Riviera and more dramatic features – from an elephant-shaped natural archway admired by Monet at Etretat to the immense bay of the Mont-St-Michel, with quicksands that have swallowed up pilgrims medieval and modern – while forests, animal conservation parks and quirky museums will lure you to the less touristy inland areas. History comes vividly alive both in the world-famous Bayeux Tapestry, recounting the invasion of Britain by Norman conquerors in 1066, and on the landing beaches that still bear the scars of the world's largest ever amphibious assault, as well as the many museums where the story of the bloody battles that followed the assault are handed down to new generations.

You'll need a car to explore Normandy fully, unless you restrict yourself to the Norman Riviera and urban centres such as Rouen, which means you'll miss out on a lot of the smaller-scale attractions that help to make Normandy so appealing. You'll also need to take account of certain cultural differences; the most difficult for me, as a new mum rediscovering France with my young sons, has been the rigid and limited restaurant opening hours, which make dining out before 7.30pm almost impossible except in a major town or resort in high season. It also takes time to adjust to everything closing down for a couple of hours around lunchtime. But it's easy enough to adapt, and when you do, you'll discover that Normandy is one of France's – indeed, Europe's – most delightful regions to discover *en famille*.

BEST FAMILY EXPERIENCES

Best Family Events The Festival International de

Cerf-Volant at Dieppe in the Seine-Maritime sees hundreds of kites in all guises and sizes, from cows to giant dragons, swooping above the beach over nine days.

Mont-St-Michel

Children can attend kite-making workshops, create wind and sound machines, explore a sound maze and more, and there's a jaw-dropping night-flying session, stilt-walkers, jugglers, street theatre and a procession. See p. 57.

In the Manche, **La Rando Baie** is a weekend of family walks and events in the stunning bay of the Mont St Michel, including Breton music and dance, a twilight stroll with actors in medieval costume, rollerblading by the beach, horse-and-carriage rides, children's workshops, storytelling sessions and more. See p. 178.

Best City Rouen in the Seine-Maritime is a medievally quaint city with a jagged roofscape said to resemble the flames that devoured Joan of Arc here in the 15th century. Half-timbered houses, a famous cathedral painted by Monet, fascinating museums and charming teashops. The tourist office has a free children's trail led by a friendly gargoyle. See p. 61.

Dieppe's Kite Festival

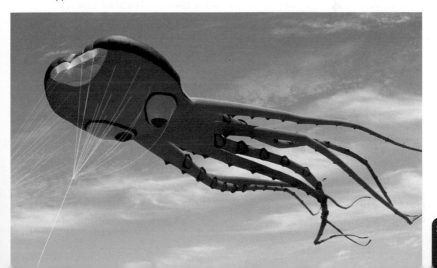

Best Natural Attractions The luminous white cliffs of the Alabaster Coast in the Seine-Maritime have dramatic natural archways, one of which looks like an elephant dipping its trunk in the water. There's also the *Aiguille* ('Needle'), which featured in a famous detective story. See p. 64.

Mainly in the Manche but extending a tongue into Calvados, the Parc Naturel Régional des Marais du Cotentin et du Bessin is a 145,000-hectare marshland park with an 'interpretation footpath', bird observatories reached by barge and wonderful family events such as evening guided walks with storytelling or bat hunts and outings to spot seals. The park is crisscrossed by walking trails and Véloroutes for family bike rides. See p. 186.

Best Animal Park Part of a wild animal rescue centre, La Ferme-Nature deep in the Calvados countryside is home to more than 60 species of domestic animals, some rare. The birdhouses are charming mini-versions of those of the species' places of origin – local varieties live in half-timbered Norman cottages, the Egyptian geese in a pyramid and so on. There are also dwarf Ouessant

Beach Huts in Deauville

sheep, bees in a transparent hive and a 'nursery' with chicks in incubators, and the circuit is dotted with displays about animal welfare initiatives. See p. 141.

Best Aquarium La Cité de la Mer in Cherbourg in the Manche, a major family attraction, includes an ocean exhibition focused around an 'abyssal aquarium' – Europe's tallest cylindrical tank (12 m deep). A walkway spirals around it from top to bottom, revealing different fish and oceanic life at each depth. There are also displays on life on the seabed and underwater exploration, and you can explore a decommissioned nuclear submarine and play at navigating one too. See p. 189.

Best Beach Resorts The Norman Riviera in Calvados, a string of resorts fashionable with weekending Parisians since the 1800s, feels like a little piece of the South of France transplanted to the Channel coast. Cabourg and Deauville have huge toddler-friendly beaches, and there's children's entertainment galore, together with some great shops, restaurants and grand seaside hotels. See p. 137

In the Manche, Barneville-Carteret includes a family

La Ferme-Nature, Orbec

Deauville Beach

resort, Barneville-plage, with watersports and a children's beach club, a smaller beach at Carteret fishing port with its shops and restaurants, and to the north, the wilder Plage de la Vieille Eglise stretching away to the north, popular for sand-yachting and speed-sailing. There's also an historic centre, Barneville-bourg, to explore, with a good weekly market. Summer frolics include rockpool trails, regattas and *pétanque* training and competitions, and there's a *train touristique* along the coast. See p. 180.

Best Island Trips to the unin-habited former plague island of **Tatihou,** 2 km (1¼ miles) off the Manche coast, are made in a wacky amphibious boat with wheels. You can come for the annual festival of maritime music or for workshops on met-alworking, pottery and prehis-toric tool-making (there were Vikings on the island), some for

children. There's also a maritime museum with items from ship-wrecks, displays on coastal nature and ecology, botanical gardens, free guided tours of the bird reserve and a bird observa-tory. See p. 181.

Best Boat Trip Day trips in *La Granvillaise*, a restored tradi-tional fishing boat, take you way out into the glorious Baie du Mont-St-Michel, often with

Forest Walk

Mémorial de Caen

stop-offs to swim, stroll and picnic in the Iles Chausey or explore Cancale in Brittany. You can help sail the craft or just sit and admire the scenery – including, if you're lucky, dolphins swimming alongside. See p. 198.

Best Forest The ravishing Fôret de Lyons in the northern Eure, known for its extremely tall beeches, was a favourite hunting spot of William the Conqueror, but you may still see deer and boar as you explore its 300 km (186 miles) of walking, cycling and riding paths. There's also a campsite. The half-timbered village of Lyons-la-Forêt in the heart of the forest is so picturesque it's often used as a film set. See p. 100.

Best Outdoor Activities The Seine-Maritime and Orne have Vélo-Rails – quirky multi-person bikes you ride along old train tracks through the heart of nature. See p. 77.

In Calvados, Gustav Eiffel's Viaduc de la Souleuvre now draws bungee-jumpers from far and wide, but there's also a 'flying fox' swing across the valley and a treetop adventure course. Nearby you can go skydiving, rafting, paragliding, climbing, canoeing and horse-riding. See p. 157.

Best Museums The Maisons Satie in Honfleur in Calvados pay hommage to eccentric local composer Erik Satie in a suitably surreal fashion, with music, *son-et-lumière* effects, images, videos and oddball objects – invisible ticking clocks, umbrellas, a giant pear with metal wings, a talking mechanical monkey and a carousel ride with nonsense instruments. See p. 149.

On a much more sober note, the Mémorial de Caen, also in Calvados, puts Normandy's experiences during World War II in the context of global conflict since 1918. There's plenty of interactive technology to get children involved but a great free crèche for under-11s too. See p. 150.

Best Château The Château de Vendeuvre in Calvados is an 18th-century castle with offbeat collections of talking mechanical figures, dogs' and cats' kennels and baskets, and miniature furniture, plus grounds with fantastical fountains, a 'nymph's grotto' and mazes. See p. 152.

Best Art Sites Artmazia in the Seine-Maritime is a unique 'art garden' based around the world's largest natural beech maze, dotted with contemporary sculptures and art installations. Children can visit a 'troll's grotto' and go on treasure hunts, and there are plenty of animals to pet. See p. 75.

In Calvados, the world-famous Bayeux Tapestry is like an early comic strip telling the story of the Battle of Hastings and the Norman Conquest, featuring everything from Halley's comet to dragons. See p. 154.

Best Theme Park Festyland in Calvados offers a light-hearted romp through the region's history, with more than 30 prehistoric, Viking, William the Conqueror and pirate themed rides and attractions. See p. 156.

Best Markets The Marché du Mardi in L'Aigle in the Orne is the third-largest in France. After browsing its hundreds of stalls of local produce, flowers and clothes, you can watch the *marché aux bestiaux* drawing livestock buyers and sellers from all over Normandy. See p. 122.

In Calvados, the sleepy little town of Cambremer comes alive every Sunday morning in summer for its *Marchés à l'Ancienne*, with stallholders dressed in traditional Norman costume, open-air folk music and dancing, and horse-and-cart rides for children. See p. 159.

Best Shops Deauville in Calvados is a chic shopper's paradise, with lots of designer clothes stores for adults and children alike. See p. 158.

In the Manche, the family-run Maison Gosselin grocery is chock-full of local gastronomic delights and interesting gifts, including old-fashioned metal toys. Don't miss the bread fresh from the oak-burning oven, or the mouth-watering array of sweets, including caramels and apple sugars. See p. 201.

THE BEST ACCOMMODATION

Most Family-Friendly Option The Château d'Audrieu near Caen in Calvados has a little wonderland of a play area with a log cabin and treehouse in its vast grounds with their resident deer. You can borrow bikes to explore the pathways and woods, and there's an outdoor pool. Rooms and suites are traditional with a modern slant, and there's babysitting, a superb restaurant with children's portions and plush drawing rooms for afternoon tea. See p. 164.

Best Grand Hotels The **Pavillon de Gouffern** close to Argentan in the Orne is an old hunting pavilion in 78 hectares of grounds and forest with resident deer, horse rides and horse-and-cart rides, golf, a fine outdoor pool, an atmospheric restaurant and stylish rooms. See p. 125.

The stately **Grand Hôtel** at Cabourg in Calvados, the very image of a Victorian French seaside hotel, inspired the novelist Proust. There are plush salons for afternoon teas, a piano bar for posh snacks and aperitifs and a restaurant with views over the lovely beach. Family rooms without a sea view make it a

Normandy Barrière, Deauville

surprisingly affordable option. See p. 161.

Best Seaside Hotels The **Normandy Barrière** a few steps from the beach in Deauville in Calvados has long been a classic among Parisian families, with its family suites, nursery, children's club, children's restaurant and babysitting service. Other facilities include an indoor pool, a fitness suite and two tennis courts, and there's access to a golf course and a range of other nearby activities, including riding, adventure sports and thalassotherapy. See p. 159.

Much more affordable, the **Villa Beaumonderie** in a handsome villa north of Granville

Grand Hôtel, Cabourg

in the Manche has luxurious amenities for its price range, including a lovely pool with a retractable glass roof, tennis and squash courts and a restaurant serving some of the best food in the area. Of the 16 rooms and suites, some with gorgeous sea views and balconies, two are duplexes with a living room and two bedrooms. See p. 204.

Best Style Hotels The port of Le Havre in the Seine-Maritime is the unlikely setting for Vent d'Ouest, a boutique-style hotel with marine décor. Its family-friendly accommodation options – suites with a double bedroom and living room with comfy sofabed, and apartments with a similar set-up plus a kitchenette and dining area – are keenly priced. See p. 82.

Vent d'Ouest's sister hotel, the Maisons de Léa in Honfleur in Calvados, is a similarly stylish proposition in a former salt warehouse. As well as rooms and suites, some with tasteful farmyard décor, there's a half-timbered fisherman's cottage in a cobbled alley a few steps away; guests there can breakfast at the hotel, have it brought to the cottage or make their own. They also have access to the hotel tearoom, library, terrace and new children's corner with games, puzzles and colouring books. See p. 162.

Best B&Bs The little-known Orne is a great place for B&Bs. La Saboterie in the stunning Parc Naturel Régional du Perche

is an organic farm with junkshop chic in its three guestrooms, one of which is in an old clogmaker's workshop. The garden has a play area, and activities can be organised, including cheese-making and cookery, mushroom-picking in the forest, astronomy and mountain-biking. See p. 123.

In the same natural park, the Moulin de Gémages is an old watermill with five delightfully rustic B&B rooms and trout ponds where guests are free to fish (there are courses for parents and children), and which often furnish the main ingredient for the optional evening meals. The occasional gastronomic evenings are accompanied by a magic show, and picnic baskets can be provided for nature outings in the grounds, which have children's play equipment. See p. 124.

Best Gîtes The Orne's Parc Naturel Normandie-Maine has a good selection of Panda gîtes – inexpensive or moderate lodgings recognised by the World Wildlife Fund (WWF) as good places for nature breaks. All offer easy access to walking trails and prolific plant and animal life, plus observation equipment such as binoculars and species identification guides. They include La Sauvagère, a four-person gîte with an owner who leads mushroom-hunting expeditions. See p. 125.

In Calvados, up by its border with the Manche, the Ferme Manoir de la Rivière is an impressive manor with a four-person, ground-floor gîte that opens onto the pretty garden with its play area. Beyond that is the farm with its friendly dogs and cows. There are also some B&B rooms. See p. 166.

Best Campsite Camping St Paul occupies a shady riverbank in the gorgeous beech forest of Lyons, combining a 'back-to-nature' atmosphere with four-star comforts, including an outdoor pool, children's games, tennis courts and mountain bike hire. If you don't want to pitch a tent, there are pretty green-painted chalets with terraces. See p. 102.

Near the family resort of Barneville-Carteret in the Manche, the modest, family-run Camping Bel Sito has lovely views over protected dunes and some of the Channel Islands and a policy of no evening entertainment, which means you fall asleep with the sounds of nature in your ears. See p. 203.

Best Views Le Moulin de Connelles in the Eure partly occupies an island in the Seine, and the best suite has panoramic views over the river and the hotel's landscaped grounds. Rooms glow with the aqueous light that entranced many Impressionist painters, and as well as outdoor and indoor pools, there's punting on a private stretch of the Seine. The excellent restaurant has a verandah with views over the water, or there are tables under the trees. See p. 102.

THE BEST EATING OPTIONS

Most Child-friendly Restaurants The Manoir du Lys at La Croix Gautier in the Orne is a half-timbered manor with a Michelin-starred restaurant offering one of the best

Manoir du Lys, La Croix Gautier

children's menus in Normandy and half-portions from its main menu. After your meal you can retire to a family pavilion on stilts in the forest, or work it all off in the play area or indoor and outdoor pools or on the forest trails. See p. 127.

Le Panoramique on a hilltop in a lovely valley in the northern Manche is famous for its sea views but ticks all the right boxes for families – all-day brasserie service, inside and outside play areas, children's menus and very good local seafood and organic vegetables. See p. 208.

Best Seafood In a pretty half-timbered building on a pedestrianised square near Honfleur's port, in Calvados, the Auberge de la Lieutenance is a great place to feast on the likes of local oysters and brochettes of scallops and prawns with creamy lime sauce and carrot purée with chives, or to share a decadent seafood platter for two. The

Shellfish

children's menu, good value given the choice and quality, includes smoked or poached salmon. See p. 168.

Also in Calvados, at Port-en-Bessin north of Bayeux, La Chenevière is an 18th-century château with a lovely dining room overlooking its park and woods. The refined but inventive fare includes pan-fried Dover sole with vanilla Bourbon and baby artichokes, and local lobster with salted Isigny butter, morel risotto and warm lobster claw salad. Children get simplified meat or fish dishes and homemade ice cream or fresh sorbet. Cooking courses here include a tour of Port-en-Bessin's fish market, and there is chic accommodation, a pool with a

Apples

Normandy for Food-lovers

It's to its lovely landscapes, lush, green and rolling, that Normandy owes much of its reputation as a culinary hotspot – they provide the region with both rich pastures for its dairy cattle and orchards for its apples. Apples and cream are, in fact, often combined in dishes described as *à la normande* (for instance, local mussels or chicken). Apples might also be teamed with partridges. Then there's Normandy's famous apple tarts, which come in slightly different incarnations in every town and village; *flan Normand*, a sort of apple pie with flaky pastry; and apples baked in pastry (*bourdelots*).

Apple tart, often served, naturally enough, with cream, is sometimes flambéed with Calvados – cider distilled to create a fiery brandy that is usually served with (or in) coffee, or as a *trou normand* ('Norman gap') between the courses of a meal (sometimes now in the form of a sorbet). Normandy's famous cider, which is lighter than the British variety, inevitably sneaks its way into the cooking pot too (try pork in cider). The 'must' or 'worst' of the cider is often mixed with Calvados to make Pommeau, a chilled aperitif; an alternative is a *kir normand* of cider (taking the place of white wine or champagne) and *crème de cassis* (blackcurrant liqueur). The prolific orchards also produce pears, the juice of which is fermented to produce perry (*poiré*). Of course, for children and those who don't drink alcohol, there's plenty of wonderful local apple and pear juice to be had.

Normandy cream, together with its butter and a number of world-famous local cheeses (Camembert, Neufchâtel, Pont l'Evêque, that

Egg Collecting at Maison du Vert

children's area, tennis courts, a croquet lawn and massage rooms. See p. 171.

Best Crêperies You can't sit down at **Marny Crêpe**, an old-fashioned food counter on Deauville's main shopping street in Calvados, but you can get cracking crêpes to munch while window-shopping or to take to the beach, or as evening snacks if you had a big lunch. There are also old-style waffles, tarts, baguettes, paninis, club sandwiches, pastries, bonbons and ice cream. See p. 170.

children's favourite Boursin, and others), is also used in lavish quantities in both savoury and sweet dishes. Vallée d'Auge chicken in a cream sauce is a reliable child-friendly dish that crops up on menus around the region, and veal and steak often come in a creamy sauce too, perhaps with morel mushrooms from the woods. The long Norman coastline also means you'll be treated to some top-notch, spanking-fresh fish, including oysters, scallops and turbot from around the Manche and sole from Dieppe (also famous for its fish stew, *marmite Dieppoise*). Inland, menus feature lots of hearty local meats, including *tripe à la mode de Caen* (tripe stew with Calvados), chitterling (tripe) sausage (*andouille*), black pudding (*boudin noir*) and *canard rouennais*, a meaty duck variety from the Seine Valley. More delicate in flavour is the melt-in-the-mouth *pré-salé* lamb from the salt plains around the bay of the Mont-St-Michel (p. 212).

For those with a sweet tooth, alternatives to apple desserts are *tergoule* (a rice pudding with cinnamon, slow-cooked in the oven), *brioches* (a buttery, slightly sweet bread made with eggs) from Évreux and Gisors, *douillons* (pears baked in pastry), Rouen macaroons and apple sugars, Le Havre marzipans, Isigny caramels and more local pastries than you can shake a stick at. Foodie families might like to follow the 'Traditions Route' through villages in the Caen area, where small-scale producers will show you how their traditional cheeses, breads, *foie gras*, honey, cider and more are made, and sell you some. For details and a map, see **www.calvados-tourisme.com**.

In the Manche, **Le Père Alta** at La Haye-du-Puits knows its stuff so well, it's got a crêpe-making school. The menu for younger children is often offered free, and they get their own 'relaxation area' with books and games. There's also an older children's menu, and crêpe and galette specialities with local farm produce, seafood and *foie gras*. See p. 209.

Best Vegetarian Food The **Maison du Vert**, a homely veggie guesthouse in an old bakery in the Orne, serves global treats

such as falafel, *röstis* and Indian *thali*s. Children can eat from the menu or have simple meals cooked to order. Stay the night in one of the cosy rooms and they can even help collect the eggs that will go into their dinner and roam the organic gardens and orchards as you enjoy tea and homemade cake or a cocktail or cider on the lawn. See p. 126.

Best Ethnic Restaurant La Suite Afghane in Rouen in the Seine-Maritime is perfect for those who've overdosed on crêpes and *steak frites*, with its shareable pick and mix *entrées* from Afghanistan, Libya, the Sahara, Sri Lanka and Thailand. Spread out at the low tables surrounded by stools and floor-level sofas, and try your hardest to save room for the sensational desserts – sliced orange with cinnamon and saffron yogurt, pannacotta with fresh mango and Thai coconut flan. See p. 87.

Best Outdoor Eating On a lakeside in a leisure park in the Seine-Maritime, the **Brasserie du Lac de Caniel** has a popular decked terrace perfect for lazy family lunches in the sunshine – choose from the likes of steak with *sauce béarnaise*, duck with green peppercorns, barbecued meats with snail butter or snackier fare such as crêpes and *croques monsieurs*. Children get their own play space, plus a children's menu (or baby food) and a surprise gift. Nearby are a large playground, pedaloes and canoes, lugeing tracks through the forest, swimming, a nature trail, picnic spots and more. See p. 86.

One of the best places for a picnic is the glorious parkland surrounding the **Haras National du Pin**, France's national stud farm, in the Orne. Try to time your visit to coincide with a *Jeudi du Pin* – a spectacular display of dressage, carriage-pulling and horseback acrobatics to a classical soundtrack – and don't forget to bring along some cheese from nearby Camembert. See p. 114.

Best Views It may not match the nature views of Le Panoramique (p. 208), but **Le Quai des Mers**, located within the old transatlantic terminal at Cherbourg in the Manche, is a good place from which to admire *Le Redoutable*, a decommissioned nuclear submarine displayed here, or to watch boats go in and out of the bay while enjoying fabulous seafood followed by Norman pannacotta with apple compôte. See p. 208.

Best Breakfasts **Dupont avec un Thé**, an award-winning Calvados patisserie with branches in Cabourg, Deauville, Dives-sur-Mer and Trouville-sur-Mer, is a fine spot for relaxed family breakfasts to an operatic soundtrack. They have delectable pastries, baguettes, *fromage frais* and red fruits and a huge range of hot chocolates from around the world. There are also wonderful chocolate fondues, afternoon teas and savoury goodies. See p. 169.

2 Planning a Trip to Normandy

NORMANDY

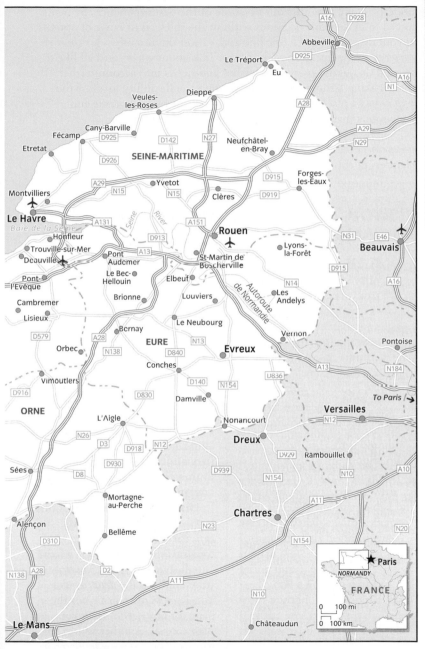

Planning any family trip is a fine art: overplan and your holiday can resemble a military expedition, or worse, a school outing; underplan and you miss out on some of the best experiences by being forced to make panic decisions without the full facts or range of options at your disposal. Tread a fine line and – most importantly – *get children involved* in the upcoming adventure. Talk about what you'd all like to see and do, taking everyone's wishes and needs into account rather than making assumptions, and maintain the flexibility to allow the *unplanned* a place in your trip – it's often unexpected events and encounters that constitute the most magical memories.

The **region** of Normandy subdivides into five administrative **départements**. For ease of planning, I have based the sightseeing chapters of this book (3–7) on these *départements*.

VISITOR INFORMATION

The **Internet** age has made researching and planning holidays a breeze. France's **official tourist board website, *www. franceguide.com***, clicks through to separate sites for 30+ countries, including ***http://uk.france guide.com*** for the UK and ***http://ie.franceguide.com*** for Ireland. Among the services they offer are online brochure ordering and a travel shop with booking for accommodation and sports activities. The tourist board also has offices, **Maisons de France**, in 29 countries, offering the same services. In the UK, there's one at 178 Piccadilly, **London** W1 (**☏ 09068 244123**), while in France there's one at 20 avenue de l'Opéra, **Paris** (**☏ 01 42 96 70 00**).

The official tourist websites let you pick the region you're heading for – including Normandy and Brittany – from a scroll-down menu, producing a page with the full contact details, including website links, of the **regional tourist board** (**Comité Régionale de Tourisme** or **CRT**), **departmental tourist offices** (**Comités Départmentales de Tourisme** or **CDTs**) and the **tourist offices** (**offices de tourisme**) of major towns and cities. Note that CRTs and CDTs aren't actual places you can visit.

The CRT website for Normandy is ***www.normandy-tourism.org***, which has translations into English and other languages. I've listed CDT websites under 'Visitor Information' in the relevant sightseeing chapters; most are translated into English and some have pages on family holidays or children's activities. They all list every tourist office, *syndicat d'initiative* (small tourist office) or *mairie* (town hall) in the *département*. You may want to print out the page for any *département* you plan to visit. Another source for tourist offices is ***www.tourisme.fr/recherche/e_main.htm***.

Child-Specific Websites

The official Normandy tourist board has a special site for families, *www.normandywithkids.com*, with accommodation recommendations, listings for child-friendly sites, events and sporting activities, and maps. Another useful resource, *www.france4families.com*, has lots of general information about France from a family perspective, plus guides to various regions, including Normandy. More general family-oriented sites are *www.takethefamily.com*, with tips, destination guides (including lots on camping in France) and a discussion board; *www.babygoes2.com*, with general tips and location reports, and *www.deabirkett.com*, a handy family travel forum for exchanging tips and views, run by the former *Guardian* children's travel specialist.

For route planning ahead of a trip, or even just general interest, *http://maps.google.com* has zoomable maps of just about anywhere, directions to and from places and even detailed satellite images – look at Deauville's racecourses from above, for instance, or even the hotel you're going to stay in! If you have the time to be really organised in advance, the excellent *www.viamichelin.com* can give you detailed directions (plus maps) from your home town to your destination in France, or between places in France, including the location of speed cameras.

Entry Requirements, Customs & Bringing Pets

Passports & Visas

Citizens of other **European Union** (EU) countries need an **identity card** to enter France – for the time being, this means a passport for UK citizens. **Non-EU citizens** need a passport but few nationalities require a **visa** – South Africans are among the few. However, **stays of more than three months** by non-EU citizens do require a visa. For French embassies/consulates around the world, see *www.diplomatie.gouv.fr/venir/visas/index.html*.

Taking Your Pet

Under the **Pet Travel Scheme** (PETS), UK-resident dogs and cats can now travel to many other EU countries and return to the UK without being quarantined. Dogs and cats are issued with a **passport** (by a vet) after being fitted with a microchip and vaccinated against rabies at least 21 days prior to travel. On re-entry to the UK, you need to get your pet treated for ticks and tapeworm (by any EU vet 24–48 hrs before being checked in with a transport company approved by the scheme). For full details, check *www.defra.gov.uk/animalh/quarantine/index.htm*.

Most French **hotels** and some self-catering properties accept animals, usually with an extra fee (averaging €7 – about £4.70).

The commercial website *www. visitfrance.co.uk* is a good source of pet-friendly self-catering options.

Coming Home

Visitors to France from other **EU countries** can bring home any amount of goods for personal use, except new vehicles, mail-order purchases, and more than 800 cigarettes, 10 litres of spirits, 90 litres of wine and 110 litres of beer. Travellers from **outside the EU** must declare all transported goods and pay duty or tax on those worth more than €175 (roughly £117 at the time of writing). All visitors leaving with more than €7600 (£5092) must declare the amount to customs. The French customs website, *www.douane.gouv.fr*, is translated into English, German and Spanish.

Money

The Euro

France – in common with 11 other countries at the time of writing – has the **euro** (€) as its currency. There are 100 **cents** in a euro, with **notes** for €5–500 and **coins** for 1 cent–€2. As of writing, the **euro–sterling exchange rate** is €1.48 to £1 (67p to €1), making mental calculations fairly easy (drop a third to get a rough figure in pounds). For current rates and a currency converter, see *www.xe.com*.

Credit & Debit Cards

Most French shops, restaurants and hotels take credit or debit cards, or at least **Visa** and **Mastercard** – **American Express** and **Diner's Club** are only really accepted in expensive hotels and restaurants. There is often a lower spending limit of €7–15 (£4.70–10) for cards. The only **places unlikely to accept cards** today are B&Bs, small campsites and inexpensive rural inns.

You now use your **PIN** number when making a purchase with your card as well as using it at a cashpoint, except at automated pumps at **petrol stations** out of hours, which, frustratingly, still refuse foreign cards.

Before you leave, tell your credit card company you're going abroad, as they sometimes put a **block on cards** that deviate from their normal spending pattern.

For **lost or stolen cards**, see p. 50.

Traveller's Cheques

These are becoming a thing of the past now cities and most towns have 24-hr ATMs, and you need to show ID every time you cash one. If you do choose to take some, if only as a backup, you can get them at some banks, building societies, travel agents and the Post Office, among other outlets. Keep a record of their serial numbers in case of loss or theft, and carry them separately from money and/or cards.

What Things Cost in Normandy	€	*£
1-litre Unleaded 95 petrol	€1.27	£0.86
Hire of medium-sized car (wk)	€200–€1350	£134–905
Taxi ride	€2 base fare; €1/km	£1.34/£0.67
City/town bus fare, adult	€1.20	£0.80
City/town bus fare, child 5 or over	same	same
Single train fare Caen–Cherbourg (120 km)	€27	£18
Single train fare child 4–11 (120 km)	€20	£13.40
Single TGV fare, Rouen–Le Havre (57 km)	€25	£16.75
Single TGV fare child 4–11 (57 km)	€17	£11.40
Single Twin Jet fare, Paris–Cherbourg (220 km)	€106–307 (inc taxes)	£71–206
Single over-2s Twin Jet fare, Paris–Cherbourg	same	same
Admission to zoo, adult	€13	£8.70
Admission to zoo, child 4–12	€6.50	£4.35
Admission to public museum	free	free
Cinema ticket, adult	€8	£5.35
Cinema ticket, child	€5.60	£3.75
British newspaper	€0.55	£0.37
Local telephone call (per minute)	€0.03–0.09	£0.02–0.06
European phone call (per minute)	€0.22	£0.15
Fixed-price menu at mid-priced restaurant	€14–18	£9.40–12
Under-12s menu at mid-priced restaurant	€9	£6
1 litre milk in supermarket	€0.78	£0.52
1 litre apple juice in supermarket	€0.78	£0.52
1.5 litre bottle still water in supermarket	€0.20	£0.14
1kg bananas in supermarket	€1.20	£0.80
Ham and cheese baguette from takeaway counter	€3.50	£2.35
Packet of 20 small Pampers in supermarket	€8.50	£5.70
330ml infant milk in supermarket	€0.60	£0.40

*Assuming a conversion rate of €1=£0.67

Cash Points

There are 24-hr cash point machines or ATMs outside all French banks and in many supermarket lobbies – even relatively small ones in out-of-the-way towns – and withdrawing cash is rarely a problem unless you've gone over your limit. You usually get a better rate at a cash point than an exchange booth (which may also take a commission), but your bank will probably charge you a fee for using a foreign cash point, so avoid withdrawing small sums every day or two as you might at home.

It's also a good idea to bring some cash into France as a backup, and to have two or more cards in case of a hiccup – you can make withdrawals from cash points using credit cards, paying interest on the advance from the moment you receive the cash.

When to Go & What to Pack

The weather in Normandy can be as **changeable** as it is on the south coast of the UK, with lightning-fast switches from glorious sunshine to pouring rain. As in the UK, winters are very cold and summers increasingly hot. Even in May you need to pack light sweaters, waterproof coats and hats and wellie boots alongside your swimming gear, or to stock up once you're here.

If you plan to eat in some of the fancier hotel restaurants during your stay, you also need to pack quite smart clothes, including shirts and trousers for men and boys.

A very helpful tool for planning days out is *www.meteo france.com*; even with only basic French (you need to know the days of the week) you get a general idea of what to expect in your area from its click-on maps. Or call ☎ *0892 68 02 XX* (XX is the number of the *département*: 76 for Seine Maritime, 27 for Eure, 61 for Orne, 14 for Calvados, 50 for Manche). A good English-language site is *http://weather.uk.msn.com*.

Since Normandy is most popular among visitors – at least French ones – for its beaches and coastal resorts, it is at its busiest, and most expensive, in **July and August**. Remember that the French holiday en masse in August, meaning congested roads and resorts – the Norman Riviera, for instance, becomes unbearable, as do big family attractions such as **La Cité de la Mer** in Cherbourg. On the other hand, this is when most **festivals and events**, including **children's beach clubs**, take place. I've listed many of these beach clubs, which are often called '*Clubs Mickey*', in the relevant sightseeing chapters; alternatively, they are detailed on tourist office websites or centrally on the national beach clubs federation's website, *www.fncp.fr*.

Otherwise, **spring, early or late summer or autumn** can be charming times to visit, when you have many animal parks and beaches virtually to yourself. But you'll need contingency plans for those days, all too frequent, when the weather lets you down and smaller attractions may not be open – save large indoor attractions such as museums and aquaria for such days.

Average Daytime Temperature & Rainfall in Normandy												
	Jan	Feb	Mar	Apr	May	June	July	Aug	Sept	Oct	Nov	Dec
Temp. (°C)	7.6	6.4	8.4	13	14	20	21.6	22	18.2	14.5	10.8	7.9
Rainfall (cm; Rouen)	5.18	4.2	4.05	4.16	4.27	4.17	4.66	3.98	4.8	5.96	5.09	6.43

Children's Kit

The following items can make travelling with babies or young children in Normandy easier or more relaxing:

Bébétel Baby Monitor: Unlike battery-powered listening devices, this is not limited by range and suffers no interference, so you can use it in all hotel-restaurants. You plug it into a standard phoneline (there are foreign adapter sets) and programme in your mobile number (you may have to add the international code); if your child gets up or cries, the monitor calls you. It costs a hefty £180 or so (see *www.bebetel.com*); a few hotels have them, but none, at the time of writing, in Normandy.

Littlelife Baby Carriers: These 'backpacks-with-children-in' – a great idea if you're doing a lot of walking or hiking and don't want to be encumbered with a buggy – include 'Voyager', with a zip-off bag for drinks, snacks and wipes, for about £170; lighter models start at half that. You can get hold of them at *www.johnlewis.com* and outdoor pursuits shops. The same firm's compact, superabsorbent **travel towels** are also very handy for travelling.

Portable Highchairs: Most French restaurants provide at least one highchair, but if they don't, or it's taken, or it's a weird old-style one without a front bar, you may be left trying to eat with one hand and hold a squirming baby or toddler with the other. Lightweight options you can carry around include the supremely compact 'Handbag Highchair' (a loop of fabric that secures your baby to the chair), the foldable Handysitt toddler seat, and The Early Years inflatable booster seat. All are sold at www.bloomingmarvellous.co.uk, with prices from £15 to £75.

Boardbug Baby and Toddler Monitor: Great for the beach (p. 27) or for shopping, this award-winning wristwatch-style monitor alerts you whenever your little one (or ones – the parent unit can be paired with up to three child units) strays from you, with adjustable distances from 2 m to 150 m. It costs about £55 from *www.travellingwithchildren.co.uk*.

Public & School Holidays

French **national holidays** are called *jours fériés*; banks and small shops close but larger supermarkets increasingly open in the morning. Most museums close but many other visitor sites stay open, as do the majority of restaurants. If there's a public holiday on a Thursday or Tuesday, many people take the Friday or Monday off as well – this is called *faisant le pont* ('making a bridge').

The main public holidays are **New Year's Day** (1st January), **Easter Monday** (March or April), **Labour Day** (*Fête du Travail*; 1st May), **VE Day** (8th May), **Whit Monday** (late May), **Ascension Thursday** (late May/40 days after Easter),

Bastille Day (14th July), **Assumption of the Blessed Virgin** (15th August), **All Saints' Day** (1st November), **Armistice Day** (11th November) and **Christmas Day** (25th December).

There are five **school holidays** a year in France: two weeks in February, two weeks at Easter, all of July and August, one week at the end of October and two weeks at Christmas. As in the UK, holidays are staggered around the country: Zone A includes Lower Normandy (Manche, Calvados and Orne), Zone B Upper Normandy (Eure and Seine-Maritime) and Zone C Paris. Most tourist sites take into account both the holiday in force in their own area and Parisian holidays, and sometimes holidays in neighbouring areas (Brittany and the Pays de la Loire to the west of Normandy are Zone A, and the Centre and Picardie regions to the south and east are Zone B).

The following are sample dates for general guidance:

18th February–6th March (A), 11th–27th February (B), 4th–20th February (C)

22nd April–9th March (A), 15th April–2nd May (B), 8th–24th April (C)

4th July–2nd September (all)

22nd October–3rd November (all)

17th December–3rd January (all)

Tourist sites and roads are busier during these periods, and hotels often more expensive, but remember that many museums, galleries and other venues host **extra children's activities** in the holidays, and resorts have children's beach clubs (p. 22) and special events and entertainment. If you do visit at a busy period, bear in mind that the French tend to go out mid-afternoon, after the lunch break, so mornings can be good times to visit the most popular attractions.

Playing with the animals at Maison du Vert

Special Events

For my pick of the best family-friendly happenings throughout the year, from kite-flying festivals to horse parades, see the 'Child-Friendly Events & Entertainment' sections of each sightseeing chapter.

Health, Insurance & Safety

Travel Insurance

Travellers to France from other EU countries now need to carry their **European Health Insurance Card** (EHIC), which replaced the E111 form as proof of entitlement to free/reduced-cost medical treatment abroad. The quickest way to apply for one is online (**www.ehic.org.uk**), or call ☎ *0845 606 2030* or get a form from a post office. You still pay upfront for treatment and related expenses; the doctor will give you a form you use to reclaim most of the money (about 70% of doctors' fees and 35–65% of medicines/prescription charges), by filling in a form you request by phone when you get home.

Note, however, that the EHIC only covers '*necessary medical treatment*', and it doesn't cover repatriation costs, lost money, baggage or cancellation, so is no replacement for **travel insurance**. Before you buy the latter, though, check whether your existing insurance policies and credit cards cover you for lost luggage, cancelled tickets or medical expenses. If they don't, an example of cover for a family of four travelling to France for two weeks, without any adventure sports, with a reputable online insurer such as **www.travelinsuranceweb.com**, is £20.49 (€30.26); an annual multi-trip policy costs £41.49 (€61.27), so is well worth it if you make more than two trips a year. Make sure your package includes **trip-cancellation insurance** to help you get your money back if you have to back out of a trip or go home early (both more likely if you're travelling with children), or if your travel supplier goes bust. Allowed reasons for cancellation can range from sickness to natural disasters or a destination being declared unsafe for travel.

Other **non-EU nationals** – with the exception of Canadians, who have the same rights as EU citizens to medical treatment within France – need comprehensive travel insurance that covers medical treatment overseas. Even then, you pay bills upfront and apply for a refund at home.

Staying Healthy

There are no real health risks while travelling in France, and you don't need vaccinations. For general advice on travelling with children, read *Your Child Abroad: a Travel Health Guide*, by Dr Jane Wilson-Howarth and Dr Matthew Ellis (Bradt, £10.95).

If You Fall Ill

For emergency treatment, doctors and chemists, see p. 49.

Bring along copies of prescriptions in case you or anyone in your family loses their medication or runs out. Carry the generic name of prescription medicines in case a local pharmacist is unfamiliar with the brand name. You should also bring along an extra pair of contact lenses or prescription glasses.

When flying, pack any prescription medicines you'll need while in the air in your hand luggage in their original containers, with chemist's labels. At the time of writing, anti-terrorism precautions require some medicines to be verified by airport chemists.

If you or your child have an illness that may make it impossible to explain what's happening to you/them, and that needs swift and accurate treatment, such as epilepsy, diabetes, asthma or a food allergy, the charity MedicAlert (*www.medicalert. org.uk*) provides body-worn bracelets or necklets engraved with the wearer's medical condition(s)/vital details, ID number and 24-hr emergency telephone number that accepts reverse charge calls, so their details can be accessed from anywhere in more than 100 languages.

Travelling Safely With Children in Normandy

France – especially outside Paris and other major cities – is generally a very safe country, with a traveller's main worry, as in most countries, the risk of being targeted by pickpockets and petty thieves – travel with your car doors locked as a precaution. As a parent, be especially wary of French drivers; many pay no heed to the speed limit, exceed the alcohol limit and drive aggressively. Virtually no one here stops at pedestrian crossings, so tell your child to wait until vehicles are motionless before proceeding.

As everywhere, hold hands with young children and don't let them out of your sight unless they are being supervised by someone you trust – they can move faster than you think. Avoid situations where your child could get swept away in a crowd, and with older children agree on a place to meet should you get parted – at the information desk at a museum, for instance. Make sure they have your mobile number and accommodation address on them, with instructions to ask for a member of the police force (*agent de police* or *gendarme*) should they not be able to find you. Their name should never be visible on their bag/clothing, and tell them the importance of never divulging their name to a stranger.

Beaches can be lethal: you lay back and close your eyes for what seems like a second, and when you open them, your child is nowhere to be seen. With the sea close by, the potential for disaster is clear. The rule is to take it in turns to flake out while one parent keeps watch. If you're alone, you have no option but to stay hyper-alert. For peace of mind, especially if you have more than one child to keep an eye on, invest in Boardbug wrist-worn monitors (p. 23) with adjustable distance alarms for children of varying ages. You could also try a set of walking reins if you have a toddler who likes to go walkabout.

Specialised Resources

For Single Parents

For a good 'Holidays' page with contact details of useful associations and operators in the UK, see *www.singleparents.org.uk*. The US-based *www.singleparent travelnet* is also good for travel advice.

One Parent Families (☎ 0800 018 5026, *www.oneparentfamilies. org.uk*) is a British charity offering information and advice for lone parents; Gingerbread (☎ 0800 018 4318, *www. gingerbread.org.uk*) is similar, with members getting regular e-mails with discounts and holiday ideas. Members of both get discounts with tour operator Eurocamp (p. 34), which has an Arrival Survival service to help lone parents unpack and settle in. Other camping operators offer discounts, as do most youth hostels (p. 41).

For Grandparents

Grandparents travelling with children are a rapidly growing market, but specialist operators tend to be US-based. Grand Travel (☎ 1-800-247-7651, *www. grandtrvl.com*), for instance, runs a 'London & Paris: Grandest Cities' tour that includes a trip to Monet's garden at Giverny (p. 98), followed by dinner at the top of the Eiffel Tower. Children of any age are welcome, but tours generally cater for ages 7–17.

Grandparents – many of whom may be retired and living in France – often holiday with their children and grandchildren in gîtes (p. 41). If you take your grandchildren on outings, remember that over-60s generally get discounts on travel tickets, museum and zoo entry and so on.

For Families With Special Needs

Many of France's historic buildings, whether museums or hotels, have limited or non-existent wheelchair access. Older town hotels, in particular, lack lifts. That said, modern facilities are up-to-scratch, and most hotels have at least a couple of accessible or ground-floor rooms. Holiday Care (☎ 0845 124 9971, *www.holidaycare.org.uk*) publishes overseas information guides (about £5) listing accommodation they believe to be accessible but haven't inspected in person. Access Travel

(📞 *01942 888844, www.access-travel.co.uk*), a specialist travel agent, offers a selection of Normandy gîtes suitable for wheelchair users, plus ferry and flight booking, car hire and more.

Remember that you stay in your car when travelling on the **Eurotunnel** (p. 32), making it easier than ferries for wheelchair users. It's also worth knowing that **Eurostar** (p. 32) offers first-class travel for second-class fares for disabled people.

The 21st Century Traveller

Mobile Phones

It's indispensable to have your mobile phone with you if you're driving with children. Luckily, these days it's usually hassle-free to use a British mobile phone in France: it will simply switch over to a **French network** when you reach France, and you can call British numbers and French numbers directly, or sometimes using the international dialling code (it seems to vary). It's wise to **check in advance with your provider** that your phone is set up for **international roaming**, and have them explain the procedure for accessing voicemails while abroad (again, this is usually trouble-free, but do double check).

Call charges to UK or French numbers will be higher than within the UK, and you will also pay for any incoming calls from your home country. If you're going to be making or receiving

a lot of calls, or go abroad often, it might be worth buying an **international SIM card** to temporarily replace your UK one; see, for instance, *www.0044.co.uk*. This will give you a local number and lower calling rates. Many UK phones are locked to their UK networks, so you can replace the SIM, although this doesn't apply to pay-as-you-go phones.

Or, if you're staying more than a few weeks or come to France repeatedly, you could just buy a pay-as-you-go mobile phone from a communications shop such as France Télécom/Orange, found in all largish town centres, or even from a large supermarket.

For those from further afield, such as the **USA**, the situation is basically the same provided you have a world-capable multiband phone on a **GSM** (Global System for Mobiles) system, with 'international roaming' activated. Again, installing an international SIM card can save you money if you use the phone frequently.

Recharge your phone whenever you get a chance (many come with travel adapters you can plug into your car's cigarette lighter).

Other Phones

For information about **area** and **international dialling codes** and **public phones**, see p. 51.

The Internet

Large cities and most towns of any size have a choice of Internet access points, whether in **cyber-cafés**, public **libraries** or the **tourist office**; tourist offices will provide you with a list, or sites such as **www.cybercafe.com** and **www.cybercaptive.com** can be helpful. A good French site is **www.cybercafe.fr**. You can also get (expensive) Internet access in some **post offices**, and some major cities have **Internet kiosks** in the street.

To **retrieve your e-mails**, ask your Internet Service Provider (ISP) if it has a **web-based interface** tied to your existing account. If it doesn't, set up a **free web-based e-mail account**, with, for instance, **www.yahoo. com** or **www.hotmail.com**. You might want to start one up anyway, as backup in case of hiccups with your existing account.

Most **hotels**, mid range and up (and sometimes also budget ones), have either a terminal where you can access the Internet for free or a small charge or means by which you can access it from your laptop. The latter could be either through a **modem connection/dataport** in your room (meaning you'll be paying as you would for a phone call, which is expensive in hotels; you may also need an adapter) or, increasingly, through free **Wi-Fi** ('wireless fidelity') access throughout the hotel. Wi-Fi access is also available in many airports and cafés. Most new laptops come already wireless-enabled; otherwise you need to install an access card, available

from, for instance, **www.shop. bt.com** or computer stores.

If you're a touch typist and need to do a lot of e-mailing, **French keyboards**, which have letters in different places, will slow you down.

Essentials

Getting There

By Plane The advent of **low-cost airlines** has opened up Normandy to air travellers. The situation fluctuates, but at the time of writing you can fly from points in the **UK** to: **Le Havre** (Seine Maritime), **Deauville** (Calvados) and **Cherbourg** (Manche). Dinard and Rennes in **Brittany** can also be quite handy for those visiting western Normandy; see the companion guide to this book, *Brittany With Your Family*.

Companies flying to Normandy from Britain are: **Skysouth** (p. 54), to Le Havre from Brighton; **Ryanair** (UK ☎ *0871 246 0000*/France ☎ *0892 232375*, *www. ryanair.com*), to Deauville from London Stansted; **Flybe** (UK ☎ *0871 700 0535/* outside UK ☎ *00 44 13 922 685 29*, *www.flybe.com*), to Cherbourg from Southampton.

As a general rule, **under-2s fly free** if they sit on your knee; older than that, they pay the same fare as you. **Fares** can start from as little as £0.01, depending on your destination and when you book, but these don't include **airport taxes and other** charges, which can add up to about £60–80 for a family of four. Also, some airlines, including Ryanair, might charge for checked-in baggage.

You can also fly to Paris from the UK or Ireland with a number of operators, including British Airways (UK ☎ 0870 850 9850/France ☎ 0825 825 4400, www.britishairways.com) and Air France (UK ☎ 0870 142 4343/ France ☎ 0820 820820, www.airfrance.com). Ryanair fly to Beauvais near Paris (p. 29). From Paris, there are flights to Cherbourg (Manche) with Twin Jet (p. 174), and to Rennes in Brittany with Air France (p. 30).

Among airlines that fly regularly between the USA and Paris are: American Airlines (☎ 800-433-7300, www.aa.com), British Airways (☎ 800-AIRWAYS), Continental Airlines (☎ 800-525-0280, www.continental.com) and Delta Air Lines (☎ 800-241-4141, www.delta.com). Air France (above) flies to Paris from the USA and Canada, and Air Canada (☎ 888-247-2262, www.aircanada.com) flies there from Toronto and Montreal.

There are currently no direct flights from Australia to Paris; most people go to London and get a connecting flight. South African Airways (☎ 0861-359722, www.flysaa.com) flies to Paris from Cape Town and other cities in South Africa.

What you can take on flights: The situation was unclear at the time of writing due to the security crisis of summer 2006, but basically, passengers flying between the UK and France were allowed one laptop-sized bag. You are only allowed to take small quantities of liquids in your cabin luggage or on your person. These liquids must be in individual containers with a maximum capacity of 100 millilitres each. You must pack these containers in one transparent, re-sealable plastic bag of not more than one litre capacity. Check with your airline prior to packing so you don't waste time repacking at the airport.

INSIDER TIP

If possible, keep children with colds grounded, as ascent and descent can be especially painful – and even dangerous – when they have congested sinuses. If that's not an option, give them an oral child's decongestant an hour before ascent and descent, or administer a spray decongestant before and during takeoff and landing.

By Car Ferries: The shortest, cheapest and most popular Channel crossings are Dover to Boulogne, Calais and Dunkerque (p. 56); they are within easy reach of the Seine-Maritime to the southwest and reasonably handy for visitors planning to tour Normandy.

Normandy's own ferry ports are Dieppe and Le Havre in the Seine Maritime, Caen-Ouistreham in Calvados and Cherbourg in the Manche. St-Malo in the Ille-et-Vilaine in Brittany is also relatively handy for western Normandy. For more details, including crossing times, see the 'Getting There' sections of the respective sightseeing chapters.

The major ferry operator between Britain and northern France, **Brittany Ferries** (UK ☎ *08703 665333*/France ☎ *02 98 29 28 00, www.brittanyferries.com*), has sailings to Normandy (Caen-Ouistreham and Cherbourg) as well as Brittany (St-Malo and Roscoff). All vessels have children's facilities, such as play spaces and entertainment, and accommodation can be surprisingly luxurious.

Though longer sailings are evidently the costliest, with small children in the car you will probably be keen to reduce your driving time. What you save in ferry fares, you may lose in petrol money (especially at current prices), possible overnight stays in hotels, countless snack stops and general shredded nerves. Try to think of a longer ferry crossing as part of the overall adventure of your holiday, not simply the act of getting there.

Prices vary widely according to whether you travel by day or night, the standard of accommodation you choose (it's obligatory on overnight sailings), the number of passengers, the size of your car and other details. It is cheaper to travel both off-season and midweek. As a rough guide, a return trip, late Aug–mid-Sept between Poole and Cherbourg for two adults and two children aged 4–15 with a standard car,

4x4 or MPV without a roof load, trailer or bike carrier, in an outside four-berth cabin, costs about £490 (€730). An outside cabin (that is, with a window) is only slighter more expensive than an inside one but makes the experience all the more exciting for youngsters. The cheapest option is an inside couchette with shared facilities. The same journey with a **motorhome** is £520 (€776), with a car and the smallest model of **caravan** £600 (€896).

The **online booking system** is generally good, with the occasional blip, and there's a £10 discount for online booking. Some people prefer the transparency of talking to an operator about the cheapest options; however, Brittany Ferries' online system does give you a colour-coded guide to the scale of prices around your preferred date, so you aren't trapped into the most expensive crossing. And make sure to play around with the buttons when getting an online quote: you may find, for instance, that a cabin with a television set is no more expensive than one without. Note that Brittany Ferries is also an award-winning **tour operator** (p. 33).

Other ferry firms operating to Normandy are **Transmanche** (Newhaven–Dieppe; UK ☎ *0800 917 1201*, France ☎ *0800 650100*, *www.transmancheferries.com*), **LD Lines** (Portsmouth–Le Havre; UK ☎ *0870 428 4335*, France ☎ *0825 304304, www.ldlines.com*), and **Condor Ferries**

(Portsmouth–Cherbourg, and Poole/Weymouth–St-Malo in Brittany; UK ☎ *0870 243 5140*, *www.condorferries.co.uk*). All have more basic accommodation and facilities than Brittany Ferries but most have children's amenities. Again, purely as a guide, in late August/early September you might expect to pay £205–277 (€302–409)for a Portsmouth–Le Havre return with LD Lines, with a four-berth outside cabin on the outward journey (overnight only; sleeping accommodation not compulsory) and standard seats on the return (daytime only), for a family of four with a standard car and no trailer.

In late 2006, LD lines introduced new 'sleeper seats', partitioned in rooms of two for privacy, in a quiet lounge with showers and toilets and free Internet access.

You might save money by booking ferries (and Eurotunnel; p. 32) through the 'one-stop shop' *www.ferrybooker.com*, but it's difficult to make direct price comparisons because its search facility may not throw up the same sailings and accommodation availability.

Eurotunnel: For some parents, **Eurotunnel**, a shuttle train taking cars through the Channel Tunnel (☎ *08705 353535*, *www. eurotunnel.com*) between Folkestone and Calais is the least painful crossing option, since the journey takes just 35 mins and you don't even need to get out of your car. Bear in mind

that Calais is only 175 km from Dieppe in the Seine-Maritime. Sample prices in late August/early September can be anything from £49 to £155 each way, with lower fares early in the morning or late at night. These are standard fares rather than more expensive Flexiplus fares, but you can still get a different train from the one you're booked on for free provided you arrive within two hours of your scheduled departure time.

By Train You can travel from London (Waterloo station) or Ashford in Kent to Calais, Lille or Paris on **Eurostar** (☎ *0870 530 0003*, *www.eurostar.com*); London–Paris takes about 2 hrs 50 mins, with fares varying according to how far ahead you book and the degree of flexibility you require regarding exchanges or refunds – they can be as low as £59 per adult and £50 per child aged 4–11 for a return ticket in standard class.

Eurostar moves from Waterloo International to its new home at St Pancras International in Autumn 2007. The new station will offer quicker journeys to France with Paris–London taking 2 hrs 15 mins.

Eurostar can also book **onward journeys** to **Normandy** – Rouen, Le Havre, Deauville-Trouville, Caen and Cherbourg. Alternatively, *www.raileurope. co.uk* offers combined booking for Eurostar tickets and onward journeys.

By Bus This is your cheapest but slowest and least comfortable means of getting to the Continent, and with children in tow you may be asking for one long headache of a journey. It may be bearable with older children, if you bring the requisite iPods, game gadgets and books.

Eurolines (☎ *08705 808080*, *www.nationalexpress.co.uk*) run from London Victoria to **Paris**, taking 7 hrs 15 mins–13 hrs depending on how long you have to wait at the port (the trip back takes from 6 hrs 20 mins). Some buses have extra legroom; all have air-conditioning and toilets. Return prices start at £28 ('funfares' for all ages from 0). There are also daily buses to **Caen-Ouistreham** in Normandy, taking about 11 hrs and costing approximately £80 return for over-26s (on overnight trips you need to pay at least £5 extra for accommodation on the ferry).

Package Deals & Activity Holidays

Package deals let you buy your aeroplane, ferry or train ticket, accommodation and other elements of your trip (i.e. car hire or airport transfers) at the same time, often at a discount. Alternatively, they may include hidden charges that you would avoid by booking direct with a hotel or carrier. The obvious appeal for parents is that they *save you time* researching and booking.

Activity holidays are roughly the same with the addition of some kind of sporting, creative or cultural activity, though sometimes you make your own travel arrangements.

Escorted tours, where you are taken around the various sites, are, to my mind, anathema to family holidays, where you need to remain flexible in case the children get bored/tired/ill. Such holidays also take away the exhilaration of getting out there and discovering your destination for yourself – one of the best lessons you can give your children.

The following are a few of the best organisers; you will find many more on the Internet and advertised in **Sunday papers**. Again, check your travel insurance (p. 25) covers you if an operator goes bust.

Brittany Ferries ★★★ This ferry company is also an award-winning tour operator, which can make parents' lives easier by booking hotels, apartments, gîtes, camping chalets, theme parks, cycling and boating holidays and so on in conjunction with travel on its ferries, not only in Brittany but in Normandy and other French regions. All properties are inspected, and – handily for those anxious about the language – there's a 24-hr hotline with English-speaking staff to deal with plumbing problems or the like. The excellent online search facility lets you refine, say, your gîte search by distance from a beach, availability of baby equipment and so on, and masses of detail is provided about each property. You can also book mix-and-match holidays that allow you to, for instance, treat yourselves to a night or two in a posh hotel after a week in a chalet. (℡ *0870 556 1600; www.brittany ferries.com).*

Keycamp This company offers tents, mobile homes and chalets at sites across Europe, including three in Normandy. All sites have children's clubs, a swimming pool or pools and a variety of play, sporting and practical amenities. You can see the attraction of this kind of holiday for those with young children – lots of readymade playmates and a range of things to do when the weather isn't so great. Expect a five-night stay in a three-bedroom mobile home without linen in late May to cost about £340, without ferry crossings (though these can be arranged, as can Eurotunnel/flydrive). You get a small discount for arranging your own travel.

Similar firms are **Eurocamp** (*www.eurocamp.co.uk*), offering three sites in Normandy; **Thomson Al Fresco** (*www. thomsonalfresco.co.uk*), with two; and **Canvas Holidays** (*www.canvasholidays.com*), with one. Some deal with the same campsites, including Camping Lez Eaux (p. 205). *Keycamp (℡ 0870 700 0740; www. keycamp.co.uk).*

VFB Holidays ★ This highly reputed and longstanding firm is a good source for gîtes in Normandy and elsewhere, plus short breaks in country hotels and river cruises (including Paris–Honfleur, stopping at Monet's garden at Giverny; p. 98). A sample price for a gîte for four plus a baby between Barneville-Carteret and St Vaast-la-Hougue in the Manche in late May/early June is £343 without crossings, which you can book at preferential rates with the company after reserving your accommodation. (℡ *01242 240340; www.vfbholidays. co.uk).*

Getting Around

By Car Though far from environmentally friendly (or cheap, given today's petrol prices), having your own set of wheels allows you the necessary flexibility when it comes to exploring Normandy, especially more rural areas.

Most visitors from the UK bring their own cars on the ferry (p. 30) or Eurotunnel (p. 32); if you're among them, you need to bring your driving licence, the original of the vehicle registration document, a current insurance certificate and, if the vehicle isn't registered in your name, a letter of authorisation from the owner. Your British insurance will give you the minimum legal cover required in France, but it's advisable to ask your insurer for a green card (international insurance certificate) – these are no longer compulsory but provide fully comprehensive cover. Get yourself some extra peace of mind by arranging **24-hr breakdown assistance** too (p. 36). Note that if you break down on a motorway, however, you can only call the official breakdown service operating in that area; there are orange emergency telephones every two kilometres (1¼ miles). They have a fixed fee of €68.60 (£46) for repairing or towing a vehicle, €85.75 (£57.45) at night (6pm–8am). Don't forget to get a receipt. You can call your breakdown service after being towed off the motorway.

Those coming into France must display an international **sign plate** or sticker (i.e. 'GB') as near as possible to their rear registration plate. Carrying a **red warning triangle** is strongly advised, even if your car has hazard warning lights, because breakdown may affect your electrics (they're compulsory for cars towing a caravan or a trailer). You should also buy a complete **spare-bulb** kit before you go, as it's illegal to drive with faulty lights. You need to **adjust your beams** for right-hand drive, which means buying special stickers to affix on your headlights. All of this gear is available at shops at the port.

The **French road system** is generally excellent. **Motorways** are uncrowded compared to British ones, though on most you have to pay a **toll** – from Rouen to Caen (127 km – 79

miles), for example, it's €7.30 (£4.90) for a mid-sized car. If you're not in a hurry, it's often preferable to take a *route nationale* (RN or N) – a main road, usually single lane, that sometimes takes you through scenic towns. Motorways have parking/rest areas every 10–20 km (roughly every 6–12 miles) and 24-hr petrol stations with basic car maintenance services every 40 km (25 miles) or so. Visa and Mastercard are accepted at tolls and petrol stations (except automated out-of-hours pumps).

The website ***www.autoroutes.fr*** (with an English version) can give you information about routes plus the toll charges, service stations, rest areas, restaurants, petrol stations and hotels along them. It even works out how much petrol you will use to get from one place to another. If you understand French, **Autoroute FM (107.7)** gives traffic information on the motorways.

Driving rules and advice: Traffic rules in France resemble those in force in Britain – the key difference is that in France you *drive on the right*. Be wary of forgetting this for a moment when you come out of a petrol station or junction. In built-up areas, you must give way to anybody coming out of a side turning on the right (the infamous *priorité à droite*); this rule no longer applies at roundabouts, where you give way to cars that are already on the roundabout. Common signs you will see are

Tips for Travelling by Car

When travelling long distances by car, it may be worth timing your trip to coincide with your child's **nap time,** or even leaving after dinner and unloading them into bed at your pre-booked accommodation. Think about investing in an **in-car satellite navigation system**; they are now relatively affordable (from about £190), and many cite them as marriage-savers. They're particularly handy for parents who are trying to map-read *and* deal with the demands of children in the back, but be vigilant about removing it from your car when you leave it parked on the street, or someone else will do it for you. Other desirables or essentials are:

- A fully charged **mobile phone.**
- **Breakdown cover/roadside assistance. Europ Assistance** (📞 *01444 442211*, *www.europ-assistance.co.uk*) has very fair prices and an excellent reputation. If you do break down, tell the operator you have children so they prioritise you, and if you're somewhere other cars could run into the back of you, such as on the hard shoulder of the motorway, it's wise to get children out of the car. If you have a **hire car**, make sure the booking includes 24-hr roadside assistance.
- **Child seats.** Under-10s must be seated in the back in France, except babies in rear-facing safety seats, though the latter must not be used if the front passenger seat is fitted with an airbag. New laws that came into force *in the UK* in September 2006 require children under 13 (or under 136 cm in height) to use a specialist

chaussée déformée ('uneven road/temporary surface'), *déviation* ('diversion') and *rappel* ('continuation of the restriction'). The official text of the **French highway code** is available in English at *www.legifrance.gouv.fr*. For **road signs**, see *www. permisenligne.com*, or your road atlas will probably picture many of them. Note that you must be at least 18, not 17, to drive in France. For **child car seats**, see above.

Don't **drink and drive** at all – apart from the safety of yourself and your children, there are

frequent random breath tests and the alcohol limit is just 0.05%. The **speed limits** are 130 km/h (80 mph) on toll motorways, 110 km/h (68 mph) on dual carriageways and motorways without tolls, and 90 km/h (56 mph) on other roads except in towns, where it's 50 km/h (31 mph). On wet roads the limits are, respectively, 110 km/h (68 mph), 100 km/h (62 mph) and 80 km/h (50 mph); in fog with visibility of less than 50 m it's 50 km/h (31 mph) even on toll motorways. For cars towing a caravan, if the weight of the seat for their age, except in certain mitigating circumstances. There is no such law in France, and the types of car seat provided by **car-hire companies** vary. Easycar, for instance, provides infant seats for babies up to 9 months (or 9 kg) and boosters for children up to 10, Europcar provides seats for the ranges 0–12 months, 1–3 years and 4–7 years. You need to reserve them when you book your car; expect to pay about €17–30 (£11–20). If that seems expensive, it's relatively hassle-free to bring your own car seat or booster by plane – they just go in the hold with your luggage (although they may come out at a separate point in the baggage hall; ask a member of staff if yours doesn't materialise). A good source of information on car seats both for the UK and abroad is **www.childcar seats.org.uk**.

- A **first-aid kit; window shades**; children's **travel pillows**; a portable **highchair** (p. 23); a **cooler box** to replenish with drinks and snacks each time you set off; **wipes, nappies** and **plastic bags** (for nappies or motion sickness); **blankets, sweaters** and a **change of clothes.**
- **Audiotapes/CDs** of your children's favourite stories or songs, **sticker books, crayons/paper** or a **magic slate**, or a **compact travel book** with games and activities, such as the *Amazing Book-a-ma-thing for the Backseat* (Klutz, £10.99 from *www. amazon.co.uk*).

trailer exceeds that of the car, the limit is 65 km/h (40 mph) if the excess is less than 30%, or 45 km/h (28 mph) if the excess is more than 30%. Speeding is supposed always to result in fines *and* a court appearance, but it's not clear what this means for foreign drivers.

Hiring cars: The best way to hire a car in France is in advance, via the Internet, so you have **proof of your booking** when you arrive – a Hertz office once denied all knowledge of a phone booking of mine despite two preliminary calls. When collecting your car, as well as your reservation printout, you need a **driving licence** for each driver, additional photo ID (your national identity card, or your British passport), your passport if you're a non-EU resident, and a credit card in the main driver's name (sometimes two cards for expensive models). Different hire firms have different **lower age limits for drivers**; it's generally 21–25, but it can depend on how expensive the model is, and you may have to pay a young drivers' surcharge. For child seat hire, see p. 36.

Car hire in France has got much less expensive in the past few years – I've been quoted as little as £119 for a week's hire of a compact four-door car at Caen railway station in early September. But prices seem to vary enormously, even between cars of a similar size, so make sure you get a few quotations from different firms – and check that they include unlimited mileage, full insurance, tax and 24-hr breakdown assistance. With some cheaper deals, you may need to buy a damage excess liability waiver so you're not liable for a considerable initial chunk of loss or damage to the car. This starts at around €6.50 (£4.35) a day. Good deals are often available if you book via low-cost airline websites (p. 29) at the same time as buying your air ticket. All of the major car hire companies operate in France, including the following. The websites will tell you which operates where.

Avis www.avis.co.uk

Easycar www.easycar.com

Europcar www.europcar.com

Hertz www.hertz.co.uk

National/Citer www.citer.com

If you bring a car hired in the UK into France (for instance if your own car is involved in an accident just before your holiday), you must inform the hire firm that the car is being taken to France to ensure you're covered there. You might need to show the French police the rental agreement to prove you have this insurance.

Motorhomes: Motorhomes are subject to the same road rules as cars. You can stop for a few hours in a motorway service area but note that toll tickets are only valid for a limited time. Nor are you allowed to stop overnight at the roadside. To find out about the 1,700 places adapted for motorhomes (i.e. providing waste disposal and water) in France, including campsites, see the French-language *Camping-car Magazine* (available at newspaper kiosks), or print out sites for your area from its website, *www.camping car-magazine.fr*, ahead of your trip.

If you're not bringing your own motorhome, you can hire one from Paris: try *www.motor home-hire-france.com*. A 4–5-person motorhome with unlimited mileage for one week in high season can cost €1000–1500 (£670–1005), with special rates for long-term rents (two months or longer). Damage excess liability waiver and 24-hr breakdown assistance are optional but highly advisable; you can also get child seats, bedding sets, bike racks, folding picnic tables and satellite navigation (with a hefty deposit).

By Plane There are no low-cost airlines operating within France. If you fly to Paris, you can continue to Cherbourg with Twin Jet (p. 174) for about €100–300 (£67–200), depending on how far ahead you book. Or you could fly to Rennes in eastern Brittany with Air France (p. 30) for about €125 (£84).

Children pay the full fare from the age of two; below that they occupy your lap.

When travelling with a baby, you may want to invest in a **Baby B'Air Flight Safety Vest**, which attaches to your seatbelt to protect lap-held little ones during turbulence, and allows you to sleep knowing your baby can't fall from your arms. It costs about £27; see *www.babybair. com*. Check first, though, that your airline doesn't already have babyholders to loan you.

By Train France's national rail system, run by the **SNCF** (*www.voyages-sncf.com*, with versions in other languages), is efficient and inexpensive compared with the British network, and a very good way of getting between cities and larger towns. Its famously zippy **TGV** (*train à grande vitesse* or 'very fast train') network is ever expanding – see *www.tgv.com*, also available in English, for an excellent click-able, up-to-date route map (it then takes you back to *www. voyages-sncf.com* to book). Normandy is much less well cov-ered by TGVs than many other regions. Still, standard trains within Normandy are good enough for your purposes. See 'Getting Around' in the sightsee-ing chapters for your options

between the main cities and towns in each *département*, with journey times. Branch lines serve some smaller towns (again, see the SNCF website), though to explore Normandy properly you really need your own wheels.

Expect to pay about €32 (£21.50) for a single ticket from Rouen to Caen (80 km/50 miles), €24 (£16) for a child aged 4–11 (under-4s travel free on a parent's lap on all trains, unless you want to pay for an extra seat). The very clear online booking system will tell you if you need a seat reservation (on some trains they're compulsory, on others you can't reserve). Note that onward tickets within France can be bought at the same time as your Eurostar ticket to Lille or Paris, via Eurostar or RailEurope (p. 32).

By Bus This is your least satisfac tory means of getting around Normandy except, perhaps, the Calvados coast (especially the Norman Riviera), which is well serviced by **Bus Verts** (p. 134). The same firm also runs a D-Day coastal route along the landing beaches. For more rural areas, it's not worth the hassle, especially for those with children. You're most likely to use French buses within large towns or cities, such as Le Havre; in this case, the basic system is that you get a ticket (about €1.20 or £0.80, under-5s free) that allows you any number of trips by bus and any other urban transport system within the following hour. That said, most Norman cities have fairly compact and walkable centres containing most of the sites, hotels and restaurants.

By Bike If you don't bring your own bikes, tourist offices can give you lists of hire outlets, or you may find that your hotel, B&B, gîte or campsite offers bike loan or hire. All hire shops have helmets, and most can also provide child seats and perhaps child trailers. My comment on French drivers (p. 26) should discourage you from riding with your family on all but the quietest country lanes. A better bet are Voies Vertes – walking, cycling, rollerblading and wheelchair-accessible tracks on former railtracks or canal towpaths. For information on Voies Vertes and Véloroutes (cycle routes), check out *http://troisv.amis-nature.org/sommaire.php3*. It also has advice on taking your bike on trains (a complex issue; you basically need to talk to the SNCF in each individual case), and in turn recommends *www.voiesvertes.com*, which has a clickable map of routes in Normandy and elsewhere. Tourist office websites also list routes in their areas.

ACCOMMODATION & EATING OUT

Accommodation

There are some stratospherically expensive hotels in Normandy, but on the whole, accommodation here represents seriously

good value to anyone used to hotel prices in the UK, which means that even if you're on a budget, you might allow yourselves an occasional splurge. I've based the price categories used within the Accommodation sections of the sightseeing chapters on the following ranges, based on lodgings per night for two adults and two children, without breakfast except in the case of B&Bs and the occasional hotel, as noted in individual reviews:

Very expensive: More than €290 (£195)

Expensive: €220–290 (£148–195)

Moderate: €110–220 (£74–148)

Inexpensive: Less than €110 (£74)

Very expensive options tend to be châteaux-hotels or grand old seaside hotels with gastronomic restaurants, swimming pools, babysitting services and more – fabulous places for the odd night or two, with a truly French feel and a welcoming attitude to children. In the expensive and moderate categories you'll find many very good seaside hotels, often with pools, though beware that most insist on half-board (breakfast and lunch or dinner in the hotel's restaurant) in high season, which can be limiting for those with children.

B&Bs (*chambres d'hôte*) split between the moderate and inexpensive categories; as a rule of thumb, the more rural they are, the cheaper they'll be. Most are cosy and welcoming; often they're on farms where children can pet the animals and sometimes join in with farming tasks. The inexpensive category also includes campsites, youth hostels and gîtes. The latter have long been the most popular option among families holidaying in France, since even relatively luxurious examples with pools, when broken down per head per night, work out very good value compared with hotels, and the self-catering facilities mean you save money on eating out too.

Campsites run the gamut from rowdy four- and five-star affairs with huge aquaparks, various sports facilities and children's entertainment to quiet sites in the grounds of historic châteaux, or green sites where the onus is on leaving a minimal 'environmental footprint'.

I've not reviewed any youth hostels in Normandy, since none are outstanding. However, if you're prepared for your accommodation to be a bit rough and ready (generally in rooms with two bunk beds, with a sink and perhaps an en-suite shower room), they can be fun places to stay, with readymade playmates on hand for the kids, communal kitchens, laundrettes and games rooms, and sometimes activities laid on. Single parents (p. 27) often get special rates. The French hostelling association, www.fuaj.org/eng/, translated (badly) into English, has links to individual hostel websites where they exist. You should expect to pay around

Breaking Journeys without Breaking the Bank

For cheap overnight stops en route, budget hotel chains Etap (www.etaphotel.com) and Formule 1 (www.hotelformule1.com) offer rooms with a double bed and a single bunk running over the top of it (suitable for over-5s) for around €37 (£24.80) a night (€28 or £18.75 in a Formule 1, where rooms have sinks but share showers and loos). Many also have enclosed car parks. If you're travelling in hot weather, it's worth finding one with air-conditioning, as they are often next to busy roads so can be noisy if you sleep with a window open.

We've used Etaps to drive far into the night with sleeping children, pulling up at the nearest when we've wanted to call it a day. If reception's closed, there are wonderful automated check-ins – you feed in your credit card and it spits out a room code. On one occasion we've found no rooms available, but we just relocated to a Formule 1 two minutes away. However, the really great thing about Etap is that you can book rooms in advance and cancel them up to 5pm on your day of arrival without paying a bean, meaning you can have the security of a reservation but back out if you fall behind schedule. Buffet breakfasts are €4pp (£2.70).

€12pp (£8) in a four-person room, including breakfast, plus €23 (£15.40) for annual family membership of FUAJ.

Just about every hotel and B&B I've reviewed in this guide offers **family rooms** for up to four people; if not, then interconnecting rooms or suites with comfortable sofabeds are available. Note that *'appartement'*, when used in the context of hotels, usually means a suite rather than a flat with self-catering facilities. **Cots** are usually provided, either free or for a small extra fee.

Breakfasts, though generally of high quality whatever the price range (almost invariably Continental or occasionally in the form of a buffet, they usually feature fresh, sometimes organic, farm produce), can get a bit monotonous – you may not think it now, but there will come a day when you can barely countenance a croissant, no matter how buttery and delicious. Hotel breakfasts, as elsewhere, can be wildly expensive.

Hotels

You're generally better off dealing directly with the 45 or so hotels and other accommodation options that I've recommended throughout this guide (or the local hotels, B&Bs, gîtes and campsites listed on **tourist board and tourist office websites)** than via a booking agency, online or otherwise. The best bet is to liaise via **e-mail**. This allows you to explain your requirements as a family and check exactly what's provided for children, from bottle warmers and cot linen to games consoles, and to have it in writing in case of queries or discrepancies when you get there. Hotels very often offer **special offers** or **last-minute deals** on their websites, but even if they don't, always ask if a better rate is available.

Where **centralised booking services** are best is in turning up late deals. For instance, *www. guidesdecharme.com* (available in English) works with a partner site offering charming inns and also more downmarket properties such as modern self-catering studio-apartments in popular resorts. The site *www.logis defrance.com* also offers reservations at approved hotels around France, including late deals, but its booking system is prone to bugs.

Hôtel-Résidences

This has been my revelation of 2006 – apartments in *résidences* attached to hotels, so you have the flexibility of self-catering but can also use the hotel facilities. An example is Le Grand Large in Granville in the Manche (p. 204), where you can get apartments with kitchenettes adjoining a three-star hotel with a lounge and bar, sun terraces, a sauna and jacuzzi, a lift to the beach, a launderette and an in-room breakfast service.

At present there aren't too many *hôtel-résidences* around,

Children's Gîtes (*Gîtes d'Enfants*)

This school-holiday programme allows children aged 4–16 to enjoy country life and outdoor activities with other children (often including the host's own family) at an establishment – usually a farm – inspected by the French department of health and social services. Activities might include butter-making, rambling, making herb gardens, picking flowers, going on picnics, dance and foreign language lessons, handicrafts, canoeing, riding and sailing. You're probably thinking you came on holiday to spend time *with* your children, not to fob them off on somebody else, but if they're independent and enjoy discovering nature and wildlife, they might enjoy doing this for a week while you stay in a hotel nearby, so you can pop in and see them every day but grab some 'adult time' and perhaps even a bit of pampering. It's generally a good idea – at least the first time – to send a child with a sibling, cousin or friend of a similar age. There are **Mini-Gîtes** for ages 4–10, generally accommodating just two to five children on a farm; **Junior-Gîtes** for six or more children aged 6–10, with the owner helped by a trained assistant; and **Clubs Jeunes** for between 12 and 35 children aged 11–16, with more active sports. Expect to pay around €285 (£191) a week; some places also offer activities by the day.

For children's gîtes by *département*, see **www.gites-de-france.fr**. Some owners speak English, where indicated, but this is obviously a great way for children who already speak some French to improve their language skills.

but I predict they'll proliferate in coming years.

Gîtes & Apartments

Many readers of this book will probably be looking for self-catering accommodation in a quaint old half-timbered Norman cottage not too far from the sea, where they can relax and feel at home abroad, with the option of cooking for themselves. You get more space and lower prices than at a hotel, your children won't disturb people in neighbouring rooms and you save money on restaurants (which children get sick of pretty quickly anyway). The downside can be a lack of things to do on a rainy day, especially if you're in a gîte without a TV/video player or covered pool – it's worth having a few contingency plans up your sleeve (save indoor treats such as aquaria for bad weather). Some gîtes can also be a bit grotty, filled with the owners' unwanted furniture. Look carefully at website photographs, and check exactly what's included – if you're there for two weeks, it's a pain to waste precious holiday hours in search of a launderette if your gîte doesn't come equipped with a washing machine.

Luckily – at least for visitors – the gîtes market is oversaturated in many parts of France, which means you get copious choice and good deals, especially if you can butch it out and wait for a last-minute deal. Good sites include *www.interhome.co.uk*, *www.frenchconnections.co.uk* and *www.cheznous.com*. With the last two you can check availability on the site but you book direct with the owner, which means they can be better value. All three offer travel discounts. The British Sunday newspapers carry ads for countless other firms arranging self-catering accommodation. Or official **French organisations** *www.clevacances.com* and *www. gites-de-france.com* have websites in English.

You can, don't forget, just type 'gîte' and the name of the area or nearest town into a search engine such as Google and see what it throws up – many owners now have their own websites. Make it easier for yourself by adding extra search-words such as 'child-friendly' or 'toddler' or 'swimming pool', though this may exclude suitable places that haven't set up their website properly (their problem, not yours).

Prices vary according to location, facilities (including pools, play areas, the availability of babysitting and so on), luxuriousness and time of year, but as a guideline expect to pay €300–500/wk (£200–335) for a gîte for four without a pool in the Caen area.

Finally, it's a long shot, but you may strike lucky at a **home-swap** site such as *www.home exchange.com*, whereby you try to match up with someone who will swap houses with you. You can sift through, say, the Normandy listings looking for someone who has listed your home country (or city) as somewhere they'd like to stay. If they like the look of your house as much as you do theirs, and you can agree on a date, you get free accommodation and someone to housesit for you while you're away. Basic annual membership of this website is US$25 (£13.18); or US$59.95 (£31.62) if you want to list your own property.

Camping

France has about 11,000 campsites, all of them listed on the excellent directory *www.camping france.com*, with versions in English and other languages and a clickable map for searches by region or a themed search facility (sites with direct beach access, scenic inland sites, sites with indoor pools or waterparks, sites with children's clubs, sites with fitness and spa facilities – and so on). It gives detailed descriptions and fees for each, and lets you book online, though it also gives telephone numbers, websites and e-mail addresses of the sites so you can do it directly. It even has mini area guides and links to tourist offices.

In the Accommodation sections of the individual sightseeing chapters, I've provided my own picks of the more than 500 campsites in Normandy; my personal preference is for smaller, 'green' sites and sites in the grounds of châteaux, but I recognise the attraction of large sites with indoor pools and children's clubs and have recommended some accordingly. For companies specialising in camping and mobile home holidays at these sorts of sites, including ferry travel, see p. 31.

Eating Out

Some people come to France for the food alone, and one of the joys of exploring this country is that you can generally walk into the most modest-looking café in any small town and be assured of getting a good meal of fresh, well-prepared food, even if it's just an omelette, a *croque-monsieur* (p. 224) or a *salad composée* (main-course salad). Normandy has a reputation for its hearty dishes, based on local dairy produce and the fruits of its many orchards; see p. 222 for a summary of Norman cuisine, and p. 221 for a French food vocabulary, including specialities of the region. Under such circumstances, it's amazing that McDonald's and other fast-food chains have been able to get a foothold here, though I admit to using the latter as handy stop-offs when on the road with my children, for their playrooms and loos.

Most French restaurants and cafés are welcoming to children, and many have **children's menus** (generally about €7.50 – £5), though often these feature little more than *steak haché* (p. 226) or ham and chips, then ice cream, and can get very repetitive. **Vegetarians** are still poorly catered for in this largely carnivorous country; omelettes, some main-course salads (above) and margherita pizzas are helpful standbys, but it's always wise to double check with your waiter that, for instance, pieces of ham won't sneak their way into such dishes. Naturally, in Normandy with its wonderful fresh **seafood**, those who eat fish but not meat won't go wanting. **Crêperies** are another godsend for both veggies and parents – in fact, crêpes are the perfect fast food – they take less than five minutes to prepare, are fairly nutritionally sound and cost next to nothing! But again, you'll get to a point where you can't face another crêpe.

Restaurants and cafés generally have at least one **highchair**, but if you're travelling by car, bring a portable one (p. 23) for places that don't or where the existing one is taken. Your only real problem as a parent in France is that mealtimes are very rigid, and you're unlikely – at least outside cities or resorts in high season – to find somewhere serving food outside standard **lunch and dinner hours** (generally noon–2/2.30pm and 7/7.30pm–9.30/10pm). For those, like me, spoilt rotten by cities such as London with their all-day eating options, this can be very frustrating. If you want to have dinner out, your only solution may be to encourage your child to have an early-afternoon nap so they can make it through to dinner without going into meltdown. **Brasseries** and **crêperies** often have all-day service (*service continu*), but again, only at the seaside in season or in larger towns. *Brasseries* can also get smoky because they have bar areas. On no account be tempted by a roadside **Buffalo Grill**; these look fun and have all the child-friendly trappings, including all-day service and sometimes even bouncy castles, but when we once succumbed, the food was so shockingly bad we tremble every time we pass one now.

I've tried to cover the whole range of options in my 'Eating Out' sections in the sightseeing chapters, recognising that if you're not staying in some form of accommodation with self-catering facilities, the cost of eating out at least once or twice a day, even in France, is going to mount up. But alongside unpretentious *crêperies*, you'll find reviews of some stunning gastronomic restaurants that welcome children – perfect for occasional treats, especially if you take advantage of **fixed-price lunch** or **dinner menus (set menus)** rather than ordering from the *carte* (à la carte menu). I've based my **price categories** on the following ranges, based on two adults and two children

consuming two courses plus drinks:

Expensive: More than €75 (£50)

Moderate: €45–75 (£30–50)

Inexpensive: less than €45 (£30)

GETTING CHILDREN INTERESTED IN NORMANDY

Involving children in planning your trip is the best way to get them interested. As well as using this book to show them what to look forward to in northern France, whether it be riding a Percheron-pulled carriage through the forest or kite-flying on the beaches of the Norman Riviera, introduce them to books such as **Bonjour France!** (Beautiful Books, £9.99), with maps, games, quizzes and activities on France for 7–12-year-olds, who can register their scores on the Young Travellers Club website (*www.youngtravellersclub.co.uk*). Its contents include 'Beach Olympics and Rainy Day Games'.

Though most of the well-loved Madeline books by Ludwig Bemelmans, about the escapades of a French schoolgirl, are set in Paris, **Madeline Says Merci: The Always Be Polite Book** (about £3 on *www. amazon.co.uk*), republished in paperback in late 2006, is a good way of getting children aged about 4–10 interested in France and in learning some French phrases.

Depending on your destination, children's ages and their/your proficiency in French, you might like to buy in advance an issue or two of **Normandie Junior** (*www.normandie-junior.com*), a quarterly French-language magazine for ages 7–12. Other possibilities are the books **Tilou au Mont-St-Michel** and **Tilou en Seine-Maritime** – two in a series of tours around France by a four-and-a-half-year-old bear who's a 'petit globetrotter', aimed at ages 4–8. Books cost €5.90 (roughly £3.95) from *www.clubtilou.com* or *www.amazon.fr*.

To get children aged about seven and up interested in the **Impressionist art** that took seed in Normandy, examples of which you will see in many local galleries (including the **Musée Malraux** in Le Havre; p. 75), get a copy of the wonderful **Linnea in Monet's Garden** (Christine Bjork and Lena Anderson), about a Swedish girl visiting Claude Monet's garden at Giverny (p. 98), with watercolours, photos and a biography of the artist, reproductions of paintings and discussion of the techniques. There's a DVD version too. Other recommended books on the subject are **The Magical Garden of Claude Monet** (Laurence Anholt), **Katie Meets the Impressionists** (James Mayhew), **Claude Monet: Sunshine and Waterlilies** (True Kelley) and **A Picnic with Monet** (Julie Merberg and Suzanne Bober). There's even one especially for toddlers, **Once Upon a Lily Pad: Froggy Love in Monet's Garden** (Kathleen Fain and Joan Sweeny), in which a frog in a pond watches Monet at work in his garden. All are available from Amazon.

On a much darker note, **D-Day Landings: The Story of the Allied Invasion** (Richard Platt) introduces children aged about 4–8 to the Allied invasion of Normandy, with photos, fact boxes and age-appropriate anecdotes from World War II. Older children (aged about 9–12) will probably be fascinated by **The Orphans of Normandy** (Nancy Amis), which tells the true story of 100 girls who were forced to leave their orphanage on the bank of the Orne when Allied forces invaded Normandy in 1944. They lived in a mine for 38 days, then walked 240 km (149 miles). The book contains reproductions of the girls' own illustrations of their experience from the joint diary they kept, and black and white photos.

For very small children, and older ones too, you can pick up locally themed **coloriage** (colouring) books in most local newsagents: topics include Normandy, Mont-St-Michel and Lighthouses.

Lastly, familiarize your family with the culinary delights of Northern France by getting a copy of *Cuisine Grandmère* by Jenny Baker and trying out some of the authentic Norman recipes.

FAST FACTS: NORMANDY

Area Codes See 'Telephone' below.

Baby Equipment Most hotels, B&Bs and gîtes provide cots, often for a charge (an average of €8–£5.35), and some offer extras such as bottle warmers and changing mats. Beware that some places don't provide linen for cots because of allergy risks. Supermarkets, especially large ones, are good for baby equipment (*matériel de puériculture*), from nappies and jarred food to baths and car seats, but if you want to go to a specialist retailer, many out-of-town *centre commerciales* (shopping parks) have baby/toddler supermarkets such as Bébe 9 (*www.bebe9.com*).

Babysitters Most expensive and some moderate hotels arrange sitters for guests, usually a tried-and-tested local (or someone from an agency) rather than one of their staff. Most need at least 24 hours' notice. You usually pay the sitter directly; rates average €8–10 (£5.35–6.70) per hour. Some gîte-owners also offer babysitting, either themselves or by a family member such as a daughter. Alternatively, *www.fr.cityvox.fr*, a 'going out guide', has 'Garde d'Enfants' *annonces* (in French, even on the English-translation pages*)* by local babysitters, but you'll need to satisfy yourself as to their credentials and references.

Breastfeeding Breastfeeding in public is much less common in France than the UK, and you may get stared at, especially if you're feeding an older infant. You may want to brazen it out, since breastfeeding is your natural right, or you might prefer to find an out-of-the-way spot.

Business Hours Shops outside large towns generally open at 9 or 10am (7 or 8am for bakeries) and close at 6 or 7pm, with a two-hour break at lunchtime (usually 12.30–2.30pm). Many also open on Sunday mornings (in conjunction with a market) but close on Monday mornings or all of Monday. Very large supermarkets often stay open until late (9 or 10pm), and larger towns have convenience stores open until late in the evening. Supermarkets increasingly open in the morning on public holidays too, except Christmas Day. Banks always close on public holidays; the rest of the time they're generally open 9.30am–4.30pm, with a lunch break in smaller towns. In the latter they may be closed on Monday afternoons but open on Saturday mornings. Most have 24-hr ATMs (p. 21). Restaurants generally open noon–2/2.30pm and 7/7.30–9.30/10pm; larger towns and resorts usually have some with *service continu* (p. 46). Public museums usually close on Monday or Tuesday and on public holidays, but most tourist sites open on public and school holidays. Some rural attractions and seaside hotels in Normandy close for part or all of the winter, and many businesses, though not hotels and rarely restaurants, close for the whole of August, when the French take their holidays en masse.

Car Hire See p. 37.

Chemists Staff at chemists (*pharmacies*), recognisable by a green cross, can provide first aid in minor emergencies. Rotas of pharmacies operating out of normal hours (9am–1.20pm and 2.30–7/8pm Mon–Sat) are posted in every chemist's window and in local papers. It's a good idea to take a first-aid course yourself; there's a CD-Rom version (about £30) developed in collaboration with St John's Ambulance: see *www. firstaidforkids.com.*

Climate See 'When to Go', p. 22.

Currency See 'Money', p. 20.

Dentists For emergency dental treatment in Paris, call ☎ *01 43 37 51 00* (SOS Dentistes); outside Paris go to your nearest hospital or health centre.

Doctors Some upmarket hotels have doctors on call, though they can be expensive private ones. Alternatively, local newspapers list doctors on call (*médécins de service*) and chemists (above) open outside

normal hours, or there may be information posted outside the local *mairie*. If you're staying in one place for a while, it's a good idea to make a list of emergency contact details and pin them up by the front door (check first that your hosts haven't already provided one in their welcoming pack).

Driving Rules See p. 34.

Electricity Electricity in France runs on 220-volt, 50-cycle AC. Visitors from the UK and Ireland need a two-pin European adapter (easily available at French supermarkets) to use their own appliances. Visitors from North America need a voltage transformer (unless the appliance has a dual voltage switch) and plug adapter. Many hotels can loan guests adapters.

Embassies & High Commissions There are embassies or consulates for the UK, Ireland, USA, Canada, Australia and New Zealand in Paris; these are your point of contact for passport and legal problems. For contact details, see *www.expatries.diplomatie. gouv.fr/annuaires/annuaires.htm.*

Emergencies Staff in most hotels are trained to deal with emergencies, so call the front desk before you do anything else. Otherwise, for an ambulance, call ☎ *15*, for the police ☎ *17*, for the fire service ☎ *18*.

Note that you will be expected to pay upfront for an ambulance and try to claim back your money later on your insurance. In rural areas it will probably be quicker to drive to the nearest **hospital** yourself anyway, unless it is dangerous to move the injured person. Note that **hospitals** are sometimes signposted *hôtel de dieu* rather than *hôpital* or *centre hospitalier*.

Holidays See p. 23.

Hospitals See above.

Internet Access See p. 28.

Legal Aid Contact your embassy or consulate (p. 49).

Lost Property Unless you know where you dropped an item and can ask there, go to the nearest police station. For important documents such as passports, contact your embassy or consulate (p. 49). For lost credit cards, see Money and Credit Cards. If you think your car may have been towed away for being illegally parked, ask at the local police station.

Mail Post offices, recognisable by their yellow signs with blue birds, are generally open Mon–Fri 8am–7pm and Sat 8am–noon. In towns and villages they tend to open Mon–Fri 9am–12.30pm and 2–5pm and Sat 9am–noon but close some afternoons. Postcards or letters to the UK weighing less than 20g cost €0.55 (£0.37) and take

1–5 days. Stamps are sold at tobacconists (*tabacs*) as well as post offices. If you need to receive mail while travelling, ask the sender to address it to your name c/o Poste Restante, Poste Centrale, in the relevant town. You will need to show proof of identity and pay a small fee.

Maps For online sources to plot your route, see p. 19. On the road, arm yourself with a good French road atlas: the Michelin Tourist & Motoring atlases (about £14; available from **www. amazon.co.uk** and at petrol stations and port shops) have the best level of detail.

Money and Credit Cards See also 'Money,' p. 20. For **lost/stolen cards**, call the relevant company immediately: for **Amex** call ☎ *01 47 77 72 00*, for **Visa** ☎ *0892 705705*, for **MasterCard** ☎ *01 45 67 84 84*, for **Diners** ☎ *0810 314159*. For emergency cash out of banking hours, you can have money wired to you online, by phone or from an agent's office via **Western Union** (☎ *0800 833833*; **www.western union.com**).

Newspapers & Magazines National **local dailies** include *Le Monde*, *Libération* and *Le Figaro*, all with online versions. The **regional newspaper** *Ouest-France* (**www.ouest-france.fr**) covers Basse-Normandie (Calvados, Manche and Orne), together with Brittany, and is a good source for local listings of markets, cinema showings and so on. For the children's magazine **Normandie Junior**, see p. 47. Otherwise, **English-language newspapers** from the UK and USA are widely available at newsstands and newsagents, usually a day old, without the supplements and at a premium price; the British *Guardian* has an international edition sold in Europe.

Police In emergencies, call 📞 *17*. For theft, file a report at a local station.

Post Offices See 'Mail'.

Safety See also p. 25, 'Travelling Safely with Children in Normandy'. The usual common-sense tips apply. Don't leave money or valuables on display on your person or in your car, and be wary of **pick-pockets** in confined public spaces. Don't allow yourself to be distracted by anyone while withdrawing money at a **cash point.** Don't walk alone in unlit open spaces such as parks (most of them are locked out of hours anyway) or even on seemingly innocuous residential streets after dark.

Taxes A 19.6% national **value-added tax** (VAT; *taxe valeur ajoutée* or **TVA** in French) is included in the price of most goods and hotel and restaurant services. Non-EU residents can reclaim most of this if they spend €175 (£117) or more at a

participating retailer – ask for *détaxe* papers and present them at the airport; the refund can go to your credit card.

Taxis In major towns and cities and at airports, taxis can be caught from ranks (look for square signs with 'Taxi' in white on a blue background); they can also be hailed in the street if the 'Taxi' sign on the roof is lit and the small lights under it are switched off. Away from main centres or airports, ask at your hotel or restaurant desk, or call a local firm – see *www. pagesjaunes.fr* (French *Yellow Pages* online) or ask at the tourist office. Check all taxis have a meter, and for airport taxis and out-of-town trips, ask the driver for an estimate before setting out. For rates, see p. 21.

Telephone Within France, all telephone numbers are 10 digits, including a 2-digit **area code** (📞 *02* in Normandy) that you must dial even if you're calling from within that area. Numbers starting with *06* are **mobile numbers** that it will cost you more to call; numbers starting with *0800* and *0805* are free to dial but are only available within France (other numbers beginning *08*, such as *0892* and *0820*, have differing rates).

To **call a French number from abroad**, you drop the initial 0 of the area code after dialling the international code (📞 *00 33* from the UK, 📞 *011 33* from the USA). To **dial the UK from**

France, you call the international code (📞 *00 44*) then the British number minus the first 0 of the area code; to call the USA, you dial *00 1* then the number. If you don't bring your mobile (p. 28), avoid using hotel phones because charges can be high; buy a phonecard (*télécarte*) from a post office, tobacconist or newsagents, prices start at €7.40 (£4.95) for 50 units. Incoming calls can be received at phoneboxes where the blue bell sign is shown.

Time Zone France is one hour ahead of British time, with clocks going forward by an hour for summertime or 'daylight saving', as in the UK, on the last Sunday in March and reverting on the last Sunday in October. France is six hours ahead of North American Eastern Standard Time (EST).

Tipping *Service compris* means that a service charge has been included on your bill, but you may wish to leave an extra tip (about 15% of the total) if service is very good.

Toilets and Baby-changing
There are public *toilettes* on the streets of most larger towns and cities, and in some smaller places. If you can't find one, bars and cafés are normally happy for you to use theirs, but for the sake of politeness, make a small purchase. Alternatively, try a large shop such as Printemps (p. 78) or a public museum. Few places, except big tourist sites such as zoos, aquaria and museums, have baby-changing facilities, so it's a good idea to be equipped with a portable folding mat.

Water French water is safe to drink. Many restaurants automatically serve you a carafe of chilled tap water (*eau du robinet*). Bottled water is *eau minérale plat/sans gaz* (still) or *gazeuse/pétillante* (sparkling).

Weather See p. 22.

3 Seine-Maritime

Untouristy, at least among overseas visitors, the *département* of the Seine-Maritime is more than likely to be your first stop during a holiday in Normandy given its proximity to Paris and the ferry ports to the north (it also has two of its own). But try not to hurry through – this is an area with an enormous amount to offer families, not least the medievally quaint city of Rouen, the *ville aux cent clochers* ('city of a hundred spires'), with its jagged roofscape that is said to resemble the flames that devoured Joan of Arc here in the 15th century, together with some fascinating museums. Then there's modern Le Havre, newly listed by UNESCO as a model of urban design, and a number of classic seaside resorts that have drawn Parisians since the fashion for sea bathing took off in Dieppe in 1824.

The natural landscapes here, especially the white cliffs of the 'Alabaster Coast' – which are the highest in Europe – and the interior dotted with placid cows and tall dovecotes, can be spellbinding, but there are countless human works of art to admire too, from Claude Monet's Impressionist paintings and the record-breaking span of the Pont de Normandie to cute, heart-shaped Neufchâtel cheese. Like the rest of Normandy, a land of gooey cheese and crunchy apples, the Seine-Maritime is a foodies' paradise – Rouen alone is fêted for its duck, its macaroons, its *mirlitons* (vanilla and almond tarts) and other pastries. And that's not to mention the seafood, which is sold on the quaysides of just about every coastal town but is especially good at Dieppe and Le Tréport, which also have great fish markets.

Essentials

Getting There

By Plane At the time of writing, Skysouth (☏ *01273 463673*, *www.skysouth.co.uk*) has just launched 45-min daily flights between Brighton on the British south coast and Le Havre airport (*www.havre.aeroport.fr*) just north of the city. There are no other flights between the UK and the Seine-Maritime, or even into the *département* from Paris, though Rouen airport (*www.rouen. aeroport.fr*), 10 km (6.2 miles) east of the city at Boos, has flights to Italy and Spain and to other French cities via Lyon, with Air France (p. 30).

Outside the Seine-Maritime but only 80 km (49 miles) from Rouen, Beauvais airport (*www. aeroportbeauvais.com*) is a possible entry point for eastern Normandy, with flights from Dublin (1 hr 35 mins), Shannon (1 hr 50 mins) and Glasgow Prestwick (1 hr 30 mins) and other European cities with budget operator Ryanair (p. 29; note that the firm refers to it as 'Paris–Beauvais').

By Ferry Following the demise of Hoverspeed, Transmanche (p. 31) is the only firm offering sailings (at least twice daily all year) between Newhaven and Dieppe, taking about 3 hours.

SEINE-MARITIME

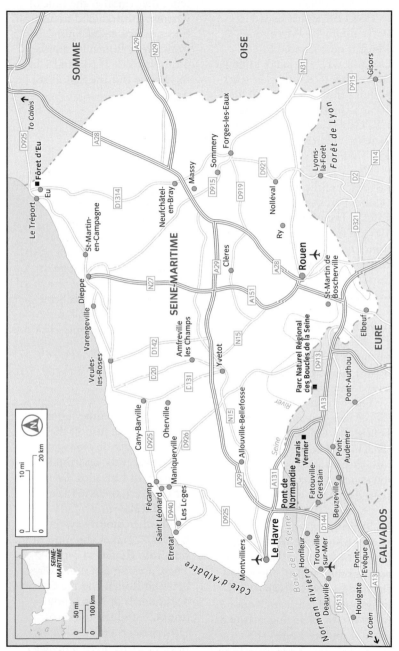

Ships are basic, but four-person cabins are available.

P&O Ferries has ceased its **Portsmouth–Le Havre** route, which is now serviced by **LD Lines** (p. 31). The single sailing a day in each direction takes 4 hrs 30 mins from France and 6 hrs 30 mins (overnight) from the UK. Cabins are quite basic but there's a children's soft play area and TV lounge showing cartoons.

Alternatively, you are within easy reach of the **shortest Channel crossings**: Dieppe is 145 km from Boulogne-sur-Mer, 175 km from Calais and 220 km from Dunkerque. At the time of writing, companies operating on these routes are: **P&O Ferries** (*www.poferries.com*, Dover–Calais, 90 mins), **Norfolkline** (*www.norfolk-line.com*, Dover–Dunkerque, 1 hr 45 mins) and the budget operator **Speedferries** (*www.speedferries.com*, Dover–Boulogne, 55 mins).

You can also take the **Eurotunnel** (*www.eurotunnel.com*, Folkestone–Calais; p. 32) through the Channel Tunnel; this takes just 35 mins and you don't have to get out of your car during the train ride.

By Train If you come into France from London or Ashford (Kent) by **Eurostar** (*www.eurostar.com;* p. 32), you have the option of purchasing good-value onward tickets to **Rouen** or **Le Havre**, changing at **Lille** or **Paris**. London–Rouen is 5 hours, London–Le Havre nearly 6 hrs. You can also take the Eurostar just to **Calais**.

There are no fast TGVs servicing the region at the time of writing, but standard trains from **Paris** to **Rouen** take just 1 hr 15 mins; from Rouen it's another 55 mins to Le Havre and 1 hr to Dieppe (for the SNCF, see p. 39).

VISITOR INFORMATION

The website of the **Comité Départemental de Tourisme** (CDT; p. 18), *www.seine-maritime-tourisme.com*, has a page with contact details of all the Seine-Maritime's tourist offices and *syndicats d'initiative*: click on 'Découvrez la Seine-Maritime', then scroll to the bottom of the page and click on the link.

Orientation

Rouen, the *département* capital, is towards its southern border with the Eure, just off the **A13** or '**Autoroute de Normandie**' motorway (toll) up from **Paris** to **Caen** in Calvados. Branching off the A13, the **A131** takes you up to **Le Havre**.

Another motorway, the **A151/N27**, takes you most of the way from Rouen to **Dieppe**. There are also fast motorways between Rouen and the **Channel ports** north of Normandy (the A28 and the toll A16). Otherwise, there's a good network of main *routes nationales* (p. 35).

Getting Around

Travelling by public transport is more feasible here than in many parts of northern France; if you need help with **train and bus schedules**, tourist offices should be your first port of call. Having said this, you will limit yourself severely in terms of what you can see and do and also where you can stay if you don't have your own wheels, missing out on lots of the Seine-Maritime's more rural (and charming) attractions and accommodation options.

If you don't bring your own, **car hire** is available at **Le Havre** (Europcar: airport and 51 quai Southampton, 📞 *02 35 25 21 95*), **Rouen** (Europcar: airport and place Bernard Tissot by the train station, 📞 *02 32 08 39 09*) and, outside Normandy, **Beauvais** airport (Avis, 📞 *03 44 05 22 50*). If you come to **Calais** on Eurostar, you can hire cars at its train station (Europcar, 📞 *03 21 96 96 50*).

Child-Friendly Events & Entertainment

Festival International de Cerf-Volant ★★★ You haven't

seen kites until you've been to Dieppe's International Kite Festival, where they are present in all guises and sizes, from cows to Indian gods and giant dragons, soaring and swooping above the beach over the course of nine days. The festival attracts about 1000 entrants from around the world. Even if you're only spectating, this makes for an awesome day out. Steer the children towards the *Espace Enfance et Jeunesse*, where they can take part in kite-making workshops, create wind and sound machines for the 'wind field', explore a sound maze in the shape of a spider's web and more. There are also demonstrations of buggy- and kite-jumping, kite-flying tuition (including for the disabled), competitions (kite battles, for instance), exhibitions on the history of kites around the world, stilt-walkers, jugglers, street theatre and a procession. Above all, don't miss the night-flying session combined with a *son-et-lumière* show – a jaw-dropping display.

Mid-September. seafront, Dieppe (📞 02 32 14 40 60 (tourist office); ***http://dieppe-cerf-volant.org****). Admission free.*

Fête du Cheval Great fun for

horsey families, this three-day festival in a scenic forest south of Dieppe features riding competitions, displays of brood mares from the Haras National du Pin at Argentan (p. 114), a parade through Forges-les-Eaux, a horse auction, sideshows with ferrets and the like, and farmers' and craft markets. Pony rides are

Norman horses

offered all day, and entertainment continues long into the evenings with the likes of country music concerts, a disco and a fireworks finale.

Late July. Bois de l'Epinay, nr Forges-les-Eaux, 55 km (34 miles) southeast of Dieppe on D915 (✆ 02 32 89 97 39 (tourist office)).

Fête Jeanne d'Arc ★ Once burnt at the stake here (p. 73), Joan of Arc is now Rouen's heroine and the subject of an annual two-day festival during which the streets radiating out from the cathedral (p. 69) come alive with theatre, music, parades, stilt-walkers, fire-eaters and minstrels. There's usually also a medieval market with craftspeople selling their wares and demonstrating their skills.

Late May. Place de la Cathédrale and around, Rouen (✆ 02 32 08 32 40 (tourist office)).

Théâtre Le Passage An energetic supporter of theatre as a way of bringing children and parents together in a shared universe of magic and poetry, this superb Fécamp theatre hosts a special *Enfantine* programme in its Petit

Théâtre, a charming old cinema. If you speak good French, you can come and enjoy shows such as *Alice in Wonderland*. Age ranges vary, but can start as low as 18 months, and many of the general performances – especially the frequent puppet shows and related 'théâtre des objets' (a very physical object-based theatre) and the operas – are deemed suitable for children aged about 10 and up.

54 rue Jules Ferry, Fécamp (✆ 02 35 29 22 81; www.theatrelepassage. fr). Open all year; show times vary. Admission prices vary; children's shows €4 (£2.70).

Village Viking ★ Every second year the grounds of the 16th century Château d'Eu, on the site of a fortress that belonged to William the Conqueror, host this 10-day festival. It includes reconstructions of scenes from everyday Viking life (including a slave market) and battles, jousting, catapulting, sporting contests, costumed parades, a mock funeral of a Viking lord, performances on reproductions of Viking instruments, replica boats, an exhibition of tin soldiers, craft demonstrations and a medieval market. Next scheduled for August 2007, it attracts more than 300 participants from Britain, Ireland, Norway and elsewhere. Taverns and food stalls provide food cooked to ancient recipes.

August, odd-numbered years. Château d'Eu, Eu, 3 km (1.8 miles) southeast of Le Tréport on D925 (✆ 02 35 86 04 68 (tourist office); www.ville-eu.fr). Admission: €4 (£2.70) adults, €1 (£0.67) children 6–12.

Joan of Arc Church, Rouen

Le Volcan, Le Havre

Le Volcan ⭑ Two volcano-shaped buildings designed by Brazilian architect Oscar Niemeyer in the 1980s, *Le Volcan* (nicknamed the 'elephant's foot') and *Le Petit Volcan* together constitute a world-class venue where you shouldn't be surprised to see big international names such as the Merce Cunningham Dance Company and the BBC Symphony Orchestra. Children's shows are generally hosted, appropriately enough, in Le Petit Volcan – the eclectic programme might include an African acrobatic circus troupe, a performance of *Pinocchio* by a Brazilian puppet company or interpretations of various tales by the Brothers Grimm. Age limits vary according to the show, but most cater for children aged eight and up.
Espace Oscar Niemeyer, Le Havre (☎ 02 35 19 10 10; www.levolcan. com). Open all year; show times vary. Admission varies; children's shows generally €5 (£3.35).

Children's Top 10 Attractions

❶ Exploring the curious shapes of the luminous white cliffs of Etretat by foot, helicopter or plane; p. 64.

❷ Snail-painting at the Ferme aux Escargots at Maniquerville; p. 66.

❸ Watching the stunning music and light show recreate Monet's famous paintings on the façade of Rouen Cathedral; p. 69.

❹ Admiring the awesome flying displays and making sound machines at the International Kite Festival at Dieppe; p. 57.

❺ Solving a mystery with a 'gentleman-burglar' at the Clos Arsène Lupin; p. 70.

❻ Discovering the sculptures and art installations at the Artmazia labyrinth; p. 75.

❼ Learning about the history of French schools though old toys, games, furniture and more at the Musée National de l'Education; p. 74.

❽ Swinging through the treetops at one of three parcours acrobatiques; p. 76.

❾ Cycling along an old railtrack on a quirky multi-person Vélo-Rail; p. 77.

❿ Staying in a cow-themed room at the unique Manoir aux Vaches; p. 83.

Towns & Cities

Le Havre ★ Known primarily to British visitors as a ferry port (p. 30), Le Havre became the proud holder of a World Heritage Site listing by UNESCO in 2005, in recognition of its reconstruction by Auguste Perret after bombing in World War II. It's a place with plenty to keep you interested amidst its wide avenues and handsome raw concrete buildings. As well as an **art museum** with one of the world's best Impressionist collections (p. 75) and an iconic **cultural centre** that hosts children's shows (p. 59), it has a central 2 km sand-and-pebble **beach** with a playground, a skateboarding track, volleyball and *pétanque* pitches, a cycleway, landscaped gardens, watersports galore and restaurants and bars.

On the outskirts, the **Parc de la Forêt de Montgeon** counts mini-zoos, children's playgrounds, a hothouse, fountains, a discovery trail, a running track, a wheelchair track, football pitches, bike hire, lakes with pedaloes and rowing boats, and lawns and meadows for lazy days and picnics amidst its 200 hectares.

Le Havre's tourist office offers **port tours** by boat, and there are scenic **flights** over nearby landmarks (p. 76). Ask at the tourist office, too, about summer French-language heritage workshops, **Raconte-moi Le Havre**, hosted for 6–12-year-olds (accompanied by an adult).

For great food shopping, head for rue Voltaire and the 19th century covered market of **Les Halles Centrales**, with stalls and little shops selling wonderful fruit and veg, cheeses, seafood, breads, coffee, wine and more, plus lots of cafés for people-watching. Most are open Mon–Sat 9am–12.30/1pm and 2/2.30–7/7.30pm.

Tourist office: 186 boulevard Clemenceau, Le Havre (☏ 02 32 74 04 04; www.lehavretourisme.com).

Le Havre Port

Rouen ★★★ Joan of Arc was burnt at the stake in the Seine-Maritime's capital, and Monet painted its cathedral compulsively. Things are less dramatic these days, but it's a lovely city in which to wander, with its different-coloured half-timbered houses – many of which are corbelled (have storeys that jut out over the one below to increase space) and have *oriols* (small stone towers poking up from the shaft of the staircase) – its teashops and its quirky little details. These include, at no.74 rue St-Romaine by the cathedral, the 16th and 17th century **maison à pan de bois** with its wooden carvings of saints battling monsters and saving children. On nearby rue Martainville, there is a 14th century plague graveyard, the **Aître St Maclou**, surrounded by ossuaries with macabre carvings, with a cat's skeleton in a glass case near the entrance (it had been embedded in one of the walls, probably to fend off bad luck).

Back west of the cathedral, the **Gros Horloge** is an elaborate giant Renaissance clock straddling the street, with two faces but just one hand on each and a bull's-eye showing the phases of the moon; come at midday to see a divinity (one for every day of the week) appear on a chariot. The clock was restored in 2006, and at the time of writing the adjacent belfry was due to reopen at the end of that same year as a museum of 14th–19th century clock mechanisms, with

stunning views over Rouen from its summit.

There are a number of other wonderful museums here too (p. 70–75), including the **Muséum d'Histoire Naturelle** (198 rue Beauvoisine, ☎ 02 35 71 41 50). Reputed to have been second in France only to the natural history museum in Paris, this closed for a vast refurbishment project in 1996 and at the time of writing was scheduled to reopen, for the most part, in spring 2007. There is also the lovely, free **Jardin des Plantes** (114 avenue des Martyrs de la Résistance, ☎ 02 32 18 21 30), with a 19th century orangery, hothouses, medicinal plants, rare trees, birds and fishponds, and children's play equipment dotted all around. Five minutes west of the city is the **Parc Animalier de la Forêt de Roumare** (☎ 02 35 52 68 10; also free), with observation posts for watching boar and interactive panels on the forest ecosystem. Two local theatrical venues, the **Centre Culturel Le**

Gros Horloge Clock

Shop Window, Rouen

Rive Gauche (☎ 02 32 91 94 93) and **Théâtre de la Chapelle St-Louis** (☎ 02 35 98 45 05) are known for their children's shows.

Practically speaking, the city hosts a weekly **fleamarket**, a big general **market** every morning save Monday on the place du Vieux-Marché, where Joan of Arc met her end and public executions were held, and lots of good **shops** (p. 78–79). A swish modern tram-style 'metro' gets you around in comfort, though the city centre is very walkable. Otherwise, in summer there's a *petit train* from place de la Cathédrale, **audioguides**, themed **walking tours** and tours by *calèche* (horse and carriage) and **boat trips** around the port. A free **children's trail**, *Mahou la Gargouille*, is available from the tourist office; in it, a friendly gargoyle brings the city to life for 8–12-year-olds, who get a free gift when they bring back the completed quiz sheet it contains. The tourist office also runs

a 2-nights-for-the-price-of-1 accommodation offer. For my hotel recommendations in the city, see p. 83.

Tourist office: 25 place de la Cathédrale, Rouen (☎ 02 32 08 32 40; www.rouentourisme.com).

Beaches & Resorts

Le Tréport A classic sea-bathing resort that still attracts its share of devotees from the French capital, Le Tréport is heaven for fish-lovers, who can buy seafood straight from the fishermen, at the fish market or in the many fish restaurants, especially along quai François Ier. Northeast along the coast from Dieppe, on the Normandy–Somme border, it has a long pebble beach and a **train routier** (road train; April to September) that ferries visitors around the town and its fishing port, over the border to see the restored seaside villas of Mers-les-Bains in the Somme, and to the charming inland town of Eu.

Dieppe holds the unlikely honour of having started the trend for sea-bathing resorts in France, after socialite the Duchesse de Berry, inspired by what the Prince Regent had made of Brighton across the Channel, began cajoling fellow Parisian aristocrats in 1824 to come and dip a toe (or more) in the chilly waters – to which they were carried, fully clothed, in sedan chairs (swimming in the sea was then considered rather *risqué*). Luxurious hotels and casinos sprung up to cater to them, and artists such as Monet and Renoir came in their wake, inspired by the quality of the light. Napoléon III and the empress Eugénie even visited; it was the latter who designed the town's long, green esplanade. The trend quickly spread around Normandy and further afield; Deauville in Calvados (p. 138) has remained one of the most chic and iconic examples.

Today, Dieppe is better known as a ferry port, but it still has decent beaches, and at the time of writing a new **station balnéaire** with indoor and outdoor pools, a fitness centre and a restaurant was scheduled to open in early 2007 as part of a larger regeneration project. There's a *petit train touristique* (April to September); a great **market** on Saturdays; the landmark **Café des Tribunaux** (1 place du Puits-Salé, ℂ *02 35 84 17 70*), excellent for people-watching; lots of art galleries; a sea museum and aquarium (p. 70) and the **Chateau-musée** (rue de Chastes, ℂ *02 35 06 61 99*), with displays on Dieppe's role as an ivory-trading and seafaring town (with a 16th century pirate, Jean Ango, as its hero). It also contains paintings of local scenes by artists such as Renoir and Braque, plus temporary exhibitions on themes such as Jean-Paul Gaultier's theatre-costume designs. While you're here, sample a bowl of *marmite dieppoise*, a creamy fish stew offered almost everywhere, including the useful **Tout Va Bien** café/brasserie/crêperie/ice cream parlour at 3 quai Henri IV. This quay is a good place for all-day eateries if you're waiting for a ferry, among them the **Mouette à Vélo** ('Cycling Seagull') crêperie at no.109. There are also beachfront cafés serving decent sandwiches and *moules-frites*.

Le Tréport Seafront

You can take half-hour **boat trips** along the cliffs, with guided commentary, and in the old prison, the **Musee du Vieux Tréport** (rue de l'Anguainerie, ☎ 02 35 86 13 36) has a 19th-century beach scene with old beach tents and prim bathing outfits, model boats, traditional costumes, fishing and lifeguard equipment and other artifacts relating to the town's history.

20 km (12½ miles) northeast of Dieppe off D925. Tourist office: quai Sadi Carnot (☎ 02 35 86 05 69; www.ville-le-treport.fr).

Veules-les-Roses ★ Popular with visiting Parisians for its beauty, this seaside town is more than just a pretty face – its seafront **Jardin d'Enfants** is a free year-round children's paradise with slides, sandpits and so on, and in high season a large paddling pool. All summer, there's also the **Crevettes Roses** ('Pink Shrimps') programme of sea-related creative activities for children aged 6–12, and a **Point Plage** (☎ 06 17 75 14 60) offering sea canoeing, sailing and more for ages eight and up. Below the cliffs, a wide plateau of rocks and sand banks is perfect for shrimping or catching *bigorneaux* (periwinkles; consult the tide tables first).

The town has two claims to fame – in 1882 writer Victor Hugo gave a banquet for its 100 poorest children, with a lottery in which all of them were winners and a fireworks display over the cliffs; and it has France's 'shortest river', at just 1.2 km

(¾ mile), where watercress is grown. You can take tours of this river, or just stroll around, checking out the tearooms, posh food shops, beach where seafood is sold fresh from the boats, Wednesday-morning market and old watermill.

25 km (15½ miles) west of Dieppe on D925. Tourist office: 27 rue Victor Hugo (☎ 02 35 97 63 05; www.veules-les-roses.fr).

Other Natural Wonders & Spectacular Views

Etretat ★★ A former fishing village that grew popular with Parisians in the 19th century and still gets busy with visitors from the capital in high summer, Etretat is best-known for its luminous white cliffs with their dramatic natural archways – they're so scenic, they drew the Impressionist master Claude Monet here several times, and the resulting paintings now sell for millions. They also gave this stretch of shore its lovely nickname, the **Alabaster Coast** (Côte d'Albâtre). Monet's favourite arch, the **Porte d'Etretat** just east of town, was likened by writer Guy de Maupassant to 'an immense elephant dipping its trunk in the water' – see if you agree (we did). The largest arch is the **Manneporte**, to the west, and there's also the **Aiguille** ('Needle'), which featured in a famous detective story by Arsène Lupin (p. 70). You can view the rocks from the Le Perrey promenade, but the tourist office can

Cliffs at Etretat

also supply itineraries for **clifftop walks** of 90 mins and up. You will discover, among other curiosities, the tiny **Musée Nungesser et Coli** (Falaise d'Amont, 📞 02 35 27 07 47), with displays on the lives of the eponymous aviators, whose plane, the *Oiseau Blanc*, was lost heading seawards over Etretat in 1927 in an attempt to cross the Atlantic. If that doesn't put you off, Le Havre airport offers **helicopter and plane trips** over the cliffs (p. 76). As souvenirs, **L'Etoile de Mer** (1 boulevard René Coty, 📞 02 35 28 02 68) sells decorative coins with images of the cliffs, plus shells and model ships.

In summer the **beach** has lifeguards and sections reserved for the use of little children and their families, and there's also the clifftop **Parc de Loisirs des Roches** overlooking the 'elephant arch', with a playground, a mini-golf course, a pool, a bouncy castle and children's pedaloes. But the resort really is best visited out of season. Either way,

you'll find some good accommodation (p. 81), a fine grocery, **Cressant** (10 avenue Georges V, 📞 02 35 27 01 56), famous for its caramels (fig, apple crumble, honey and other scrumptious flavours) and glorious sunsets.

25 km (15½ miles) northeast of Le Havre on D940. Tourist office: place Maurice Guillard (📞 02 35 27 05 21; www.etretat.net).

Aquaria & Animal Parks

There's an aquarium in Dieppe's **Estran, Cité de la Mer** (p. 70).

Ferme Au Fil des Saisons ★
This is a working farm where you can bring the children to feed sheep and ducks, meet Coquette ('Flirt') the mare, pigs, cows, rabbits and chickens, go for donkey-and-cart rides, learn to fish and join storytelling walks or suppers led by the farmer himself. You, meanwhile, might like to see the displays and video on linen production and *clos-masures* (rectangular Norman farm enclosures within

Norman Cows

high banks). All the family will like the discovery circuit dotted with games designed to 'awaken the senses' of young and old alike, taking in plants, orchards and ponds busy with wildlife, from bees and frogs to geese, with panels bearing explanations. You can also buy products both from here and neighbouring farms, including vegetables, honey and cider, and eat *tartines* (bread with garnishes) in the *tartinerie*.

Yémanville, Amfreville les Champs, 35 km (21¾ miles) northwest of Rouen off D142 (℘ 02 35 56 41 46). Open Mon, Fri and Sat 1.30–7pm, Sat 9.30am–noon. Admission free; guided walks and suppers €5–9 (£3.35–6).

Ferme aux Escargots ★★

Probably only in France would you get the opportunity to visit a working snail farm, so don't miss the opportunity to come and observe (during a French-language guided tour) how the slimey critters are bred and raised. You learn, among other fascinating facts, that snails

hibernate for 4–6 months of the year, awakening from their slumber in spring (the centre is closed all winter); that grease and black soap are placed around their enclosures to stop them escaping; that they are hermaphrodites; and that specimens raised in artificial conditions such as this, with optimal warmth and nutrition, are fully mature when they hatch – a process that takes two years in nature. Children get the chance to make snail paintings by dipping their bases in food colouring and letting them loose on a piece of paper, and to pet the other animals – rabbits, ducks and horses – on the farm. There's a kitchen where snail recipes are demonstrated, and a garden where you can picnic. On your way out, if you have the heart, you can buy freshly cooked or frozen snails, plus other farm produce and homemade ready-cooked meals. Or you can stay the night in a B&B room here, and sample some of the proprietress's gastropod-based treats.

La Hêtrée, Maniquerville, 10 km (6.2 miles) southwest of Fécamp on D79 (℘ 02 35 29 25 93). Guided tours April to August Sun–Thur 11am. Admission: €4 (£2.70) adults, €2.30 (£1.55) children aged 4–14.

Parc de Clères ★

This 13-hectare park set around a Renaissance castle and adjoining manor in a magnificent valley was set up by celebrated traveller Jean Delacour in the 1920s, partly as a research and conservation centre (it's now owned by

Room to Roost

The Pays du Caux – roughly, the stretch of countryside between Veules-les-Roses and Etretat – is famous for its distinctive giant **dovecotes or colombiers,** built in a variety of shapes (cylindrical, square or polygonal), topped with pigeon weathervanes and in some cases even matching the architectural style of the manor house to which they belonged (aristocrats used to keep pigeons to eat and to provide fertiliser). A good way to see some of the best examples is by following the 55-km (34-mile) walking/cycling **Route des Colombiers Cauchois** (available in map form from local tourist offices, or downloadable from *www.ot-bolbec. fr/colomb.htm*). There's also a **Musée des Colombiers Cauchois** (**℡** *02 35 96 69 69*) at Oherville to the north of Yvetot, actually inside the restored dovecote of the 15th–16th century Manoir d'Affay, with colourful mosaic brickwork, a spiral staircase leading to the 1470 *boulins* (roosting holes), display panels and a video.

the natural history museum). It counts some of the world's rarest birds among its 220 bird and seven mammal species, many of whom wander freely on its lawns, wooded slopes and lake-islands. They include flamingos and Hawaiian geese. You can also wander in the English-style garden, admire the medicinal plant beds and botanical collection, and in summer enjoy art exhibitions, indoors and out, on

Flamingos

animal, vegetable and mineral themes. Within the grounds are the ruins of a 9th century castle, a picnic area and a café.

32 avenue du Parc, Clères, 40 km (24.8 miles) south of Dieppe off N37 (**℡** *02 35 33 23 08). Open daily March to November 10am–7pm; October 10am–5.30pm; November 1.30–5pm (last admission 1 hour before closing time). Admission: €4.60 (£3.08) adults, €3 (£2) children aged 3–16.*

La Valaine This goat farm based around an 18th century manor house has a jovial owner who loves showing people round in the language of their choice (French, English or German; Italian and Spanish group tours are also available). Tours last roughly an hour, during which time you see the 60 dairy goats and two rams close up (don't be surprised if they come and nuzzle you) and learn about breeding, feeding, milking and modern cheese-making. Inevitably, there's a shop selling farm produce – goats' cheese plus homemade goats'-milk chocolates in eight flavours, ice cream, goat terrine with Calvados and cider.

Manoir de Cateuil, route du Havre, Etretat (☎ 02 35 27 14 02). Guided tours 11am Easter to June and September to mid-November Sun and public holidays; 11am, July and August Sat–Wed and public holidays.

Nature Reserves, Parks & Gardens

There's a lovely big city park in **Le Havre** (p. 60).

Le Jardin de Louanne This collection of themed gardens is great for a peaceful hour or so *en famille*, with its own special children's section, the *Jardin des Lutins* ('Pixies' Garden'), containing a little wooden house with a cottage garden. It's a place for listening to and contemplating nature, let it be stressed, rather than running amok. There's also an exotic water garden with tame carp who feed from your hands, rabbits, a mini-farm with goats and a waterfall. The tearoom, serving ice creams, has a lovely terrace beside the carp pool.

Le Moulin Bleu, Fécamp (☎ 02 35 28 94 81; www.lejardindelouanne. com). Open May Mon and Wed–Sat 9am–noon and 2–7pm, Sun 2–7pm; June to August Mon–Sat 9am–noon and 2–6pm, Sun 10am–noon and 2–6pm; September, October and April Mon and Wed–Sat 9am–noon and 2–6pm. Admission: €4.50 (£3) adults, €2.50 (£1.68) children aged 3–18.

Parc Naturel Régional des Boucles de la Seine Normande ★ The ravishingly

named 'nature park of the Seine's curls' covers 800 km² of marshland and forested riverside where France's best-known river meanders crazily between Le Havre and Rouen. It's a great place to walk (there are signposted footpaths), cycle or canoe. For equipment hire, as well as information on the park's other attractions (three old abbeys and various other ruins, a nature reserve and some little museums and small-scale food producers), contact, or better still, visit the **Maison du Parc** (below). This also hosts fun exhibitions on relevant themes (with an ecological bent) and organises nature outings, demonstrations in an old Gallo-Roman pottery and so on. Staff will also tell you about the crossings you can make in old barges at five points along the river.

Note that some of the park, including the Vernier marsh, is in the Eure (p. 95).

Maison du Parc: Notre-Dame-de-Bliquetuit, 45 km (28 miles) east of Le Havre on D490 (☎ 02 35 37 23 16; www.pnr-seine-normande.com). Information point: rue André Bourvil, Allouville-Bellefosse, 30 km (18⅔ miles) southeast of Fécamp on D33 (☎ 02 35 96 01 65). Open April to June, September and October Mon–Fri 9am–6pm, Sat and Sun noon–6pm; July and August Mon–Fri 9am–6.30pm, Sat and Sun 10am–6.30pm; November to March Mon–Fri 9am–6pm. Admission free.

Historic Buildings & Monuments

Cathédrale de Rouen ★★★

Painted by Monet more than 30 times, Rouen's world-famous gothic Cathédrale de Nôtre-Dame (to give it its proper name) is a must-visit for a number of reasons. It has the tallest spire in France, over the transept of the Tour de Beurre, at 151 m (495 ft). It contains the preserved heart of Richard the Lionheart, buried in its spooky crypt. And on summer evenings, its façade is used as the canvas for a stunning light show in which Monet's colours and angles are recreated by digital artists, with projections of the original works and a musical soundtrack. These wonderful free events began in 2004 to celebrate the end of a 60-year external restoration project. Children of a ghoulish bent will also like the carved monsters on the choir stalls, the stained-glass windows of St Julien L'Hospitalier killing his own parents (let's hope it doesn't give them ideas) and a

Rouen Cathedral at Night

tomb showing a decomposing body. When you're done, make sure you go and see one of Monet's views of the cathedral in the Musée des Beaux Arts (esplanade Marcel-Duchamp, ☎ 02 35 71 28 40), which has one of France's best Impressionist collections and a lovely sculpture garden.

Place de la Cathédrale, Rouen; for tourist office, see p. 56. Open April to October Tue–Fri 7.30am–7pm, Sun and public holidays 8am–6pm; rest of year Tue–Fri 7.30am–noon and 2–6pm, Sun and public holidays 8am–6pm. Admission free.

Riding High

If you're heading out of the Seine Maritime into the more touristy *département* of Calvados (p. 131–172), there's no more thrilling way to do it than via the **Pont de Normandie** rising over the Seine estuary between Le Havre and Honfleur. When it was built, in 1995, it claimed the world record as the world's longest cable-stay bridge, with a central section stretching 856 m (2808 ft) and an overall length of nearly 2 km (1¼ miles). Despite losing its crown to a bridge in Japan, it remains one of the region's biggest tourist attractions, and is well worth the small toll charge (€5, about £3.35, at the time of writing).

Site Archéologique du Bois l'Abbé

This important Gallo-Roman site on a plateau in the beautiful Eu forest near the Norman border first underwent excavation work in the 18th century, but research resumed in recent years. You can go on fascinating (if long, at 2–3 hrs) guided visits with one of the archaeologists, who will introduce you to theories about the site, as well as the team's work methods, and show you the artifacts uncovered to date. The entire site, believed to cover at least 30 hectares and contain many structures that have not yet come to light, includes a theatre, temples and public baths.

Bois l'Abbé, 4 km (2½ miles) southeast of Eu via D49 (℡ 02 35 50 23 24; **www.ville-eu.fr/site-archeologique. php)**. *Guided visits mid-June to mid-September Tue 2pm. Admission: €4.50 (£3) adults, €3 (£2) children aged 10–16.*

The Top Museums

Clos Arsène Lupin, Maison Maurice Leblanc ★★

This wholly unique attraction takes you on a 45-minute trail of discovery about the famous fictional 'gentleman burglar' Arsène Lupin and his creator Maurice Leblanc, created by the latter's granddaughter in his summer villa at Etretat. A costumed guide greets you with an audio guide (French or English) that leads you first into Leblanc's study and then through six more scenes, with shadowy images projected onto walls and a soundtrack of creaking doors and whispering voices. The commentary is ostensibly narrated by the burglar himself, whom you help solve the mystery of *L'Aiguille Creuse*, one of Leblanc's best-loved novels, in which one of Etretat's curious rock formations (p. 64) becomes the hiding place for some stolen jewels that Lupin returns to their rightful owners – the French royal family. If you're hooked, the shop stocks books, videos and other Lupin goodies.

You might stop at the **Lecoeur** patisserie/tearoom (47 rue Alphonse Karr), where Leblanc often came to work on *L'Aiguille Creuse*. Try one of its orangeflower and almond/marzipan specialities: perhaps a *rayon vert*, named after the green flash that occurs when the sun disappears behind the horizon.

15 rue Guy de Maupassant, Etretat (℡ 02 35 10 59 53; **www.arsene-lupin.com)**. *Open daily 10am–5.45pm April to September; daily 11am–4.45pm early February to early March; Fri, Sat and Sun only for the last 3 wks in March and the first 3 wks in October; daily for the last week in October, two days in mid-November and the second half of December. Admission: €6.50 (£4.35) adults, €4 (£2.70) children aged 6–16.*

Estran, Cité de la Mer ★★

Part aquarium, part museum of the sea, Estran will appeal mainly to children because of its breeding tanks full of baby fish, and its touching pool with the usual rays and turbots, plus spider crabs and dogfish. There are also seahorses, hermit crabs and sea urchins for them to coo over. Though it might sound rather dry in comparison, the Naval Construction section is actually more worthy of a visit. It has a Lego corner where children can make boats from diagrams, large models of wooden Viking ships and fascinating reconstructions of two ships' bridges – one from the early 20th century and the other from the present day – full of mind-boggling, state-of-the-art technology. Further galleries house an unexpectedly interesting exhibition on local cliffs and pebbles, with explanations (in French, as elsewhere) of how chunks of cliff break away and are slowly shaped by the tides into smooth round pebbles, and displays about local fishing techniques. In addition, there are good temporary exhibitions on subjects such as lighthouses, and a programme of events that includes summer discovery walks along four local beaches, taking 2 hrs.

37 rue de l'Asile Thomas, Dieppe (📞 02 35 06 93 20; http://estrancite delamer@free.fr). Open daily 10am– noon and 2–6pm. Admission: €5 (£3.35) adults, €3 (£2) children aged 4–16.

Galerie Bovary/Musée d'Automates

The fictional town of Yonville in Flaubert's *Madame Bovary* was said to have been based on Ry just east of Rouen (its main character, Emma, was almost certainly inspired by a local woman), and of the 300 miniature mechanical figures that spring to life in this former cider press in the town, more than two-thirds play out scenes from the novel. Though it helps to have read (and loved) the story, the little figures are delightful – dressed in period costume against painted backgrounds – and each scene is 'explained' by panels with extracts from the book (in French). They were made by a local jeweller and clockmaker more than 30 years ago, who still takes visitors round.

You won't fail to notice how the rest of the town has muscled in on the literary connection, with the Chez Emma grocery and Hôtel Bovary. Teenagers studying the novel at school or college might like to ask at the tourist office for the **Promenade au Pays d'Emma Bovary** map. This highlights other local sites said to have inspired locations in the novel, including the wet nurse Rollet's farm, the Marquis de Pomereu's château at Le Héron, where Emma danced all night,

Emma, Madame Bovary

and the house in Héronchelles where Hivert the coachdriver was born.

Place Gustave Flaubert, Ry, 20 km (12½ miles) east of Rouen on D13 (📞 02 35 23 61 44). Open 2.30–6pm May, June, September and October Sat, Sun and public holidays; July and August Tue–Sun. Admission: €5 (£3.35) adults, €3 (£2) children.

Musée des Arts et de l'Enfance

It was in Fécamp, in 1894, that Doctor Léon Dufour, godfather of modern nursery nursing, founded his *Goutte de Lait* ('Drop of Milk') project that went on to save thousands of malnourished babies through a daily delivery of babies' bottles combined with weighing sessions and medical visits. The 'Childhood' section of this eclectic museum is made up in large part from the doctor's collection of feeding bottles from ancient times, many made from ceramic, plus some modern versions. Other items from the doctor's museum of childhood in the region are here too, including old cots, baby-walkers and some toys and games, and there is a current drive to expand the section further. The rest of the museum has archaeological artifacts from the town, the capital of the first Dukes of Normandy, local furniture, traditional jewellery and ceramics, ancient weaponry and historical and landscape paintings. However, at the time of writing the museum was closed after having reached bursting point, with reopening scheduled for 2008 in a new

combined building with the **Musée des Terre-Neuvas et de la Pêche**, on Fécamp's history as a fishing port.

1 quai Jean Recher, Fécamp (📞 02 35 28 31 99). Call for new opening times and admission rates.

Musée Découverte du Chocolat

Let slip to the children that there's a chocolate museum in the area and there'll be no keeping away, but there's an educational aspect to this attraction. As well as watching chocolate being made (this is part of the Hautot factory) and enjoying a free tasting, you can see displays and a video on its history going as far back as the Maya culture of South America. The Mayans ate and drank it in spicy ceremonial drinks more than 2500 years ago, and decorated their temples and palaces with carved cocoa pods. Displays include waxwork dummies, old boats, period packaging and machinery, and English translations are available. It'll take about an hour to work your way round.

851 route de Valmont, Fécamp (📞 02 35 27 62 02; http://www.chocolats-hautot.com). Open Mon–Sat 9am–noon and 2–6.30pm. Admission: €3 (£2) adults, €2 (£1.34) children aged 4–17.

Musée Flaubert et d'Histoire de la Médecine ★★

Not one for the squeamish or for little children, this unusual combined literary and medical museum in the city's former main hospital (now municipal offices) came about as a result of the fact that writer Gustave Flaubert was born here while his father was its chief surgeon. The former quarters of the Flaubert family consist mainly of busts and old furniture, though you can see the stuffed Amazonian parrot that Flaubert borrowed from Rouen's natural history museum to help him describe 'Loulou' in his story *Un coeur simple*. The museum covering medicine from the 12th to 20th centuries is vastly more entertaining, albeit in a rather gruesome way. In its 10 rooms you'll find anatomical models made of wax, plaster or *papier mâché*, 19th century amputation instruments used on battlefields, 70 phrenological heads (including ones of the painter Raphaël and the writer the Marquis de Sade) dating from the time when some believed you could 'read' a person's character from the shapes and bumps on their skull, a strange six-person hospital bed (ah, those were the days), a reconstructed pharmacy and an utterly bizarre wooden statue of Sainte Agathe, patron saint of wet nurses, proffering a breast on a plate. The *pièce de résistance* is the museum's unique 'childbirth machine' – a fabric model complete with umbilical cord that midwife Madame Corday used to demonstrate childbirth and its possible complications all over France in the 18th century. A recent X-ray of it revealed it to be constructed around a real pelvis. The €6 (£4) French-language museum guide will help

you make the most of your visit, which may coincide with one of the temporary exhibitions on the likes of dental medicine. A free fun booklet for children is available at reception.

After all that, find some calm amidst the beds of medicinal plants in the garden, where Flaubert played as a boy and which contains a big marble monument to him.

51 rue de Lecat, Rouen (☎ 02 35 15 59 95; www.chu-rouen.fr). Open Tue 10am–6pm, Wed–Sat 10am–12pm and 2–6pm, but call ahead for closures, especially Sat. Admission: €2.20 (£1.48) adults, under-18s free, large families €1.50pp (£1).

Musée Jeanne d'Arc Call it tacky, but Rouen's waxworks museum in an old cellar can be a good way of introducing younger children to the story of 'the Maiden' – Joan of Arc – who, from the age of 14, heard the voices of saints urging her to lead the French troops against the English during the Hundred Years' War, which she did – clad in white armour. After her luck failed, she was imprisoned in Rouen's castle and tried for witchcraft and heresy, then burnt at the stake a few steps from this site. She was just 19. The museum traces Joan's life through old-fashioned waxwork scenes, culminating in her burning against a backdrop of Rouen buildings. There are also scenes featuring local writers Flaubert and Corneille. Visits normally take about 45 mins–1 hr, with free audio guides and quiz sheets available in French, English, German and Italian.

33 place du Vieux Marché, Rouen (☎ 02 35 88 02 70; www.jeanne-darc.com). Open daily mid-April to mid-September 9.30am–1pm and 1.30–7pm. Rest of year 10–noon and 2–6.30pm. Admission: €4 (£2.70) adults, €2.50 (£1.68) children.

Musee National de l'Education ★★

One of five state 'scientific' museums, the national education museum is a serious-minded institution charged with keeping the French educational heritage of the last five centuries alive. Which is not to say that it isn't good fun – amidst its stunning collection of almost a million items are old games and toys, children's literature, school furniture, photos, paintings, engravings and prints and work by pupils. For parents or grandparents it's a trip back in time, for children a fascinating insight into what life used to be like. The toys include dolls and dolls' houses, tin soldiers, jigsaw puzzles, marbles, diabolos, skittles, optical games such as Chinese shadows, alphabetical tarot cards, musical and babies' toys, train sets, Meccano, role-playing games and toys from abroad, including African and Japanese toys and mahjong sets. You'll find some of them available in reproduction form in the little shop, together with postcards. Everything is lovingly maintained and beautifully laid out.

185 rue Eau-de-Robec, Rouen (☎ 02 35 07 66 61; www.inrp.fr/musee). Open school holidays Tue–Mon 2–6pm. Rest of year Mon and

Wed–Fri 10am–12.30pm and 1.30–6pm; Sat and Sun 2–6pm. Admission: €3 (£2), under-18s free.

Musée des Traditions Verrières

Set in a valley in which 80% of the world's luxury perfume bottles are produced, this is a small but interesting museum on glass production from its origins in ancient Egypt about 7000 years ago. It contains a Turkish glass furnace from 1500 BC, displays and videos on local glassworks and the world's first semi-automatic glass-making machine, dating from 1930. The highlight for little princesses in love with glitter and sparkle is the wonderful room full of glinting perfume bottles from around the world, in all kinds of shapes and sizes – including animals and female figures – and bearing such glamorous brand names as Chanel and Yves Saint-Laurent. There are also mice and other little crystal animals, and occasional glass-blowing demonstrations.

Quartier Morris, Eu, 3 km (1.8 miles) southeast of Le Tréport on D925 (☎ 02 35 86 21 91) Open Easter to November Tue, Sat, Sun and public holidays 2.30–6pm, plus Wed in July and August. Admission: €3 (£2), under-12s free.

Salon des Navigateurs

Surely one of France's most eccentric 'museums', this is actually a barber's shop that the owner, who once worked on a cruise liner, has partially transformed into a showcase of transatlantic sailing and hairdressing history. If he's not busy cutting hair, dressed as a sailor, Monsieur Le Compte will talk to you about the ships' models, photos, paintings and other marine objects, and then, in the back room, his collection of scissors, razors, combs, brushes and shaving bowls, including some antiques. He and his wife are also happy to share their knowledge of things to do and see in Le Havre.

1 rue du Petit Croissant, Le Havre (℃ 02 35 42 12 71). Open Tue–Sat 10am–6pm. Admission free.

Arts & Crafts Sites

Artmazia ★ ★ **FIND** This one-off attraction – an 'art garden' based around a natural beech maze (the world's largest) dotted with contemporary sculptures and installations by artists from around Europe – was conceived by British-born Geoff Troll, whose sense of humour is evident in the presence here of a 'troll's grotto' for children. There's also a three-legged toad called Robert and treasure hunts. Troll, an artist himself, used to lead therapeutic art courses at Dieppe hospital and believes in its importance in the lives of children too (the place has been an enormous hit with school groups). There's also a gallery with an annual exhibition, lakes, a cider orchard and apple press, a cottage garden and lots of animal life – geese, fish, frogs and two goats, Pistache and Caramel – plus a gîte with a double and a single room (from €220, about £147, per week).

25 route du Neufchâtel, Massy, 30 km (18⅔ miles) southeast of Dieppe off D915 (℃ 02 35 93 17 12; www. decouvertefrance.com). Open May

to September Mon–Wed 2.30– 6.30pm. Admission: €5 (£3.35) adults, €3 (£2) children.

Musée Malraux ★ This wonderfully light-flooded 1960s glass building right by the sea, refurbished in 2006, houses France's second most important collection of Impressionist art (after the Musée d'Orsay in Paris) and is the perfect setting for some of the greatest works to have been inspired by the surrounding coastline. These include Monet's *Les falaises à Varengeville*; his *Impression, Soleil Levant*, painted right in front of where the museum now stands, and so iconic it gave its name to the Impressionist movement, is now in Paris. Among five other works here by Monet are one of the Houses of Parliament in London and one of the waterlilies in his garden at Giverny (p. 98). The artist, in fact, came to live in Le Havre at the age of five, and met his first teacher, Eugène Boudin, here. Boudin liked working in the

Sculpture outside the Musée Malraux, Le Havre

open-air on Normandy's beaches, and you can see how he influenced Impressionism in some of his works on display here, notably *Etudes de ciel* (a cloud painting) and *Dame en blanc sur la plage de Trouville*. You can also see some Renoirs, Pissarros, Sisleys, Dégas and a Manet, with special signposting for adults and children helping you find your way around. Afterwards, there's a library with 6000 books, catalogues and art reviews, plus CD-Rom terminals, a shop with postcards, posters, books and souvenirs, and a café with views over the entrance to the port.

INSIDER TIP

The tourist board offers Impressions du Havre weekends including a 'walk in the footsteps of the Impressionists', entry to the Musée Malraux, bed and breakfast in a three-star hotel and cream teas.

Boulevard Clémenceau, Le Havre (02 35 19 62 62). Open Mon–Fri 11am–6pm, Sat and Sun 11am–7pm. Admission: €3.80 (£2.55) (€5 (£3.35) during temporary exhibitions), under-18s free; free to all on the first Saturday of the month.

Child-Friendly Tours

Survols des Falaises d'Etretat

★★ Your bank manager may never forgive you, but if you want to be really blown away by the stunning coast of the Seine-Maritime (or sights further afield), book a helicopter for up to four people. Departing from Le Havre, you head north along the coast, past the Cap d'Antifer

to the cliffs of Etretat (p. 64), returning over the Pays de Caux countryside. Alternatively, swoop over the lovely *Boucles de la Seine* (p. 68) east of Le Havre, with their three impressive bridges, including the modern Pont de Normandie (p. 69), returning via Honfleur. You can even go as far as the landing beaches in Calvados (Chapter 6) and the Manche (Chapter 7). Another firm at the airfield offers flights in a light aircraft over the Etretat cliffs, Baie de Seine (the Pont de Normandie and Deauville) and landing beaches, with the opportunity (for adults, and at the pilot's discretion!) to take the controls for a while.

Aéroport Le Havre-Octeville, rue Louis Blériot, Le Havre: Hélistar (08 20 20 02 25; www.helistar.fr); Aviation Service Normandie (02 35 44 89 95; www.aviationservice.fr). Prices from €90pp (£60) for the shortest helicopter trip (30 mins; Etretat); from €99 (£66) for a 30-min plane ride, then €20 (£13.40) per additional person and €10 (£6.70) per child under 10.

For Active Families

See also 'Beaches & Resorts', p. 62–64.

D'Arbre en Arbre ★ This tree-top adventure course is a great way of getting close to nature – as well as experiencing 2 km (1¼ miles) of rope bridges, rope-swings, climbing nets, log walkways, tunnels and ford crossings, you can meet the park's own animals – llamas, kangaroos, reindeer and more. Age limits depend on the different stages, but generally you need to be a minimum of eight (or 1.2 m tall – that's about 3 ft 11 in).

Those who are too young can play in the 'Ludi-parc' with its playground equipment, pedal tractors, and so on, and there's also a children's farm with donkeys, pigs, poultry, guinea pigs and very friendly dwarf goats; ask at reception for the free French-language information and quiz sheets. Artwork dots the forest, which children can explore on pony-rides (either with parents or a member of staff).

Ask about outings: hikes, bike rides or boat trips towards Etretat, for example, with picnic stops, followed by a day at the park. The park has a canteen with family fare, picnic tables and even 'nomadic' accommodation in the form of yurts (circular tents) with shared shower blocks: family ones for 4–6 have beds and Oriental-style furniture, or adults can get a two-person yurt to themselves and 2–3 children can share another, with prices from €55 (£36.85) per night for 2–4, including park access.

Avenue Mal de Lattre de Tassigny, Fécamp (℡ 02 35 10 84 83; http:// arbreenarbre.free.fr/). Open daily April to September 10am–7.30pm. Rest of year 10am–5pm. Prices from €5 (£3.35) adults, €3.50 (£2.35) children aged 6 and over.

Etretat Aventure ★ Another acrobatic course across the tree-tops, this time set in the grounds of a manor house, Etretat Aventure offers five routes

through the oaks and beeches, though you can just stroll through the lovely six hectares of forest if you don't have a head for heights, or hire mountain bikes and follow paths that bring you out near the famous *Aiguille* (p. 70). The advantage of this course is that the routes include a 20-min *Parcours Baby* for children as young as three, and a *Parcours Famille* that a family with children aged eight and up can do together. Adrenaline-junkies, meanwhile, opt for the *Parcours Rouge – Frisson.*

The park has a snack bar and quite posh (and expensive; from €300/night – that's £200) hostel-style accommodation in the manor (14 three- and four-person rooms with shared bathrooms and kitchen, and wooden floors) and the 'Loft', an outbuilding with three bunkbed rooms for three, four or six people and shared facilities.

There's yet another *parcours acrobatique*, **Arbr'en ciel**, at Préaux near Rouen (℡ 02 35 02 10 00; *www.arbreenciel-aventure. com*), with hanging ball nets for ages two and up and a route for 3½ –7-year-olds among its options.

Route de Gonneville, Le Château du Bois, Les Loges, 6 km (3¾ miles) east of Etretat on D940 (℡ 02 35 29 21 76; www.etretat-aventure.fr). Call for opening times. Admission from €12pp (£8).

Vélo-Rail ★★ A quirky idea for a family day out, the Vélo-Rail consists of multi-person bikes rigged up to travel along an old train track. Each can fit 2–5 people; there's no minimum age requirement for the three passenger seats, but the people in the two cycling seats have to be at least 10 or 11 to be able to reach the brake pedals, and one rider has to be an adult. For 20–30 mins you ride downhill through a green valley between Les Loges and Etretat (6 km – 3¾ miles), then you pedal back uphill (this takes about 45 mins) or hop aboard a *train touristique* for the return journey. Booking is essential for the bikes but not the train (which you can take as a return-trip independently of the Vélo-Rail), and you need to arrive 20 mins before your booked slot for a safety briefing.

Old train station, Les Loges, 6 km (3¾ miles) east of Etretat on D94 (02 35 29 49 61; www.train-fr.org/unecto/ ttepac). Open July and August daily, call for times; September and October Sat 2 and 3.30pm, Sun 10.30am (bikes only), 2 and 3.30pm. Price €22 (£14.75) for four people with return by train.

Shopping

Colette There are only six ivory carvers in France, and this family business dating back to 1870 counts two of them – 87-year-old Jean and his daughter Annick, the sole female carver. Before you object, know that the raw material is sourced from stocks left over from before the 1976 ban on ivory imports and would have been burnt if it wasn't used in this traditional Dieppe craft, examples of which you can also see in the Château-musée (p. 63). In the little shop and workshop that has produced pieces now displayed in the Musée National des Arts et Traditions Populaires in Paris, you'll find everything from jewellery and model boats to cute little owls, pigs and cows, with prices starting at about €10 (£6.70).

3 rue Ango, Dieppe (02 35 82 36 97). Open Tue–Sat 10am–noon and 2–6pm.

Fnac Eveil et Jeux ★ Part of the very good countrywide book and media chain, Fnac Eveil et Jeux are outlets specially conceived for children aged 0–12, stocking thousands of carefully selected and rigorously tested (by parents and grandparents, nursery teachers and so on) games, toys, books, records and films, most costing less than a tenner (€16). Like its other stores, the one in Rouen is a consciously fun and colourful environment fitted with children's furniture and lots of products unwrapped and laid out so young shoppers can try them out before buying.

There's also a general Fnac in Rouen, at 8 allée Eugène-Delacroix, Espace du Palais (02 35 52 72 00).

11–13 rue Beauvoisine, Rouen (08 92 35 06 66; www.eveiletjeux.com). Open Mon–Sat 10am–7pm.

Printemps Department stores, traditionally held to stock 'everything under one roof', are a good family bet precisely because of their range, which means just about everyone can find something to please. The Rouen

Say Cheese

Creamy **Neufchâtel** – claimed to be the oldest cheese in Normandy – is often sold in the shape of a heart, a custom said to have begun in the Middle Ages, when a local farm girl wanted to proclaim her affection to an English soldier across the language barrier. You can buy it, including the mild Coeur de Bray, at Neufchâtel-en-Bray's large Saturday **market**, which has a dairy section in the Halle au Beurre. Or ask the tourist board for their free 'Route des Fromages' leaflet listing local farm outlets.

The perhaps more child-friendly **Petit Suisse**, a mass-produced *fromage frais* that's particularly good served with jam, honey, fruit and nuts, also originated from near Neufchâtel, not Switzerland – the inventor's dad was Swiss.

branch of this institution can't match its Paris sister in size or prestige, but it does have good stationery, toy and children's wear sections and men's and women's fashion departments, the latter stocking such desirable teenagers' labels as Quiksilver, Lulu Castagnette and Cimarron. Accessories are always good for a browse with teen girls, as is the beauty hall, and there's a useful branch of **Le Pain Quotidien**, a Belgian chain that serves breads, pastries and salads around communal tables.

Neufchâtel Heart-shaped Cheese

There are also Printemps stores in Le Havre (p. 60); Evreux in the Eure (p. 101); and Caen and Deauville in Calvados (p. 158 and p. 138).
4 rue du Gros Horloge, Rouen (↳ 02 32 76 32 32). Open Mon–Sat 9am–7pm.

Roussel Chocolatier On a street full of gourmet food shops, this master chocolate maker stands out. Set in a magnificent old baker's shop retaining much of its original décor and selling around 60 kinds of plain, dark, milk and praline chocolates, it doubles as a charming tearoom, Les Coulisses du Chocolat. Here you can enjoy a wonderful array of teas, coffees and hot chocolates from around the world, inside or on a pretty terrace. The genial owner even gives chocolate-making demonstrations on occasion, and informal talks on the history of chocolate.
115 Grande Rue, Dieppe (↳ 02 35 84 22 75). Open Mon 2–6pm, Tue–Sat 10am–6pm.

FAMILY-FRIENDLY ACCOMMODATION

Dieppe & Around

MODERATE

Douce France ★ ★ **VALUE** This beautifully restored old coaching inn – the name of which translates as 'Soft France' or 'Mild France' – sits by Veules-le-Roses' famously diminutive river (p. 64), amidst charming pedestrianised streets. An enclosed garden scented with rose and honeysuckle and a tearoom with a waterside terrace are among its assets, but the rooms won't leave you wanting – quite luxurious, with tasteful beige and cream décor, they have separate living areas and kitchenettes. Five are four-person apartments, varying in size but all with one twin and one double bedroom, a large living room and a view over the charming paved coach yard and jumble of village rooftops. For smaller families there are 2–3-person (one-bedroom) suites: seven 'Grand Large' ones in the eaves, with balconies, and 14 'Large' ones with river or courtyard views, four of them over two levels. Beds are large and very comfortable, but note that a few rooms have shower-only bathrooms. Still, it's exceptional value, especially if you take up the 4-nights-for-the-price-of-3 year-round offer.

It's all the more of a good family option given the lovely afternoon tearoom and terrace where you can enjoy homemade patisseries, crêpes, ice cream, fruit juices, 20 varieties of tea and old-style hot chocolate. That's if you have room to spare after the generous buffet breakfast (€11 – £7.40 – adults, €7 – £4.70 – children aged 3–12), including homemade jam, farmyard cheeses and freshly squeezed juice. Later on in the day, the genial staff will be happy to recommend local eateries to suit your mood and wallet.

13 rue du Docteur Girard, Veules-les-Roses, 25 km (15½ miles) west of Dieppe on D925 (℡ 02 35 57 85 30; www.doucefrance.fr). 26 rooms. Suites €95–180 (£63.50–120), apartment €214 (£143.40). Cot free. Amenities: tearoom; terrace. In room: satellite TV, telephone.

Villa Florida **FIND** This light-flooded house is a comfortable option for those coming in or out of Dieppe by ferry, with muted Oriental styling in some of the rooms and a chatty resident parrot called Bonjour, and set apart from the noise and bustle of the centre of town (2 km/1¼ miles away), on a road leading down to the sea. Of the four rooms, Golf has a double room and a little mezzanine with a single bed, plus a terrace looking over the garden and neighbouring golf course. Or there's Yoga, another two-level room for three or four, with a terrace overlooking a little wood. Those with babies will need their own travel cot. Continental breakfasts, served in a pleasant salon or in the landscaped garden, may be a little late for some, at 9–10.30am, but the amenable staff may serve you a bit earlier if you ask.

24 chemin du Golf, Dieppe (☎ 02 35 84 40 37; www.lavillaflorida.com). 4 rooms. Double €66 (£44), 4-person duplex €105 (£70.35). Amenities: garden. In room: TV, Wi-Fi Internet access, terrace (some).

INEXPENSIVE

Domaine Les Goélands This well-maintained four-star campsite half a kilometre from the sea in a village halfway between Dieppe and Eu has spacious tent and caravan plots and mobile homes for up to six people, available on a weekend or midweek basis as well as weekly. Spread over a terraced four hectares, its facilities run to a tennis court, a mini-golf pitch, good, well-fenced-off playgrounds, *boules*, billiards and TV rooms, bike hire and a large communal barbecue. There's also a baby-changing/bathing room, a launderette and ironing room, a shop and an ice-cream counter. A nearby leisure centre makes up for the lack of a pool, and also has slides, a skating rink and a fitness suite.

rue des Grèbes, St-Martin-en-Campagne, 12 km (7½ miles) from Dieppe on D925 (☎ 02 35 83 82 90; www.camping-les-goelands.com). Rates: pitch for 4-person tent/car €21–24 (£14–16); mobile home for 4 €350–490 (roughly £234–328). Closed November to March.

Le Havre & Around

EXPENSIVE–VERY EXPENSIVE

Hôtel Le Donjon ⭐ This turreted little Anglo-Norman castle and adjoining seaside villa in large grounds overlooking Etretat's famous cliffs (p. 64) is the kind of place to come either with tiny babies or slightly older children – say, from five and up – and not with chaotic, tantrum-prone toddlers. Indeed, if you've just had a baby, there's an *Escapade avec Bébé* offer including breakfast, dinner, gifts for mum and tot and a room fitted with practical items: a changing station, bottle warmer, baby bath, cot or Moses basket, revolving nightlight and even nappies. Prices start at €114 (£76.40) per night per adult; for an extra fee you can avail yourselves of the services of a daytime nanny, allowing you to go for a splash in the outdoor pool.

Rooms and suites are divided into various categories of luxury; a family of four is limited to a Junior Suite with a salon fitted with two extra beds for children aged 5–12 (€220–280 – roughly £147–188 depending on season), or two interconnecting 'Confort' (medium sized) rooms (€130–190 – roughly £87–127). The décor in all is sumptuous: a palette of rich siennas, reds and chocolates, or a refreshing white with pale-striped wallpaper. Some have decorative teddy bears, a dozen or so have the option of soothing background music. Elsewhere, there's a poolside patio for breakfast or lunch during the summer, five restful salons and a library. Rates include Continental breakfast.

Chemin St Clair, Etretat (☎ 02 35 27 08 23; www.ledonjon-etretat.fr). 21 rooms. Double €90–250 (£60–167.50), suite €220–330 (£147–220). Cot free. In room: satellite TV, telephone, hairdryer, complimentary mineral water.

MODERATE

Vent d'Ouest ★★ **VALUE** This
boutique-style hotel with its
fashionable marine décor –
striped fabrics, painted wooden
furniture, model ships, and
carved seagulls – comes as a surprise in gritty Le Havre, all the
more so given its well-priced,
family-friendly accommodation
options. There are double rooms
that can fit a single or double
sofabed or two extra beds, and
have a shower or bath; interconnecting doubles with showers;
one suite with a double bedroom, living room with sofabed
and bathroom with bath; or
three apartments, each with a
similar set-up to the suite plus a
kitchenette, small dining area
and flat screen TV and DVD
player. The latter allow you the
freedom of self-catering with the
perks of staying in a hotel –
though this one doesn't have a
restaurant, cold platters are provided on request and good
Continental breakfasts (€12
(£8)/free under-12s) are served
in a pleasant salon/bar, where a
highchair is available. The efficient staff are also happy to
advise on local eateries.

*4 rue Caligny, Le Havre (℡ 02 35 42
50 69; **www.ventdouest.fr**). 38
rooms. Double €88–115 (£59–77),
two interconnecting doubles €155
(£104), suite €130 (£87), apartment
€135 (£90.50). Extra bed €15 (£10),
cot free. Amenities: salon/bar; cold
meal service. In room: TV, telephone,
Wi-Fi Internet access, kitchenette
(some).*

INEXPENSIVE

Ferme de Bray ★ For those
who like their holidays to come
with dollops of authentic rural
charm, this is the real deal. As
well as offering five B&B rooms
warmly decorated with gleaming
old wooden furniture, the owners have restored large sections of
this 17th century farm, which
has been in the family for an
astonishing 18 generations and
which you are free to explore
(non-guests have to pay a small
admission fee). They include a
mill, a bread oven, a dovecote, a
poultry barn and some cider-
making buildings, all with tools
and machinery that were used to
make Neufchâtel cheese (p. 79)
as well as cider and flour. Black-
and-white photos of people using
the equipment bring the
'museum' to life, and animals still
wander around. Basic but sweet,
and affording views over the surrounding fields, the accommodation inside the ivy-clad brick
farmhouse includes a family
room with two double beds. The
resident cockerels will ensure
you're up in time for Continental
goodies served in the wood-
panelled breakfast room.

The village of Sommery also
has ponds where you can trout-
fish without a permit. Rods can
be hired (€16.30 – £11 – for
half a day for one adult and child
aged 8–12) and bait is sold, and
there's a barge, mini-golf, picnic/
BBQ areas, and a *friterie* (chip
stand).

*Sommery, 6 km (3¾ miles) from
Forges-les-Eaux on D915 (℡ 02 35 90
57 27; **http://ferme.de.bray.free.fr**).*

5 rooms. Double €44 (£29.50), family room €88 (£59). Amenities: farmyard and museum.

Rouen & Around

Le Manoir aux Vaches ★ FIND

In a region known for its bovines, what could be more natural than a cow-themed hotel? It's a wonder no one's thought of it before! Opened in 2006, the hotel is the result of one woman's 50-year love affair with cows, and the rooms are decorated with the collection of more than 1600 model cows she has amassed from around the world, including India, Peru and Africa, in everything from ceramic to wood and clay. Some even sing or dance. Don't worry: they're safely displayed behind glass, away from meddling fingers. Rooms vary in size, but all have a mezzanine that can be used as an extra two-person bedroom, plus a veranda for breakfast (free) when it's fine – you won't be surprised to see cows decorating plates of farm produce or bowls of milky tea. Each room is named after a type of cow; *L'Abondance* is a 'robust', high-yield one for families of up to six. Surprisingly, the décor couldn't be less rural: all creams and whites, it has a boutique-style chic that wouldn't be out of place in London or Paris, and that comes as a surprise after the plain façade of this modern, one-storey building in an unremarkable town inland of Veules-les-Roses.

rue Félix Faure, Yvetot, 40 km (24.8 miles) east of Le Havre on N15

☎ *02 35 95 65 65; www.manoiraux vaches.com). 9 rooms. Double €96–106 (£64–71), 4-person room €136–146 (£91–98). Extra bed €20 (£13.40), cot free. Amenities: car park €7 (£4.70). In room: telephone.*

Chez Mills This child-friendly, Brit-owned place offers both B&B and self-catering in tranquil rural surroundings not far east of Ry. The former is available in two cosy beamed attic rooms in the friendly owners' timber-framed cottage, Les Quatre Oiseaux, and a breakfast of croissants and jam made with fruit from the garden is served in their living room with its woodburning fire. With advance booking, you can also share an evening meal (€18 – £12 – with drinks) with them, including home grown fruit and veg. There is, however, an independent entrance via a guests' sitting room with a TV, video player, books and games. The twin room has an en-suite shower room, the double a shower and basin in the room and a toilet just outside; a folding bed is available if you want to share one room between three. Outside is a *pétanque* pitch, a giant lawn-chess set, a barbecue and plenty of space for picnicking. The resident animals – Klovis the collie, Cipo the donkey and Utah the goat – love attention from children, for whom a cot and highchair are available. In August, a two-night stay is required.

Les Quatre Oiseaux, Chez Mills

Two kilometres (1¼ miles) away, **Le Chaudron**, named after the old cooking pot adorning its kitchen, is a gîte in a traditional Norman one-storey dwelling with very low beams, with en-suite bedrooms (one double and one twin), a living area with an open fire, TV, video and CD players, a dining-kitchen, a washing machine and heating. From the terrace you have clear views over the fields, and there are large front and back gardens. Bedlinen is provided but not towels.

INSIDER TIP »

If you're going to Rouen, ask the owners for a copy of the guide they wrote themselves. Former teachers in Africa, they now run a charity for children in Uganda, to which you might like to make a donation.

St Lucien (Nolléras), 20 km (12½ miles) east of Rouen off N31 (℡ 02 35 90 51 95; www.chezmills.co.uk). 2 rooms + gîte. Rates: B&B double/ twin €42–45 (£28–30), extra bed €12 (£8), cot free. Gîte: €230–325

(£153–217) per week. Amenities: B&B: dinner by request; garden; games; books; TV lounge; animals; BBQ equipment. Gîte: garden; kitchen; washing machine; TV; video player; CD player; BBQ equipment.

Hôtel de la Cathédrale ★

VALUE In a half-timbered building on a cobbled street behind the cathedral, this hotel couldn't look quainter, and that's before you see the delightful paved inner courtyard full of lush plants, flowerpots, statuary and wrought-iron furniture – a civilised place for a cup of tea or cold drink when the weather permits. The rooms, which include three- and four-person rooms with baths (extra beds mean up to five can be accommodated), could do with an overhaul, but they do have exposed beams and a kind of worn charm, and prices are great given the location. Some of the three-bedders are available in 'Supérieure' versions, meaning they're larger and have a little sitting area. You do tend to get squirreled away in the depths of the hotel as a family, which is not necessarily a bad thing in terms of not disturbing or being disturbed, but you then have to carry your luggage up lots of stairs and along narrow corridors – this is in addition to not being able to unload your luggage right in front of the hotel because the street is pedestrianised (for parking, there's a secure underground lot on the street parallel, and this being France it is affordable). Breakfasts (€7.50 – £5/free under-6s) are a decent cold buffet in a beamed dining room.

*12 rue St Romain, Rouen (02 35 71 57 95; **www.hotel-de-la-cathedrale. fr/**). 25 rooms. Double €52–89 (£35–60), family room for four €105 (£70). Extra bed €15 (£10). Cot free. Amenities: courtyard tearoom; free Internet access. In room: cable TV, telephone, hairdryer.*

FAMILY-FRIENDLY DINING

Dieppe & Around

For eating suggestions in **Dieppe** itself, see p. 63.

MODERATE–EXPENSIVE

Auberge de la Rouge Set in a quiet garden with a bubbling fountain (beside which you can lunch in summer), this pretty inn is known for its local seafood and duck – and most of all for its delicious *soufflé chaud Bénédictine*, a hot soufflé made with a liqueur unique to the nearby town of Fécamp. Other

adventurous specialities on the *menus* (there's no *à la carte* option) are starters of duck's liver with slices of Granny Smith apple and cinnamon caramel, or thinly sliced seabass with masala curry and a wasabi madeleine, and mains of turbot roasted on a bed of sea salt with seasonal vegetables and reduced oyster cream, or wild duck with *foie gras* sauce and stuffed potato. The children's menu (€11 – £7.40) is a simple but good-value affair starting with a platter of cold meats or *crudités*, followed by beef or fish with sautée potatoes then ice cream.

Above the restaurant are eight garden-view rooms with mezzanines perfect for children; a room for four without breakfast costs just €74 (£49.50), but there's also a good bargain to be had in the form of the *Séjour Gastronomique*, whereby two adults and two children get two nights' lodging, breakfast and dinner for €242 (£162).

*Route du Havre, Saint Léonard, 2 km (1¼ miles) south of Fécamp on D925 (02 35 28 07 59; **www.auberge-rouge.com**). Menus €19–53 (£12.75–35.50). Highchairs available. Open Tue–Fri 12.15–1.30pm and 7.15–9pm, Sat 7.15–9pm, Sun 12.15–1.30pm.*

INEXPENSIVE

Un Jour d'Eté With its beach-chic décor, deep armchairs and newspapers, this delightful tearoom in an old fisherman's house is a handy spot not only for delicious homemade cakes and pastries (including a famous chocolate fondant), and a huge range of teas and coffees, but also for its light meals served at lunchtime and in the afternoon. Light *assiettes de pays* feature local marinated herrings and rabbit *rillettes* and savoury tarts. Try to bag a table on the lovely terrace when the weather's fine.

25 rue Victor-Hugo, Veules-les-Roses, 25 km (15½ miles) west of Dieppe on D925 (02 35 97 23 17). Main courses €6–9 (£4–6). Open 11am–7pm Sat, Sun and school holidays. Closed January and February.

Le Havre & Around

INEXPENSIVE–MODERATE

Brasserie du Lac de Caniel ★

FIND Ideally situated for a lazy family lunch, on a lakeside in the Eau et Nature leisure park just inland, this place knows what parents need for a relaxed meal – as well as a basic *Formule Enfant* (€7.50 – €5; ham, steak, breaded fish or nuggets with chips, dessert and drink) and a *Formule Bébé* (€5 – £3.35; pot of baby food and yogurt or fruit compôte), it offers children up to six a surprise gift and has recently introduced a play space for 3–8-year-olds. While they play, you can choose from well-prepared classics such as steak with *sauce béarnaise*, duck with green peppercorns, barbecued meats with snail butter, Breton-style squid, skate wing with capers, salmon lasagne and *moules-frites*. Snackier fare includes ham crêpes and *croques monsieur*. Among the desserts, the rhubarb and raspberry tart

stands out. Get here early if you want a table on the decked terrace in summer.

The leisure park offers bowling (available as part of a lunch *formule*), billiards, *boules*, mini-golf, a large playground, bouncy castles, waterskiing, pedaloes and canoes, lugeing tracks through the forest, bungy-trampolining, swimming (with a lifeguard in July and August), a nature trail, fishing and picnic spots.

Lac de Caniel, Cany-Barville (02 35 97 40 55; www.lacdecaniel.fr). Main courses €5.50–17 (£3.70–11.40). Open July and August daily 11am–10pm, April to June, September and October Wed, Sat, Sun and public holidays noon–3pm and 6–10pm.

Le Cardinal With its long opening hours, warm décor and wide-ranging menu, this is a good spot for family dining in the heart of Le Havre and within easy reach of both the ferry terminal and the train station. Although there's a decent enough *Menu Bambino* for under-10s (€8.50 – £5.70; *steak haché* or *jambon blanc* with chips or tagliatelle, or tagliatelle carbonara, followed by *crème caramel* or ice cream), it's a bit redundant given the ample choice of more interesting dishes – homesmoked salmon with toast, poached eggs with salmon and asparagus, hearty salads (including Montagnarde with local ham, Emmental, lardons, tomatoes and croutons), *croques* in a number of guises, omelettes and pasta dishes. There's a good range of more substantial steaks and fish dishes, including a delicious seafood gratin with leeks, all served with green salad, green beans, chips, tagliatelle, steamed potatoes or rice.

107 boulevard de Strasbourg, Le Havre (℡ 02 35 43 45 45). Main course €5–18 (£3.35–12). Open Mon–Sat 9am–10pm. Highchairs available.

INEXPENSIVE

La Grange This rustically decorated little place with its seafront terrace describes itself as a crêperie and tearoom, but it's got far more on offer than pancakes and cups of tea, including mussels in Normany cider and other guises, main-course salads, ice creams and – from September to May, when a log fire often roars – fondues. The *Petit Breton* menu for under-12s (€6.90 – £4.60) is an unnecessary but good-value option featuring steak or ham with chips or ham crêpes, then ice cream or a crêpe with sugar, chocolate or jam. For parents, there's a good choice of drinks, from local cider and Belgian beer to cocktails. If you're on the way to the beach, you can drop by for takeaway crêpes and drinks.

Seafront, Etretat (℡ 02 35 28 17 31). Main courses €4–9 (£2.70–6). Open July and August and school holidays daily noon–9.30pm. Rest of year Wed–Sun noon–2.30pm and 6–9.20pm.

Rouen & Around

MODERATE

L'Hirondelle Named after the stagecoach that carried Emma from Rouen in the classic novel *Madame Bovary* by Flaubert, which many claim to have been set in this little town (p. 61), L'Hirondelle is a surprise oasis of south-eastern French cooking in Normandy – hence the red chillies strung from the beams in this restaurant complete with huge fireplace, old well, sundial and pleasant terrace. Specialities include duck with *cèpe* mushrooms, pork pie (quite unlike the English version), *cassoulet*, *pipérade* (Basque scrambled eggs with peppers and tomatoes) and ewes' milk cheese with black-cherry jam – a favourite with children. It's all very informal: there's no children's menu but a good choice of simple dishes such as omelettes, crêpes and salads. On some evenings you can enjoy humorous *café-théâtre*, music concerts and other themed events.

40 Grande Rue, Ry, 20 km (12½ miles) east of Rouen on D13 (℡ 02 35 02 01 46). Main courses €6–15 (£4–10). Open Tue 7–10pm, Wed–Sat noon–2pm and 7–10pm, Sun noon–2pm. Highchairs available.

La Suite Afghane ⭐ All warm red and aubergine walls, low lighting and banquette seating, this 'Oriental lounge' lures you in with its tempting aroma of not only Afghani dishes but also specialities from Libya, the Sahara, Sri Lanka and Thailand. It's a fresh choice for a family fed up of crêpes and *steak frites*, especially if you sit at one of the low tables surrounded by little stools and floor-level sofas with huge cushions. Though there's no children's menu, it's the kind of place where you can pick and mix a number of *entrée* dishes to share – perhaps the hummus, the fish, potato and aubergine pakoras, the chicken, cheese and spinach pie, and the Thai mixed mini-brochettes with satay sauce, with pitta breads or a bowl of saffron and cumin rice to mop up. The French don't tend to like their food very spicy, so you don't need to worry unless your children are really fussy, though the solicitous staff are happy to guide you. Follow it all up with a selection of the sensational desserts, including fine slices of orange with cinnamon and saffron yogurt, Afghani cream with almonds, pistachios and cardamom, havla, baklava, pannacotta with fresh mango, Thai coconut flan or banana ice-cream with cardamom. The drinks list includes strawberry juice, tea with cinnamon, cardamom and saffron, French and north African wines, and *boukah*, a firewater made from figs. If you want a quiet meal, come at lunchtime or early in the evening; DJs often take to the decks later on, to spin some Oriental mixes. If you're self-catering, dishes can be ordered as takeaways at a discount of 10%.

3–5 rue des Augustins, Rouen (02 35 15 42 52). Main courses €10.50–12.90 (£7–8.60). Open Mon 7–10.30pm, Tue–Thur noon–2.30pm and 7–10.30pm, Fri and Sat

noon–2.30pm and 7–11.30pm.

INEXPENSIVE

Au Temps des Cerises Despite the famously deplorable service, this institution among Rouen's student community is worth highlighting because it specialises in cheese – if your children are anything like mine, too much cheese is never enough. Younger diners also go a bundle for the kitsch décor of cow paintings, cheese boxes and other dairy-themed knick-knacks. Bestsellers include Norman fondue, *truffade* (a shredded-potato pancake with tomme cheese), *tartiflette* (potato gratin with strong Savoy cheese), baked Camembert with cherry jam, and *fromage blanc* and caramel ice cream (if you want a dessert, don't get a starter – portions are generous, even for the salads). Avoid weekends, when it gets packed, hot and smoky; the terrace is a better bet (though there is also a non-smoking room). On the other hand, the fact that this huge place can be noisy means you don't need to worry about your own little banshees.

4–6 rue des Basnage, Rouen (02 35 89 98 00). Main courses €7–12 (£4.70–8). Open Mon and Sat 7–10.30pm, Tue–Fri noon–2pm and 7–10.30pm

4 Eure

Low on most visitors' agendas, and even then only really well known for Monet's house and garden at Giverny, this landlocked *département* is rich in history, rural charm and unspoilt towns and villages with half-timbered buildings. It's also easily accessible from the French capital: indeed, parts of the eastern Eure have been described as a Parisian suburb, and many day trips run from Paris, including boat rides up the Seine.

The Seine zigzags through sections of the Eure to create some of its most appealing landscapes and best leisure sites. Its banks are wonderful spots for leisurely family walks, especially around Les Andelys, home to Richard the Lionheart's now-ruined castle, built to protect Rouen and the Duchy of Normandy from the French kings. William the Conqueror, a previous Duke of Normandy and invader of England, used to hunt in the stunning Fôret de Lyons in the Eure's north-eastern corner – another great spot for outdoor activities and home to one of France's prettiest villages, Lyons-la-Fôret. You could feasibly base yourself in or around Rouen in the Seine-Maritime, on the Norman Riviera in Calvados or even in Paris while you're exploring some of the Eure's charms, but the region has some regal châteaux-hotels, old coaching inns and low-key B&Bs that make it a good place for a relatively inexpensive stay. The town of Gisors is famous for its sumptuously buttery brioches, but you'll be spoilt for choice amidst the superb country produce served in the Eure's restaurants.

ESSENTIALS

Getting There

By Plane There are no airports within the Eure, but Ryanair flies to Beauvais airport about 75 km (46.6 miles) east of Les Andelys from Ireland and Scotland (p. 29), or you can fly into Paris with many carriers, such as British Airways (p. 30) and Air France (p. 30).

By Ferry Depending on where you are, the nearest Channel ports are Caen-Ouistreham in Calvados (p. 30) and Le Havre and Dieppe in the Seine-Maritime (p. 32). Caen-Ouistreham is about 80 km

(50 miles) west of Bernay, Le Havre 100 km (62 miles) north-west of Evreux and Dieppe 85 km (53 miles) north of Les Andelys. The northernmost ports of Boulogne, Calais and Dunkerque are within about a 2 hr 30 min drive.

By Train No TGVs run here but Evreux and Bernay are only 1 hr 90 mins from Paris St Lazare respectively by normal train (both on the Caen line), and there are trains from St Lazare to Vernon (45–60 mins). St Lazare is within easy reach of the Gare du Nord, where Eurostars (p. 32) from London and Ashford (Kent) arrive.

EURE

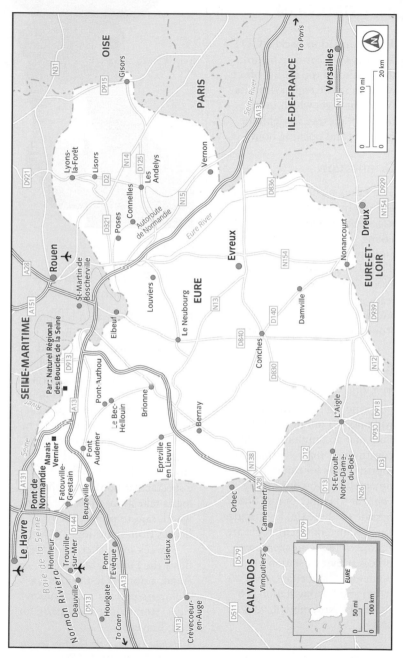

VISITOR INFORMATION

The information-packed CDT website, *www.cdt-eure.fr*, links through to all the tourist office websites in the region from its *Nos Liens* page, which in turn has their addresses, telephone numbers and opening hours.

Orientation

The Eure's main town, **Evreux**, is roughly in the centre of the *département*, with the main **N13** taking you from there to **Bernay** and then to **Caen** in Calvados. The N13 splits off the toll **A13** Paris–Caen motorway, which leads up past **Vernon** and **Pont-Audemer** in the north (via **Rouen** in the Seine-Maritime).

Getting Around

Travelling around the Eure by **bus** is possible but means you will miss out on the rural attractions and accommodation that constitute its main charms; ask at tourist offices for routes and timetables. If you don't bring your car to France or hire one outside the Eure (in, for instance, Paris, Rouen or Caen), there are **Europcar** (*www.europcar.com*) offices at **Evreux** station (4 boulevard Gambetta, ℓ *02 32 39 09 43*) and **Bernay** station (16 rue du 11 Novembre, ℓ *02 32 43 50 49*).

Donkey

Child-Friendly Events & Entertainment

Feu de St Clair ★ A bit like a French bonfire night but far less commercialised, this ages-old festival in the village of La Haye-de-Routot in the Parc Naturel Régional des Boucles de la Seine (p. 95) involves a ritual procession of villagers carrying a 15 m (49 ft) pyramidal tower covered with flowers and topped by a cross, which is set alight to create a spectacular bonfire. At the end, locals take away a piece of burnt wood, said to protect their homes from lightning.

A week or so later, La Haye hosts the **Fête de la Saint Anes**, a donkey festival with a children's/parents' race, donkey rides, storytelling and a prize for best 'brayer'.

Mid-July. La Haye-de-Routot, 15 km (9⅓ miles) north-west of Pont-Audemer off D139 (ℓ 02 32 57 30 41 (mairie)). Admission free.

Les Château-Gaillard-Andelys

Journées Médievales ★ In celebration of its medieval history, the town of Les Andelys, famous as the site of Richard the Lionheart's Château-Gaillard (p. 96), holds themed events over one weekend in June. As well as a market with medieval recipes and crafts, these include falconry displays, a night demonstration of equestrian skills by knights in armour, a medieval feast and street entertainment by jugglers, fire-eaters, stilt-walkers and the like.

Mid-June. Les Andelys (☎ 02 32 71 04 75). Admission: €8 (£5.35) adults, £5 (£3.35) children.

Vièvre, Terre de Mystères ★ This night spectacle presents local history from Neolithic times to the World War II through a stage show involving up to 180 actors, singers and extras together with horses and carriages. It's held at the suitably

atmospheric Manoir de la Fortière; the best bits are the giant images of knights and the like projected onto the castle walls, plus the fireworks finale. Although the 2-hour show doesn't kick off until 10.30pm, you can arrive from 7pm for snacks or proper meals (the latter with advance booking) and a crafts market.

8 nights in July. Manoir de la Fortière, Epreville en Lieuvin, 12 km (7½ miles) north of Bernay off D834 (☎ 02 32 43 32 08 (Bernay tourist office); http:// vievre-mysteres.ifrance.com/). Admission: €18 (£12) adults, €6 (£4) children.

WHAT TO SEE & DO

Children's Top 5 Attractions

❶ Exploring the marshlands of the **Parc Naturel Régional des Boucles de la Seine** with their

Camargue Horses

birdlife, quirky museums and outdoor activities; p. 95.

❷ Investigating Richard the Lionheart's Seine fortress, **Château-Gaillard**; p. 96.

❸ Finding out about local ghosts and legends at the **Musée des Fantômes et Légendes**; p. 97.

❹ Riding Mardi Gras, Halloween and Christmas trains along the **Chemin de Fer de la Vallée d'Eure**, or canoeing along the Eure and returning by train; p. 99.

❺ Getting active amidst the deer and boar of the **Fôret de Lyons**; p. 100.

Beaches & Resorts

Base de Loisirs de Léry-Poses ★
The closest you'll get to a resort in the landlocked Eure, this massive leisure base has colonised two of northern Europe's largest artificial lakes, nestled within a 'curl' of the Seine not far south of Rouen (Seine-Maritime). The first, the **Lac des Deux Amants**, has a supervised

beach, waterskiing, pedalo, catamaran, canoe and windsurfer hire, mini-golf and an 18-hole golf course, fishing, a football pitch, tennis courts and *pétanque*. There are also snack bars and picnic areas, and 4–6-person chalets can be hired year-round. The **Lac du Mesnil** offers climbing, caving, archery, mountain-biking, canoeing and rowing, and there's a nearby dam with an observation room for watching fish go through the *passe à poissons*, and a bird reserve with guided visits.

rue de Savoie, Poses, 7 km (4⅓ miles) south-east of Rouen (Seine-Maritime) off N15 (02 32 59 13 13). Open all year; call for times of various activities. Admission free to Base; fees vary for different activities.

Animal Parks

Les Bois des Aigles – Naturama ★
As the name suggests, 'Eagles' Wood' has lots of birds of prey – up to 40 species in aviaries dotted throughout the woods – displays of hunting techniques they use and costumed horseback falconry displays. But

there are other animal shows too, including a 'fly-over' by cormorants and a sheepdog display – or rather, a dog learning to herd a gaggle of geese – plus some friendly donkeys to pet. For your entry fee you're guaranteed three or four shows a day, assuming you stay that long – you might bring a picnic to eat in the grounds, and there's a bar and a shop. The park hosts various events, including a celebration of animals in film, a festival of Camargue horses and medieval and Halloween festivals.

N12, Bâlines, Verneuil-sur-Avre, 35 km (21¾ miles) south-west of Evreux on D840 (02 32 32 14 75; www. lesboisdesaigles.com). Open mid-March to October daily 10am–6pm. Admission: €10 (£6.70) adults, €7 (£4.70) children under 15.

Nature Reserves, Parks & Gardens

Parc Naturel Régional des Boucles de la Seine ★★
Partly situated in the Seine-Maritime (p. 68), the 'nature park of the Seine's curls' is named for the way this mighty river winds its way between Le Havre and Rouen. The section of the park in the Eure includes the Marais Vernier, a marsh famous for its birdlife, with observation towers and lookouts on the Grande Mare lake. There are also some quirky sights, including, in Ste-Opportune-la-Mare, a former smithy hosting demonstrations and the Maison de la Pomme, an old cottage with displays about apples, tastings of cider, apple juice and the

like, and occasional markets selling apples and other marsh products. To the east, La Haye-de-Routot has an 1845 village four à pain with bread-making demonstrations on Sundays (March to October; (02 32 57 07 99), after which you can take a fresh loaf home, and a curious clog museum (Musée du Sabot; (02 33 25 75 96).

As in the Seine-Maritime, you can walk and cycle here: the Maison du Parc (in the Seine-Maritime) has leaflets outlining a Route des Chaumières, looking at local cottages with irises growing along the top of their thatched roofs, and a Route des Fruits. Ask, too, about donkey and pony rides and canoe hire.

Northern Eure. For the Maison du Parc, see p. 68.

Historic Buildings & Monuments

Château de Fleury la Forêt ★
The main draw of this 17th century château at the end of a sweeping driveway lined with ancient lime trees, at least for young girls, is its Musee de Poupées, a collection of old dolls and dolls' houses and furniture. If you come in mid-October, there's even a *Salon des Poupées* where you can buy antique and hand-crafted dolls for a pretty penny. Otherwise, come for egg hunts at Easter (ages 2–16), an old car meeting in early May, magic shows, detective trails and a mini-zoo in summer, or to see the cellars, chapel and old laundry year

round. Two quite smart and very spacious double B&B rooms, plus the Suite Mathilde (€115/£77) with its double and twin rooms, huge bathroom with a bath and wooden floors, mean you can stay over.

Lyons-la-Forêt, 35 km (21¾ miles) east of Rouen (Seine-Maritime) on D321 (02 32 49 63 91; www.chateaufleury-la-foret.com). Open 2–6pm daily mid-June to mid-September; Sat, Sun and public holidays only mid-September to November and March to mid-June. Admission: €6 (£4) adults, €5 (£3.35) children.

Château-Gaillard ★★ In a spectacular position on a clifftop overlooking a loop in the Seine, this stronghold of Richard the Lionheart, King of England and Duke of Normandy, was built to intimidate King Philippe-Auguste, whose territory extended to Galllion 10 km (6.2 miles) away, and stop him invading Normandy. Today it lies in ruins but is all the more atmospheric for that. Looking at the site and realising the scale of the fortress, you will be astonished to learn that it was built in one year (1197–1198) – a feat that required more than 6000 workers. Architectural innovations conceived by Richard include a circular rampart with an embossed wall that gave less purchase to projectiles, and arrow slits through which one could shoot diagonally. In the inner part are two wells that descend right through the rock down to groundwater 120 m (394 ft) below – imagine being one of the labourers who had to dig those beauties.

As you learn on an excellent guided tour (French, English or German, mid-March to mid-November), Richard, nicknamed 'Coeur de Lion' for his bravery in the Crusades, died of a crossbow wound a year after the completion of the castle he called his 'daughter'. As Philippe-Auguste launched the conquest of Normandy, the 1700 inhabitants of Les Andelys fled inside the castle. French soldiers entered seven months later, some say by the toilet window, others by the chapel. After the surrender, Normandy was made part of the

Château de Fleury la Forêt

Kingdom of France in 1204. The repaired castle went on to play a role in the Hundred Years' War, until Henri IV had much of it demolished in the 16th century. The keen-eyed may spot some unusual flowers on the site, brought back from the Orient by the Crusaders.

Don't miss the equestrian statue of Philippe-Auguste clad in shiny armour in Les Andelys, colonised rather beautifully by grass and plants, or the town's annual **festival** in celebration of its medieval heritage.

Les Andelys (℡ 02 32 54 04 16). Open Wed–Mon 10am–1pm and 2–6pm. Admission: €3 (£2) adults, free under-10s (grounds free).

The Top Museums

There's a **doll museum** at the Château de Fleury la Forêt in Lyons-la-Forêt (p. 95).

Chocolatrium ★ **FIND** This new museum is part of Cluizel, which has been famous for its chocolates for generations (it has shops in Paris and New York, no less), and recounts the history of cocoa and chocolate through texts (in French), photos, artefacts and machinery. In contrast to the reconstructed workshop with its old tools, there's a modern workshop where you watch chocolates being handmade, plus a little cinema with a film showing how a cocoa bean is transformed into chocolate, and teaching you how best to taste it – you get a gift at the end and can also stock up in the adjoining shop. Children go

mad for the *Sucettes* – milk-chocolate lollies filled with praline, decorated with animals, Halloween and mountain scenes (snowmen, St Bernard dogs and so on). There's also the Chocolatrium's own comic-strip book (€25, about £16.75). Allow 75 mins for a visit.

Chocolaterie Cluizel, avenue de Conches, Damville, 18 km (11 miles) south of Evreux on D51 (℡ 02 32 35 60 00). Open Mon–Sat 10am–6pm (last admission 4.45pm). Admission: €5 (£3.35) adults, under-6s free.

Musée des Fantômes et Légendes ★ Strange things have been afoot inside this ruined abbey and its surviving outbuildings for centuries – the sound of footsteps in empty corridors, objects moving by themselves, disruption to attempted archaeological digs and crossed telephone lines among them. The abbey's Museum of Ghosts and Legends tells the story of the 'white lady' (William the Conqueror's granddaughter Mathilde), the 'she-wolf' and the four monks, all said to haunt the place, the latter after being massacred in the

Chocolatrium, Damville

cellars during the Revolution. Comprised mainly of paintings, weird photos and *son-et-lumière* projections that recreate the legends and other spooky beings from the region as a whole, the museum forms part of a 45-minute guided tour, which also takes in some rooms furnished with period décor and the cellars, with old tools, a bread oven, a monk's cell and the *Fontaine des Célibataires*, where the monks used to wash their faces, hands and feet before meals – now visited by girls hoping to meet the love of their life by throwing in a hairpin or coin. Afterwards, you can go for a short spin around the little lakes rich with birdlife on the *petit train*.

Periodic events here include a **Richard the Lionheart festival** (the English king was a visitor to the monastery), with a play and puppet show; a **medieval festival**; and a **teddy bear salon** for collectors and enthusiasts.

Abbaye de Mortemer, Lisors, 3 km (1.8 miles) south of Lyons-la-Forêt

off D2 (✆ *02 32 49 54 34;* **http:// mortemer.free.fr/**). *Guided tours: May to August daily 2–6pm, rest of year Sat, Sun and public holidayss 2–5.30pm. Grounds (ruins, dovecote): daily 1.30–6pm. Admission: €7 (£4.70) adults, €6 (£4) children aged 6–16.*

Arts & Crafts Sites

Fondation Claude Monet à Giverny
A pilgrimage site for art lovers from around the world, the house and gardens that belonged to Impressionist master Claude Monet from 1883 to 1926 and that inspired some of his most famous works, the waterlilies (*nymphéas*) series, are best visited out of high season to avoid the coachloads of visitors from Paris only 70 km (43½ miles) or so away. Despite its popularity, though, it has retained its charm. You can tour the pink house with its restored, colourful interiors hung with the artist's collection of Japanese woodblock prints and copies of some of his own canvases (no originals), and the

Monet's Garden, Giverny

The Seine at Vernon

gardens, reworked to their original state, with a *clos normand* of geometric flowerbeds, climbing plants and the famous Water Garden with its Japanese footbridge. There's also a gift shop in the restored studio that was built to store the huge waterlilies paintings that heralded 20th century abstract art.

The foundation is adjoined by **Les Nymphéas** (**&** *02 32 21 20 31*), a pretty restaurant and tearoom offering sandwiches and drinks (to eat in or take away) as well as full meals all day. Another good spot for breakfast, lunch and afternoon tea is the airy **Terra Café** with its shady terrace in the garden of the **Musée d'Art Americain** (**&** *02 32 51 94 65;* ***www. maag.org***), devoted to American painters and photographers who came to work in Giverny or France as a whole.

84 rue Claude Monet, Giverny, 2 km (1¼ miles) south-east of Vernon on D5 (**&** *02 32 51 28 21;* ***www.***

fondation-monet.com). *Open April to October Tue–Sun 9.30am–6pm. Admission: €5.50 (£3.70) adults, €3 (£2) children aged 7–11.*

Child-Friendly Tours

Chemin de Fer de la Vallée de l'Eure ★ ★ These trips on the old Rouen–Orléans line by 1950s electric rail-car or carriages drawn by a historic engine, starting at Pacy, allow you to see the attractive scenery of the Eure river south of Rouen (Seine-Maritime) towards Evreux. You can disembark at Breuilpont to look around a *wagon-musée* with its restored engines and displays on the line's history, or at Cocherel for a guided walk in the footsteps of local celebrities Bertrand du Guesclin (a famous soldier) and Aristide Briande (former French PM and Nobel Peace Prize winner). At 2 hrs 30 mins, the latter is a bit long and heavyweight for young children (the Breuilpont

trip, at 1 hr 15 mins, is best). On some days Pacy's platform hosts a farmers' market; other events include a winter Galette Express trip with pancake tastings, a Mardi Gras fancy-dress train with gifts for children, haunted Halloween trains, Christmas trains with presents from *Père Noël*, and – if you have a babysitter – Beaujolais Nouveau tasting trains. Best of all are the guided trips along the Eure by canoe followed by a return trip on the train.

For **canoe hire** alone, try the Base Nautique des Tourelles ((06 61 77 20 27) at nearby Vernon. This is also the starting point for 90-minute **river cruises along the Seine** ((02 32 51 39 60), with audio guides (in English for those who want it), that point out the houses of painter Pierre Bonnard (a friend of Monet) and influential publisher Gaston Gallimard, amidst a landscape of pretty valleys dotted with willows, poplars and birdlife, including cormorants and herons.

Pacy-sur-Eure station, 10 km (6.2 miles) south-east of Vernon on D181 ((02 32 36 04 63; www.cfve.free.fr). Open May, June and September Sun and public holidays; July and August Wed, Sat, Sun and public holidays; call for times. Tickets: €8–10 (£5.35–6.70) adults, €6–10 (£4–6.70) children aged 6–16.

For Active Families

See also '**Beaches & Resorts**', p. 94.

Fôret de Lyons ★★ Covering nearly 11,000 hectares in the northern Eure, this ravishing beech forest is known for its extremely tall trees. William the Conqueror came to hunt here, but you may still see deer and boar as you explore its 300 km (186 miles) of marked walking, cycling and riding paths. For maps and details of guided nature walks, bike/mountain bike hire and stables, contact the tourist office at the gorgeous half-timbered village of **Lyons-la-Forêt** in the heart of the forest – a place so picturesque and seemingly untouched by modern life it's often been used as a film set, including by Claude Chabrol for his recent version of *Madame Bovary*. The composer Ravel was also inspired by its peacefulness. Stop off at **La Boutique des Quatre Fermières** (22 rue de l'Hôtel de Ville, (02 32 49 19 73) for wonderful local farm produce. For the forest campsite, see p. 102.

Lyons-la-Fôret tourist office: 20 rue de l'Hôtel de Ville ((02 32 49 31 65; www.lyons.tourisme.free.fr/).

La Voie Verte The latest section of this bucolic 40-km (24.8-mile) walking and cycling route on and beside an old railway line between Evreux and Le Bec-Hellouin, via Le Neubourg and Brionne, was completed in summer 2006. A short stretch north of Le Bec-Hellouin to Pont-Authou will be added in the not-too-distant future. It's a great place for walking, hiking, jogging and cycling, and you'll also see children rollerblading, skateboarding and scootering. Buggies and

Cycling in Normandy

wheelchairs aren't a problem either. For bike hire, including mountain bikes, folding bikes, children's bikes and babyseats, try **Mab Location** at the golf course (☎ *02 32 26 79 73*).

Fvreux tourist office: 1 place de Gaulle (☎ 02 32 24 04 43; www. ot-pays-evreux.fr/).

Shopping

There's a branch of **Printemps** (p. 78) in Evreux (place Armand Mandle, ☎ *02 32 33 02 49*).

Chocolatier Pâtissier Auzou This place is famous throughout the Eure and beyond for its sugary specialities, which include *pavés d'Evreux* ('Evreux paving slabs' – chocolate- and nougat-covered almonds), *pommes de Normandie* (bonbons with Calvados), *zouzous d'Auzou* (macaroons), *Number 1s* (filled chocolates) and *caprices des Ursulines* (delicious little cakes that were originally made by the town's nuns). You can even take

the children into the workshops to see the goodies – which are expensive but worth it – being made.

34 rue Chartaine, Evreux (☎ 02 32 33 28 05). Open Tue–Sat 9.30am– 12.15pm and 2–7pm, Sun 9.30am– 12.15pm.

Le Panier à Nature ★ **FIND** If you care about the environment and the effect of global trade, as well as what you put into your own and your children's bodies, this little shop, opened in mid-2005, is for you. It offers only local produce and organic and Fair Trade products sourced from small-scale producers within a 50-km (31-mile) radius. Among the award-winning goodies are farm yogurts, jams and honeys, fruit juice (try the refreshing red apple juice), beer (including Richard Coeur de Lion beer from Tosny) and wine, organic bread and meat, snails and ready-made dishes. The best time to come is Saturday morning, for free tastings.

4 place Adolphe Barette, Vernon
(📞 02 32 54 67 42). Open July and
August Mon–Sat 9.30am–12.15pm
and 3–7pm, Sun 10am–1pm; rest of
year Mon–Sat 9.30am–12.45pm and
2.40–7pm, Sun 10am–1pm.

FAMILY-FRIENDLY ACCOMMODATION

Around Les Andelys

MODERATE–VERY EXPENSIVE

Le Moulin de Connelles ★★
One of Normandy's most stunningly situated hotels, partly occupying an island in the Seine, this 19th century, half-timbered manor offers quite smart accommodation that differs wildly in price according to the view from your window. The best of the five suites, for up to four people, has panoramic views over the Seine and the hotel's landscaped grounds, plus a jacuzzi; it costs more than double the cheapest suite, which looks over the car park. The décor could be more exciting (unless you have a thing for washed-out pastels), but rooms glow with the river light that entranced many Impressionist painters. Outside there's a pretty swimming pool, punting on a private stretch of the Seine, *boules,* table tennis and mountain bike hire; there's also an indoor pool, jacuzzi and sauna. The excellent restaurant has a non-smoking verandah with views over the Seine plus refined regional cuisine such as red mullet salad with basil and olive oil, snails with champagne butter and green apple sorbet

with Calvados. Children can choose a starter, fish or meat main course with vegetables and dessert for €12 (£8) – perhaps John Dory with courgettes and thyme, roast lamb or gratin of Charlotte potatoes, then apple and almond cream tart or chocolate shortbread and praline cake with vanilla sauce. Even better than the verandah, in fine weather, are the tables set out beneath the trees – a beautiful spot to spend a summer evening while the children run around.

*D19, Connelles, 15 km (9⅓ miles)
south-east of Rouen (Seine-Maritime)
via D126 (📞 02 32 59 53 33; www.
moulindeconnelles.com). 13 rooms.
Double/twin €120–278 (£80–186),
suite for two €145–383 (£97–257)
then extra bed €27 (£18) (free under-
12s). Cot free. Amenities: restaurant;
indoor and outdoor pools; jacuzzi;
sauna; grounds. In room: satellite TV,
minibar, safe, jacuzzi (some).*

MODERATE

There's good accommodation at the **Château de Fleury la Forêt** (p. 95).

INEXPENSIVE

Camping St Paul ★ This campsite is on a shady riverbank in a gorgeous beech forest (p. 100) that you can explore on foot, by bike or on horseback, but its 'back-to-nature' atmosphere comes combined with some four-star comforts: an outdoor pool, children's games, football and *pétanque* pitches, tennis courts and mountain bike hire. The pool and tennis courts require an extra fee but there's 50% off for campers. There are also special

Lyons-la-Forêt

sanitary blocks for the disabled. If you don't want to camp, there are some pretty, green-painted 4–5-person chalets with terraces, available for midweek or weekend as well as weekly stays; guests in these get free use of the pool and 50% off the tennis courts and mountain bike hire.

Lyons-la-Forêt, 35 km (21¾ miles) east of Rouen (Seine-Maritime) on D321 (☎ 02 32 49 42 02). 100 pitches. Pitch and car: €13 (£8.70) for two then €3 (£2) per extra person aged 3 and over. Caravan/motorhome pitch: €15 (£10) for two then €3 (£2) per extra person aged 3 and over. Chalet: €250–350 (£167–235) per week. Amenities: outdoor pool; games; sports facilities. Closed November to March.

Around Evreux

EXPENSIVE

Château de Brécourt ★ This storybook château surrounded by moats and wooded 20-hectare grounds is a good place to unwind *en famille*, with its smart and incredibly spacious accommodation, including four family 'apartments' (interconnecting rooms), and its indoor pool and outdoor tennis court. There's a restrained elegance to the décor, both in the guestrooms and the plush restaurant, **Le Grand Siècle**, with dark woods and fresh colours predominating. Menus in the restaurant start at €42 (£28) and might include carpaccio of smoked monkfish with herbed winkle salad then roast seabream with seasalt, crushed lemon-scented aubergine and a black-olive samosa, followed by apricot mousse with pistachio ice cream. For children there is a €14–€18 (£9.40–12) menu of smoked salmon or a cold meat platter, then fillet of sole *meunière* or fillet of beef accompanied by crushed potatoes or fresh tagliatelle, followed by ice cream or sorbet. The good Continental or buffet breakfasts (€14 – £9.40/children's prices according to age and by arrangement) can be enjoyed on the lovely terrace in summer.

Route de Vernon, Douains, 7 km (4⅓ miles) south-east of Vernon off D181 (☎ 02 32 52 40 50; www.chateau debrecourt.com). 29 rooms. Double €90–172 (£60–115), 'apartment' for four €270 (£180). Extra bed €30 (£20), cot €14 (£9.40). Amenities: restaurant; indoor pool; tennis court; grounds. In room: satellite TV, telephone, hairdryer.

INEXPENSIVE–MODERATE

In Evreux, the **Hôtel de France** offers good inexpensive accommodation. *www.hoteldefrance-evreux.com.*

Broc Fontaine This 300-year-old half-timbered farmhouse and its outbuildings is set in lovely grounds with a medieval-inspired rose and herb garden and a colour-coded organic fruit and vegetable garden – blue leeks, purple kale, scarlet chard and berries of all hues are just some of the ingredients you might find in your optional evening meal, during which you can enjoy the likes of pork with sage and cider and goats' cheese potato gratin (€25–30/£16.75–20); children can get smaller portions of the same dishes or special meals according to their personal tastes. Breakfasts (bread, brioche, warm croissants, farm butter and homemade jams) are similarly tempting, and you can indulge in afternoon tea by a trout-filled brook. Of the three pretty and homely B&B units, one is a double/twin, one is a two-bedroom suite for 3–6, and the last – and best, with views over the orchard – is a separate cottage with two bedrooms for a total of four. The French-American owners have French-and English-language books and magazines on gardening, gastronomy and Impressionism – and if you've been inspired by a visit to Monet's house (p. 98) 30 minutes away, they will even supply you with art materials. Or you can take turns at the piano in the cosy living room.

36 rue St-Fiacre, Brosville, 9 km (5½ miles) north of Evreux on D52 (02 32 34 61 78; http://giverny.org/hotels/ pivain/). 3 rooms. Double/twin €70 (£47), suite for four €125 (£83.75). Cot free. Amenities: gardens; living room with piano; evening meals with advance booking.

Around Bernay

MODERATE

Le Domaine du Soleil d'Or ★

Rooms in this stern-looking building, set in an unremarkable but pleasant little town in the Risle valley, vary wildly: some are rather chintzy and old-fashioned, others more up-to-date, with muted colours, new wooden floors and even flat-screen TVs. In addition to double rooms, there are a suite and an 'apartment' in a separate manor half a kilometre away: both have two double bedrooms, but the suite has a bathroom with a jacuzzi and shower, while the apartment has only a shower room (albeit one with multijets). These have the advantage of being set away from the hotel's 'lounge-restaurant', **So Café**, which has a lively bar with a billiards table and a busy programme of music concerts. Its wildly eclectic, tapas-style menu should have something to please everyone, be it plates of Oriental or Corsican specialities, *ramon ibérico* (Spanish ham), lamb and aubergine tagine, Tunisian *brik* (filo pastry) with chicken and coriander, or even traditional French dishes, followed by the likes of almond tart with roast figs or rice pudding. The under-12s menu (€10/£6.70) comprises *croque monsieur*, ham or steak with sautée potatoes, market vegetables or homemade pasta, followed by ice cream in wacky flavours (Nutella, chewing gum or Carambar – a French

Le Bec-Hellouin

caramel) or waffle with sugar or Nutella.

*1 chaussée du Roy, Thibouville, 15 km (9⅓ miles) north-east of Bernay off N13 (02 32 45 00 08; **www. domainedusoleildor.com**). 14 rooms. Double €54–90 (£36–60), 'apartment' for four €180 (£120), suite for four €210 (£140). Amenities: restaurant and bar. In room: TV, telephone, minibar (some).*

INEXPENSIVE

Abbey Stone House and Cottage Located in a small hamlet surrounded by water-meadows and woods by the River Risle, these two gîtes overlook Le Bec-Hellouin and its Benedictine abbey, and are believed to have been built with stone from the original 11th century abbey. Sharing a big garden, both can fit up to eight at a squeeze. The 'house' has three double bedrooms (one with a balcony, one with a shower unit), and there's a sofabed downstairs in the living room. The modern bathroom is also downstairs, though there's a loo with a washbasin upstairs. The kitchen has a contemporary styling quite rare in French gîtes. The 'cottage', a converted barn, has two double bedrooms, a bunkbed room and a sofabed in the living room with its open fireplace (wood can be provided, though there's central heating too; the heating supplement is a rather expensive €65/wk – that's £43.55). You can request a cot and an extra mattress to use on the floor. In July and August you can also rent Edelweiss, a very pretty half-timbered house on a hillside overlooking a peaceful valley near Pont Audemer, with four bedrooms for up to seven. Up a notch in luxury, it has a well-equipped kitchen with a dishwasher, a washing machine, a TV with DVD and video players, a badminton court and a large enclosed garden.

*5 rue St Nicolas, Le Bec-Hellouin, 15 km (9⅓ miles) south-east of Pont Audemer on D130 (02 32 44 90 02; **www.abbeystonecottage.com**).*

Pont Audemer

3 rooms. Rates: €600–872 per week (£400–585). Cot free. Amenities: garden; badminton court (one). Gîtes: kitchen; TV with DVD and video (one); books; dishwasher (one); washing machine (one); heating (extra fee).

Le Phare ★ One of the most unusual places to stay in northern France, this B&B is in an old lightkeeper's dwelling, and you have your breakfast in the adjoining 33 m (108 ft) lighthouse. On clear days, the latter offers lovely views over the Seine estuary and the Pont de Normandie (p. 69). The five basic en-suite rooms include a family room for two adults and two children under 15 (in two double beds). Baby equipment, including a cot and bottle-warmer, is available, and there's a courtyard garden and a communal living room with a TV and hi-fi.

Fatouville-Grestain, 3 km (1.8 miles) south-east of Honfleur (Calvados) off D180 ☎ 02 32 57 66 56; www.

locationhonfleur.com). 5 rooms. Double €50–65 (£33.50–43.50). Family room €80 (£53.60). Extra bed €15 (£10), cot free. Amenities: communal TV room; garden.

La Venise Normande ★ This B&B in Pont Audemer – dubbed the 'Norman Venice', hence the name – is handy for the Marais Vernier and the Parc Naturel Régional des Boucles de la Seine (p. 95) as a whole, occupies a former butcher's shop, it's so bright and welcoming. This being, in part, a 17th century building, rooms tend to be on the cosy side, but they're lovingly decorated, with beams and a palette of warm siennas and sunny yellows. The best is Bianca with its tailor's dummy and view of a bell tower; this can sleep a family in a double and two single beds, with space for a cot too, and has a restored antique bathtub. The other rooms (doubles) look over the delightful cobbled courtyard, set with tables and chairs for summer breakfasts of homemade breads, crêpes and jams. Evening meals are sometimes available, and a highchair is provided. There's also a homely salon with a piano. Alternatively, you can book an adjoining wooden chalet for up to five (including a baby), available on a B&B basis or as a self-catering gîte.

9 rue Sadi Carnot, Pont Audemer ☎ 02 32 56 82 53; www.venise normande.com). 4 rooms. Double €55–70 (£37–47), suite for 4/5 €100 (£67). Cot free. Amenities: salon with piano; courtyard; Internet access; evening meals (occasional). In room: telephone, hairdryer.

FAMILY-FRIENDLY DINING

Around Les Andelys

MODERATE

Les Lions de Beauclerc A restaurant, tearoom, hotel and antiques shop all rolled into one, set in one of France's prettiest villages (p. 100), Les Lions has a smart dining room decorated with items from the shop and a pretty courtyard where you can enjoy daily specials based on market produce, or good galettes and crêpes – ideal for those times when the children need simple and reassuring fare but you want something a little more interesting. Children can also get small portions of steak and ham with chips. Note, though, that there's no highchair.

The five **rooms**, only recently introduced, include a family suite for four, which at €89 (roughly £59.60) is great value given the luxurious modern bathrooms. Breakfasts are a delicious affair including freshly squeezed orange juice and homemade jam and hot chocolate, served until late in the morning.

7 rue de l'Hôtel de Ville, Lyons-la-Forêt, 35km east of Rouen (Seine-Maritime) on D321 (℡ 02 32 49 18 90; www.lionsdebeauclerc.com). Menus €11–26 (£7.40–17.50). Open noon–2pm and 7–9.30pm Wed–Sun.

INEXPENSIVE–MODERATE

Le Paris Plage Named after a 'beach' by the Seine that drew weekending Parisians to this area, this is a cheerful joint with tropical motifs in its slightly canteen-like dining room. Usefully, it's open throughout the day, for a flexible array of eat-in or take-away food – snacks, salads, pizzas (including one with snails and garlic butter), seafood platters or traditional French dishes. There's a good-value children's menu at €6.50 (£4.35), offering *steak haché* with a fried egg, sausages or ham with chips, followed by an ice-cream cone, *fromage blanc* or fruit salad, but there are also pasta dishes and some omelettes and *croques*. In fine weather, it's good to sit on the large terrace; on Thursdays, Fridays and Saturdays you'll be treated to magic shows, musical concerts or karaoke sessions, relayed onto a big screen that's also used for special sporting events such as World Cup matches.

6 place de Paris, Vernon, (℡ 02 32 51 48 54). Main courses €4–15.50 (£2.70–10.40). Open Tue–Sun 9am–1.30am, plus Mon when a public holiday. Food served 11am–12.30am, takeaways 11am–3.30pm and 6.30pm–12.30am. Highchairs available.

Eureux & Around

EXPENSIVE

The **Château de Brécourt** (p. 103) has a very fine restaurant.

INEXPENSIVE–MODERATE

Restaurant de la Voie Verte A surprising location for good lunch cuisine as well as snackier fare, this restaurant is set in a golf clubhouse at the start of the Voie Verte (p. 100) and has lovely views from its terrace. You choose from 'posh' dishes such as *foie gras* with *cèpes* or figs, roast pike with orange sauce and courgettes flavoured with star anise, and *crème brûlée* with orangeflower, large salads, or a brasserie menu with seafood crêpes, mushroom and ham galettes, omelettes, and *croques madames* – the latter are a little expensive, at €11 (£7.40), but include a drink/coffee. Better-value *formules* include the Birdy (starter and main/main and dessert €17, or £11.40). You can also enjoy sandwiches (€3.50/£2.35) at the bar. If the children don't find anything to please amidst all that, there's a fallback children's menu (€7/£4.70) with a drink, *steak haché*, fish fillet or Parisian ham, and ice cream.

Chemin du Valème, Evreux (℡ 02 32 62 51 16). Main courses €10–12 (£6.70–8). Open Mon–Fri noon–3pm, Sat and Sun noon–6pm. Highchairs available.

Around Bernay

La Pommeraie ★ This restaurant in a rural setting not far from Bernay is a relaxed spot for refined local produce, with an elegant dining room with a roaring fire in winter and a very pretty riverside terrace for milder days. House *foie gras* is the speciality, cooked, for instance, with apples and gooseberries, but if you don't approve or want something lighter, the fish dishes, which include turbot with king prawns, are excellent, and the dessert of Calvados apple sorbet superb. Children are consulted by the efficient waiting staff as to what

they might like, but basically get melon or *crudités*, followed by fish with vegetables, steak with chips or a small portion of anything on the main menu – perhaps seabass with crunchy vegetables or duck with apple chutney – for a good-value €10–12 (£6.70–8).

N138, St Quentin des Isles, 3 km (1.8 miles) south of Bernay on D33 (℡ 02 32 45 28 88). Main courses €18–28 (£12–18.75). Open Tue–Sat noon–2pm and 7.30–9.30pm, Sun noon–2pm, plus Mon when a public holiday. Highchairs available.

Le Domaine du Soleil d'Or (p. 104) has an interesting global menu.

Papa Joe's If you've worked up an appetite exploring the nearby 'curls of the Seine' (p. 95), this is a handy if basic option where you can enjoy grills, pasta dishes and salads in small or large portions. The main attraction, though, is the authentic crisp-based pizzas, which you can also get to take away: highlights are the Normande, with ham, egg and cream, Attomica, with mince, garlic, parsley and oregano, the *calzone soufflée* and – for parents – the Orientale with spicy merguez and chorizo sausages. Desserts include good ice creams.

70 rue Constant Fouché, Beuzeville, 15 km (9⅓ miles) west of Pont Audemer on N175 (℡ 02 32 57 82 44). Main courses €6–14 (£4–9.40). Open daily noon–2pm and 7–9.30pm (closed Mon and Tue evening in August). Highchairs available.

5 Orne

ORNE

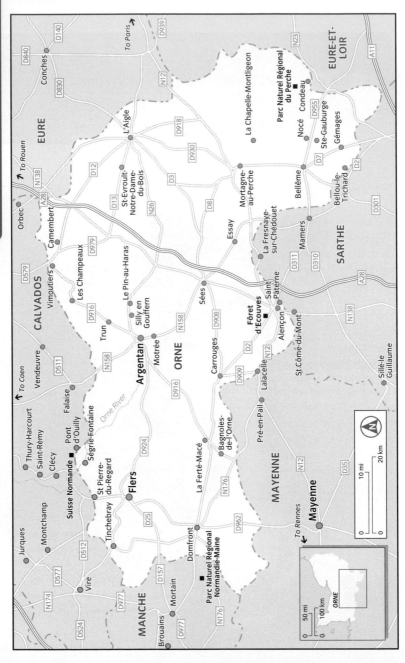

Largely overlooked by tourists, the Orne is ideal for active holidays in the heart of nature, far from commercialised forms of tourism and surrounded by animals. As well as the long-lashed cows who provide the ingredients for the Orne's most famous export, Camembert, the area is well known for its Percheron horses – handsome beasts of burden who you may have seen pulling streetcars at Disneyland. And the forests clothing much of the *département*, which is home to portions of two national regional parks, teem with wildlife.

In spite of its relative obscurity, however, the Orne is home to some truly sensational places to stay that can make it a very good-value alternative to the more touristy Calvados over the border – from moated castles to cosy farmhouse B&Bs. Many of them have their own restaurants serving superb local produce; others run a variety of nature-based courses and activities that make them the perfect base for the kind of family that gets twitchy after a couple of hours on the beach. Your only problem, in fact, will be deciding between them.

Essentials

Getting There

By Plane There are no airports within the Orne. Depending on which part of the *département* you're heading for, your nearest air entry points are **Le Havre** (p. 54), about 65 km (40.4 miles) from Vimoutiers, **Rennes** about 100 km (62 miles) from Domfront in Brittany (see the companion to this guide, *Brittany with Your Family*) and **Paris** (p. 56) about 120 km (74½ miles) from L'Aigle.

By Ferry Again, depending on where you're going, the ports of **Caen-Ouistreham** about 60 km (roughly 37 miles) from Argentan, **Le Havre** (p. 60) about 65 km (40.4 miles) from Vimoutiers and **St-Malo** about 100 km (62 miles) from Domfront in Brittany are quite convenient.

By Train The TGV network doesn't serve any part of the Orne, but there are direct trains to **L'Aigle** from **Paris-Montparnasse** (on the line to Granville in Manche), taking between 1 hr 15 mins and 1 hr 40 mins. **Argentan**, meanwhile, is 40–50 mins from **Caen** on the line to Le Mans. For the **SNCF**, see p. 39.

VISITOR INFORMATION

The informative CDT website, *www.ornetourisme.com* (which has an English translation), has a page with contact details of the *département*'s tourist offices and *points informations* – click on 'Useful addresses'.

Orientation

Alençon, the largest town in the Orne, is near its southern border and about 165 km (102½ miles) from **Paris** on the main N12 (small parts of which are motorway), which goes via **Mortagne-sur-Perche**; this road also takes you on to **Rennes** in eastern Brittany, via the Mayenne. Alençon is also about 140 km (87 miles) from **Rouen** in the Seine-Maritime on the **A28** toll motorway down to Tours.

From the north, the fastest road is the **N158** from **Caen**, past **Argentan** to **Sées**, where you can join the **N138** or **A28** to Alençon. Otherwise, there are a handful of other *routes nationales* and *départementales* and lots of country roads.

Getting Around

Bus and train services are sketchy in this very rural *département*, and though tourist offices will advise on routes and timetables, the only real way of exploring the Orne is by car. In the unlikely event that you don't bring your own or hire one elsewhere (for instance, Caen, Rouen or Paris), there is **car hire** two minutes from the station at **Alençon** (Europcar, 3–5 rue Demées, ☎ *02 33 28 91 11*).

Child-Friendly Events & Entertainment

For the spectacular **Jeudis du Pin** horse shows at the Haras du Pin, see p. 114; for the **Percheron** day in the Parc Naturel Régional du Perche, see p. 116.

Les Musilumières ★ Subtitled the 'book cathedral', this show held inside Sées's medieval cathedral tells the story of its construction, architecture, sculptures and stained-glass windows, and recounts the life of several saints, through hi-tech sound and light effects, including giant images of faces, animals, plants and more projected onto the inner walls, resembling huge frescoes. Unlike many *son-et-lumière* shows, it's a perfect length for children, at just 45 mins, although you still have to wait until it gets dark – 10.30pm in July, 10pm in August and 9.30pm in September.

Fri and Sat July to mid-September. Cathédrale, Sées, 20 km (12.4 miles) north-east of Alençon on N138 (☎ 02 33 28 74 79 (tourist office); www. musilumieres.org). Admission: €12 (£8) adults, €5 (£3.35) children aged 10–18.

Sées Cathedral

Perche, Terre de Legendes

Another of the nocturnal spectaculars the French seem so keen on, this show – held on 10 nights over the course of a month in summer – relives local history and legends through a stage show involving actors, Percheron horses and *son-et-lumière* effects. Like most such events, it's not inherently unsuitable for very young children, but they will probably have difficulty staying up so late – the show begins at 10.30pm. The website has lots of details of local restaurants offering special menus, including children's meals, on show nights.

Mid-July to mid-August. Parc de Vigan, Bellême, 40 km (24.8 miles) east of Alençon on D955 (☎ 02 33 25 23 23 (tourist office); www.perche-passion.com). Tickets: €10 (£6.70) adults, €8 (£5.35) children aged 12–18, €4 (£2.70) children under 12.

WHAT TO SEE & DO

Children's Top 5 Attractions

❶ Watching an equestrian show at the Haras du Pin national stud farm; p. 114.

❷ Meeting the horses, donkeys and cows or making rustic toys at the Maison du Parc and riding a Percheron-pulled carriage through the Réno-Valdieu forest in the Parc Naturel Régional du Perche; p. 116.

❸ Browsing at L'Aigle market, the third biggest in France, then watching the livestock auctions; p. 122.

❹ Staying in a family pavilion on stilts in a forest clearing at the Manoir du Lys, and eating in its Michelin-starred restaurant; p. 130.

❺ Flyfishing with Mum or Dad at the Moulin de Gémages, before a gastronomic dinner accompanied by a magic show; p. 124.

Beaches & Resorts

Base de Loisirs La Ferté-Macé
If you can't make it to the seaside, the 65-hectare leisure base centred around La Ferté-Macé's large lake is a more-than-acceptable alternative. Among the amenities are a beach that has lifeguards in July and August, a play area for children, volleyball pitches and a bar. You can also hire pedaloes, electric boats, windsurf boards, sailboats and canoes, and enjoy mini-golf, archery, orienteering, *pétanque*, model boating and fishing, or pitting yourself against the climbing wall. It's also a good spot for picnics.

Boulevard de la Forêt d'Andaine, La Ferté-Macé, 18 km (11 miles) east of Domfront on D908 (☎ 02 33 38 99 00). Open all year; reception 2–7pm May and June Wed, Sat, Sun and public holidays, July and August daily. Admission free (fees for some activities).

Other Natural Wonders & Spectacular Views

La Roche d'Oëtre ★★
This 118 m (387 ft) cliff, which looks like a human face and has wonderful views over the

La Roche d'Oëtre

surrounding countryside, is the main attraction of the Suisse Normande (p. 140), most of which is in Calvados. In the past the region was notorious as a refuge for all sorts of outlaws, who hid in caves and other secret spots such as the *Chambre aux fées* ('fairies' chamber').

In 2006 a new visitor centre, the **Pavillon de la Roche d'Oëtre**, opened here with displays on local geology, plants and wildlife, which includes green lizards. This is the starting point for various walking paths – those recommended for families are *Le sentier des corniches*, which is basically a 10-minute nature stroll around the top of the cliff, and *Le sentier des gorges*, a 1-hour walk suitable for children aged 7/8 and up, taking you down alongside the Rouvre waterfall (it's a fairly steep descent, so you need good shoes).

The reception desk and shop have a general map, available in French and English, plus 12

larger foldout maps, and there's a restaurant with non-stop service (Easter to November) from noon to 10pm, whether you fancy a gastronomic meal or a sandwich and ice cream.

At nearby St Pierre-du-Regard you can ride four-person **Vélo-rails** (📞 *02 31 69 39 30*) along old railway tracks, similar to those in the Seine Maritime (p. 77), and see displays in some old postal carriages.

St Philbert-sur-Orne, 20 km (12.4 miles) north-east of Flers off D25 (📞 02 31 59 13 13/02 33 62 80 70; www.normandie-montagnes.fr). Admission free to site; centre: €5 (£3.35) adults, €2.50 (£1.68) children aged 6–16. Site open all the time; centre July to late November daily 10am–7pm.

Animal Parks

Haras National du Pin ★★
France's national stud farm is well worth visiting at any time, but try to come on a Thursday at 3pm (June to September) for the *Jeudis du Pin* – spectacular displays involving dressage by English and Arab thoroughbreds, carriage-pulling by local Percheron horses (p. 117) and horseback acrobatics to a classical soundtrack in the splendid Cours Colbert (note: you need to arrive at 2.30pm: gates close at 3pm sharp for security reasons). In July and August there are also 45-minute tours of the research centre (Mon 3–6pm), 30-minute demonstrations by the blacksmith (Tue 3–5pm) and 30-minute saddle-making displays (Fri 2–4.30pm). From

mid-July to the end of August (Wed 3–5pm) there are 30-minute paddock tours when you can see the horses relaxing and working outdoors. General guided tours take place year round and, in addition to introducing you to the working stables and exhibitions of old carriages and saddles, they take you inside a new *parcours découverte* or museum space with interactive displays on horse anatomy, breeds, reproduction and use, plus the history of the Haras. There are also films, photos, drawings and artifacts.

Out of season (September to May, Thur 2–5pm) you can also take guided visits of the castle, nicknamed the 'Versailles of the horse', with its 17th century artwork and furniture. A new café, Degas, serves light meals and snacks, but the surrounding parkland is also a wonderful spot for a family picnic.

Le Pin-au-Haras, 12 km (7½ miles) east of Argentan on N26 (✆ 02 33 36 68 68; www.haras-nationaux.fr). Open for guided tours daily early October to March 2–5pm (plus 10.30am–noon in school holidays), April to early October 9.30am–6pm. Admission: €4 (£2.70) adults, €2.50 (£1.68) school-age children, €1.50 (£1) children under school age. Research centre tour €2 (£1.34); blacksmith/saddlery demonstration €2 (£1.34); paddock session €2 (£1.34); Jeudis du Pin €4 (£2.70).

La Petite Boderie ★ This 10-hectare site with its orchards, woods, pond and walking paths is a lovely place to bring little children, who can ride donkeys

Haras National du Pin

or a New Forest pony, go for a jaunt in a cart pulled by two Normandy cobs, or pet the goats and sheep. Donkeys can be hired for anything from an hour to a day, with or without a guide.

Ste Honorine-la-Chardonne, 10 km (6.2 miles) north-east of Flers on D25 (✆ 02 33 65 90 46). Open Mon–Wed and Fri; booking required. 1 hour donkey ride €10 (£6.70).

Nature Reserves & Parks

Parc Naturel Régional Normandie-Maine ★★
Covering much of the southern section of the Orne (plus parts of the Manche – p. 173 – and Mayenne and the Sarthe outside Normandy), this regional park is heavily forested over a quarter of its 235,000 acres, and includes deer, boar and hares among its abundant wildlife. Come in late September or early October to witness the dramatic annual stag rut. On some of its plains you can even seen rare sundews (*Drosera*), a carnivorous plant

that exudes a nectar to attract the insects it feeds on. Flora and fauna aside, it's an excellent place for walking, orienteering, rock-climbing, mountain-biking, horse-riding and fishing. The **Maison du Parc** on the edge of the Fôret d'Ecouves can provide details of all activities, and also sells Topoguides' walking, riding and mountain-biking maps and runs various nature sorties. For World Wildlife Fund **gîtes and B&Bs** in the park, see p. 125.

*Maison du Parc: Carrouges, 25 km (15½ miles) north-west of Alençon on D2 (✆ 02 33 81 75 75; **www.parc-naturel-normandie-maine.fr/**). Open Mon–Fri 9am–noon and 2–6pm. Admission free (fees for some activities).*

Parc Naturel Régional du Perche ★★ Known for its sturdy but agile Percheron horses (p. 117), the Perche area east of Alençon forms part of another French regional natural park (the rest is in the Eure-et-Loir outside Normandy). A landscape of forests, rivers, hills and marsh-land, this is home to a host of animal and plant life and is another good place to cycle and walk. To get a bite-size taste of it, visit the **Maison du Parc** in the 15th century Manoir du Courboyer at Nocé, which has a tourist information point, exhibitions, a shop selling regional produce and a restaurant serving local dishes, plus 65-hectare grounds with Percheron horses, Norman donkeys and cows and 8 km (5 miles) of themed walks with viewing points. The best time to visit is July, when there's a

Cycling in the Forest

Percheron day including carriage-pulling and dressage competitions organised by the Haras National du Pin (p. 114), plus burlesque shows involving Percherons pitted against Shetland ponies. For the rest of the year the Maison runs guided nature walks and work-shops for adults and children (including making rustic toys), farmers' markets and more.

*Maison du Parc: Courboyer, Nocé, 18 km (11 miles) south-east of Mortagne-au-Perche on D9 (✆ 02 33 85 36 36; **www.parc-naturel-perche.fr**). Open daily June to October 10.30am–6.30pm, November to March 10.30am–5.30pm, April and May 10.30am–6pm. Admission free (manor €2/£1.34; guided visits €3/£2; free under-16s).*

Historic Buildings & Monuments

Abbaye de St-Evroult-Notre-Dame-du-Bois Particularly atmospheric at sunset, when it glows a reddish hue, this ruined 13th century abbey on the site of

Gentle Giants

The symbol of the Perche region, **Percheron horses** are known around the world for their size (they're up to 1.72 m or 5 ft 7 in tall and a tonne in weight) and strength – they're used to pull streetcars at the Disney theme parks in France and the States. Yet they're a friendly and placid breed said to have been mixed with Arab horses after the battle of Poitiers in 732 AD. You can meet some dappled grey or black specimens at the Maison du Parc in the Parc Naturel Régional du Perche (p. 116) and the Haras du Pin (p. 114), but better still, since 2006 you've been able to take **horse-and-carriage rides** pulled by Percherons in the Réno-Valdieu forest, including a 2-hr 4.7 km (2.9 miles) circuit around La Chapelle-Montligeon. For information, ask at the Maison du Parc (p. 116), which also sells the brochure *A la découverte du cheval percheron*. Additionally, you can see displays on Percherons and take part in an annual Percheron festival at the **Musée des Arts et Traditions Populaire du Perche** (℡ *02 33 73 48 06, **http://ecomuseeduperche. free.fr***) at Ste Gauburge to the southeast of Bellême. The museum houses a collection of farm and craft objects ranging in date from the 19th century to the 1960s.

one dating back perhaps as far as the 6th century was used by Luc Besson (who lives in the next village) as the location for some of the scenes in his *Joan of Arc*, shot

Horse-drawn Carriage

in 1998. It's a pleasant place to wander around, and when you've had your fill of ancient history, you can swim or fish in pretty Saints-Pères lake in which the ruins are reflected, with its small beach, boat and pedalo hire, play equipment, a mini-golf pitch and tennis courts. You're also on the edge of the Forêt de St-Evroult, where you can walk, ride or mountain-bike, and the town has a campsite.

St-Evroult-Notre-Dame-du-Bois, 10 km (6.2 miles) north-west of L'Aigle on D13 ℡ *02 33 34 93 12 (mairie)). Open all the time. Admission free.*

The Top Museums

Exposition de la Météorite de L'Aigle The meteor shower that struck the little town of L'Aigle in 1803 was so scientifically

Abbaye de St-Evroult

significant – a report written by leading mathematician Jean-Baptiste Biot after studying the incident supported emerging theories that rocks could fall from the sky – that today there are fragments from the fall in almost every collection around the world, including in Paris, London and New York.

Unsurprisingly, perhaps, the town took the bicentenary of the shower as an opportunity to open a special exhibition on the subject. Here you can learn, among other facts, that 2000–3000 rocks fell from the sky that day, the largest weighing 9 kg, and see some of the fragments, on loan from Paris's natural history museum. French-language panels explain the phenomenon of meteorites, and there are also some displays on Biot, who had a crater on the moon named after him.

In the same building is the **Musée Juin 44**, with unintentionally hilarious talking waxworks of General de Gaulle, President Roosevelt, British PM Winston Churchill and others helping to relay the history of World War II, with special reference to events in Normandy. An **archaeology exhibition** and a small **musical instruments museum** are also here.

Musée Muncipal, Place Fulbert de Beina, L'Aigle (☏ 02 33 84 16 16). Open April to October Tue, Wed, Sat and Sun 2–6pm. Admission: €3.60 (£2.40) adults, €1.80 (£1.20) children aged 7–15 (inc entry to Musée Juin 44 and archaeology exhibition; instrument museum is free).

Musée du Camembert This little museum tells the story of one of France's most famous exports – the stinky cheese created by a farmer's wife, Marie Harel, in the nearby village of Camembert (p. 121) in the 18th century. Near the town market is a statue of Harel presented by an American cheese-maker after the old one was destroyed in World War II. At the museum itself you learn about traditional production methods (from milking through moulding to packaging), see a reconstructed cheese dairy and admire a collection of Camembert posters, boxes and labels. A stroll around will take you about half an hour, but leave double that if you want to enjoy a tasting (extra €2.50/£1.68).

If you're a real fan, ask staff about the 'Camembert route' through picturesque local villages, with stops at working farms and buildings of historical interest.

10 avenue du Général de Gaulle, Vimoutiers, 25 km (15½ miles) northeast of Argentan on D916 (℡ 02 33 39 30 29). Open April to October Mon 2–6pm, Tue–Sat 9am–noon and 2–6pm, Sun and public holidays 10am–noon and 2.30–6pm, November to March Mon 2–5.30pm, Tue–Sat 10am–noon and 2–5.30pm. Admission: €3 (£2) adults, €2 (£1.34) children.

Musée du Jouet This rather old-fashioned museum in a former town baths presents toys and games from the 19th and 20th centuries, displayed in the main in glass cases away from meddling fingers. Divided into several thematic sections that help paint a portrait of French life in days gone by, they include musical instruments, robots, optical games such as magic lanterns and shadow theatres, Meccano sets and dolls made from an amazing variety of materials – wood, *papier mâché*, porcelain, wax, celluloid and even metal. Though it's not

Camembert

worthy of a special trip, it does make for a good interlude if you're spending the day at the town's **Base de Loisirs** (p. 113) or coming for its Thursday-morning **market**.

32 rue de la Victoire, La Ferté-Macé, 18 km (11 miles) east of Domfront on D908 (℡ 02 33 37 04 08). Open 3–6pm daily July and August; Sat, Sun and public holidays in April to June, September and October. Admission: €3.25 (£2.20) adults, €1.55 (£1) children of school age, children under 6 free.

Arts & Crafts Sites

Musée des Beaux Arts et de la Dentelle
Craftworkers began making lace in Alençon in the 1800s, after Catherine de Médici introduced it to France in the 16th century, and Alençon lace – especially *point coupé* (snipped thread) – is now the most famous type in the world, dubbed 'the queen of lace'. As well as housing the town's fine-arts collection and a roomful of Cambodian artifacts, this museum tells the story of the evolution and technique of Alençon lace through videos and a collection of very fine pieces. As you look at them, bear in mind that it takes two to three working days to make one postage-stamp-sized piece. If

Antique Lace Hats

that doesn't put you off and you are staying in the area for a while, ask about courses.

You can wander freely around the museum, or ask for a **guided tour** by one of the dozen or so remaining lace-workers from the Atelier National du Point d'Alençon, set up in the 1970s to preserve the tradition. Twice a week in summer there are also lace-making **demonstrations**; call for times. If you're truly bitten by the lace bug, ask at Alençon's tourist office (below) about the 'Lace Route', which takes in other towns known for their lace – Argentan and La Perrière in the Orne, Caen and Courseulles in Calvados, and Villedieu-les-Poêles in the Manche.

Between rue du Collège and place Foch, Alençon (℃ 02 33 80 66 33 (tourist office)). Open Tue–Sun 10am–noon and 2–6pm (daily July and August). Admission: €3 (£2) adults, children under 14 free.

For Active Families

See also 'Beaches & Resorts', p. 113, and 'Nature Reserves & Parks', p. 115.

Poney-Club de la Moynerie
A well-respected riding school, La Moynerie is unusual on two counts – it offers pony rides for children as young as two, and it has some English-speaking staff among its friendly team. Situated just north of Argentan, it runs treks in the surrounding countryside of meadows and hills, away from traffic, plus courses in the likes of equestrian circus tricks, and a few non-horsey activities too, such as trampolining and monocycling.

Coudehard, near Trun, 15 km (9⅓ miles) north-east of Argentan off D16 (℃ 02 33 35 78 11). Open all year. Prices vary.

Shopping

Ferme Biologique de Cutesson The chief attraction

of this pretty little organic farm in a green valley 10 minutes outside the town of Vimoutiers is that while you shop for excellent ciders, *poiré* (p. 228), *pommeau* (p. 233) and Calvados (oh, and apple juice too), little ones can be outside petting the cows and calves, sheep and farmyard animals. On your way in or out, clock the Char Tigre, a restored tank in the spot where it was abandoned by the Germans in World War II, and one of only two to remain in existence.

Route de Gacé, Vimoutiers, 25 km (15½ miles) north-east of Argentan off D916 (☎ 02 33 39 18 53). Open Mon–Sat 9am–noon and 2–6pm, Sun 9am–noon.

La Maison du Camembert

Shaped like a half-open circular Camembert box, this shop is in the tiny village where one of France's most famous cheeses was first made. It's owned by mass-market producer Président, who also run the Ferme Président opposite, which is not a farm at all but a museum on cheese production through the ages, very similar to the one in nearby Vimoutiers (p. 118). As well as having a cheese bar where you can taste Camembert and other local cheeses, including Pont L'Evêque, Livarot and Neufchâtel (p. 79), the shop sells cheese in a variety of guises and related paraphernalia such as boards and knives.

Just down the road is the last farm producer of Camembert in Normandy, Fromagerie Durand (La Heronnière, ☎ 02 33 39 08 08).

It's generally only open to groups of 20 or more with advance booking, but if you're passing by in July or August, it's worth calling in to see if the farm gates are open to visitors, allowing you to see Camembert being made and buy farm products.

Camembert, 18 km (11 miles) north-east of Argentan off D916 (☎ 02 33 12 10 37). Open 10am–6pm Wed–Sun February to April and September; daily 10am–6pm May to August.

Maison des Métiers de Carrouges

Half exhibition space, half shop, this was set up to promote local produce and crafts, so you get to see demonstrations by craftspeople and enjoy free tastings while you browse the stalls of cider, pâtés, honey, jams, chocolates, biscuits, cheese and so on. The helpful staff will also give you information on local producers and working farms selling to the public. Come at weekends, when there is more entertainment, or Christmas, when there's a gift fair selling famous local

La Maison du Camembert

lace from Alençon (p. 120) and other gifts.

Maison du Parc, Carrouges (℡ 02 33 82 82 75). Open mid-July to mid-August 11am–12.30pm and 2–6.30pm, second half of August Mon–Fri 2–6pm, Sat, Sun and public holidays 11am–12.30pm and 2–6.30pm.

Marché du Mardi ★★ The Tuesday-morning market in L'Aigle, a town said to have got its name from an eagle that watched over the building of its first castle in the 11th century, is the third-largest in all France, with hundreds of stalls taking over the town centre. You'll find fish and dairy stalls on rue de l'Abreuvoir, butchers and cold meat stalls on the place St Martin, poultry on place de Verdun, fruit and vegetables on place Boislandry, and a flower market on place de la Halle; then there's fabrics, clothes and more on place de l'Europe, rue de Bec-Ham and rue de Gambetta. When you've shopped until you want to drop, sit and watch the bustling livestock auction (*marché aux bestiaux*), which attracts buyers and sellers from all over Normandy to trade in cows, horses, sheep and other animals.

L'Aigle (℡ 02 33 24 12 40 (tourist office)). Open Tue 8am–1pm.

FAMILY-FRIENDLY ACCOMMODATION

The Perche

EXPENSIVE

Domaine de Villeray ★★ This moated castle and mill complex in extensive grounds is perfect for a relaxing few days, but staff will try to tempt you from the cosy salons or poolside to take part in a whole host of activities, including canoeing on the Huisne, horse-riding, horse-and-carriage rides, mountain-biking, touring local manors or even

Marché du Mardi, L'Aigle

flying in a hot-air balloon. There are also tennis, table tennis and *pétanque* facilities, and, when the children are tucked up for the night, wine-tastings in the plush mill restaurant with its excellent seasonal dishes and river views. Here you might enjoy such sophisticated fare as Perche black pudding with compôte of apples, seabass with truffles, cream of broccoli and asparagus tips, and mango and pineapple roasted with passionfruit and an orange reduction. Children's meals (€10/£6.70) take into account their preferences, but typical offerings are melon with smoked ham or tomato and mozzarella salad, cod fillet or grilled steak with green beans, pasta with tomato sauce, rice or sautée potatoes, and sorbets, fruit tart or chocolate mousse; there are several highchairs.

From May to October, you have to stay half-board at an extra €47–70 (£31.50–47) a day for two adults. Children aged three and under stay here free all year (except for meals); you have the choice of 'apartments' (interconnecting rooms) for four in the castle or mill buildings, and there's another room for 3–4 in the mill. There's not much difference in price; the mill is more rustic and flowery in feel than the château with its refined pinks and pastels. Good Continental breakfasts (€13/£8.70 adults, €8/£5.35 children) can be served in one of the salons, on a terrace in good weather, or in your room.

The Perche

Condeau, 25 km (15½ miles) south-east of Mortagne-au-Perche on D10 (☎ 02 33 73 30 22; **www.domaine devilleray.com**). 41 rooms. Double €90–170 (£60–114), 'apartment' for four €230–250 (£154–168). Cot free. Amenities: restaurant; bar; salons; grounds; outdoor pool (May to October); tennis court; games; canoe and mountain-bike hire; activities; babysitting service. In room: satellite TV, telephone, hairdryer.

INEXPENSIVE–MODERATE

La Saboterie ★★★ It's hard to decide between these B&B rooms/gîtes in the stunning Parc Naturel Régional du Perche (p. 116) and those at the Moulin de Gémages below. Where at the Moulin you are at a trout fishing centre, here you are on an organic farm that provides the goodies for healthy but delicious breakfasts and optional evening meals (€17–24/£11.40–16; over-fives €15/£10). With its junkshop chic, La Saboterie has the edge on style. The three B&B rooms consist of two doubles and a vast old clogmaker's workshop with space for 5–8 in two double and three single beds, plus its own dining area in a lovely conservatory. You can book all the rooms out to form a gîte for 8–10, with an added kitchen (with washing machine) and a cottage garden, or one of the doubles (the one with a sitting/dining room) with an extra children's bedroom (beds are available for children up to six, 6–12 and in their teens) plus the kitchen, for a total of four. Outside there's a garden with a play area for children and various activities, including cheese-making and cookery on the farm, mushroom-picking in the Fôret de Bellême, astronomy, nature walks, mountain-biking and oddities such as trips to look at sundials in the Perche or restoration courses at the Musée des Arts et Traditions Populaire (p. 117). The hosts will lend you maps if you're heading out alone.

La Haute Blatrie, Bellou-le-Trichard, 40 km (25 miles) south-east of Alençon off D2 (℡ 02 33 83 25 98; http://bellou61.free.fr). 3 rooms. Double €50–70 (£33.50–47), suite for five €150 (£100), gîte for four €250–300 (£168–200) per week (weekends also available). Amenities: garden with play area; evening meals by request; farm with animals; kitchen with washing machine (in gîtes); courses and activities.

INEXPENSIVE

Moulin de Gémages ★★★
Another lovely option in the Parc Naturel Régional du Perche, this old watermill counts 12 trout ponds among its 15 hectares, where guests (including beginners and children) are free to fish, and which often furnish the main ingredient for the optional evening meals (€25/£16.75; €17/£11.40 children under six). Other wonderful homely dishes might include goats' cheese quiche, rabbit in cider, stuffed curds and chocolate profiteroles to follow, and there are occasional gastronomic evenings accompanied by a magic show. Picnic baskets can also be provided for days out or in the grounds. Accommodation comes in the form of five delightfully rustic B&B rooms and an attached gîte for six; four of the B&B rooms have one double bed and one single. There's plenty of space to run around outside, where tables are set under a tree with a swing.

The flyfishing ponds have their own lodge with a bar serving snacks and hot meals (the latter by advance booking) and a shop with rod hire and repair and fishing material and accessories for sale. There are regular one-day fishing courses, including ones for parents and children, and ones strictly for ladies and for couples! If fishing's not your bag, there are other activities and courses, including ceramics and nature outings looking at plant and animal life within the grounds.

Gémages, 25 km (15½ miles) south of Mortagne-au-Perche off D7 (℡ 02 33 25 15 72; http://moulindegemages. free.fr/). 6 rooms inc gîte. Room for three €80–90 (£54–60). Gîte €270–390 (£181–260) per week (weekends

possible outside school holidays).
*Amenities: trout fishing courses;
nature outings; optional lunch and
evening meals. In room: hairdryer.*

Around Argentan

EXPENSIVE

Pavillon de Gouffern ★★★
Handy for the Haras du Pin
(p. 114), this 18th century hunting pavilion in 78 hectares of
grounds and forest with resident
deer stands out for its stylish
rooms newly fitted with
flatscreen TVs and granite, teak
or stone bathrooms. Families can
bag a cute cottage with a living
room with a sofabed on the
ground floor and a double room
and bathroom on the first, or
there's a triple in the main
building. If you don't feel like
venturing into the surrounding
countryside, there's heaps to do
on site – horse rides in the forest, horse-and-cart rides (you can
even drive them yourselves),
mountain bike hire, fishing in

the hotel pond, golf (a three-
hole training area was introduced in 2006) and a fine
outdoor pool. There are also seasonal events such as Easter egg
hunts, Mothers' and Fathers'
Day lunches and concerts by the
floodlit pool. At lunchtime you
can enjoy light meals of salads
and grills beside the pool, while
for evenings there are three
salons with leather armchairs
and an atmospheric restaurant
serving the likes of shrimp ravi-
oli with lemongrass consommé,
tarte Tatin of black pudding with
a honey *jus* and caramelised
apple, and vanilla waffle with a
minestrone of red fruits. Children
get €8 (£5.35) and €12 (£8)
menus – both feature *steak haché*
or turkey escalope with chips, ice
cream and a drink; the first
offers a starter of a cold meat
platter or *crudité* salad, the second smoked salmon or melon
and proscuttio salad in season.
A highchair is provided.

Bear Necessities: Staying in a Panda Gîte

In common with other *parcs naturels régionaux/nationaux,* the **Parc Naturel Normandie-Maine** (p. 115) is home to some World Wildlife Fund (WWF)–labelled Panda gîtes – inexpensive or moderate lodging (usually self-catering) that offers *séjours nature* with easy access to walking trails and prolific plant and animal life plus observation equipment such as binoculars and species identification guides. There are several close to Alençon: the **Château des Villiers** at Essay, a moat-encircled castle with five B&B rooms and a gîte for six to eight; **Le Tapis Vert**, an old hunting lodge at Lalacelle, with three- and eight-person gîtes plus music and theatre courses and concerts; and **La Sauvagère**, a four-person gîte at Mortrée with an owner who leads mushroom-hunting expeditions. For details, contact **Gîtes de France** (☎ *02 33 28 07 00*; *www.gites-de-France.fr*).

Silly en Gouffern, 7 km (4⅓ miles) east of Argentan on N26 ☎ 02 33 36 64 26; *www.pavillondegouffern. com*). 21 rooms. Doubles €80–180 (£54–120), family 'cottage' for four €200 (£134). Cot free. Amenities: outdoor pool (June to September). In room: satellite TV, Internet access, radio.

INEXPENSIVE

Maison du Vert ★★ **VALUE** An anomaly in a carnivorous country such as France, this vegetarian guesthouse in an old bakery is a wonderful spot for animal-loving families, with its organic gardens and orchards full of rabbits, ducks, geese, chickens, turkeys and sheep that children can pet and help to feed, a pond full of koi carp, an ever-increasing cat population, and wildlife such as kingfishers, herons and woodpeckers. Children can even help collect the eggs, which British owner and chef Debbie puts to good use in the kitchen, along with fruit and veg from the garden. Your optional evening meal in the homely restaurant might include such globally inspired veggie (and vegan) treats as falafel with hummus, *röstis* (panfried potato and onion cakes), an Indian *thali* plate, and coconut and ginger ice cream. Main courses are around €12 (£8). Children's meals are cooked to order – jacket potatoes and pasta with tomato or cheese sauce, followed by ice cream, tend to be most popular, but they can eat from the menu too. If it's not too busy, the friendly young waiting staff may offer to keep an eye on your children in the

Maison du Vert

cosy neighbouring salon with its books and games while you linger at the table.

The rooms are excellent for the price, if not huge. Two are doubles and one is a family room with a double and a single bed; all can fit an extra bed or a cot. The family room has a bath in the bathroom; the other rooms have showers (one of them across the hall). Not that you'll spend too much time in them – while the children play, you can enjoy a cup of tea and a slice of homemade cake, or a cocktail, cider or Calvados, at one of the tables set out on the lawns. You can also eat your Continental breakfast (€6.50/£4.35, €3.50/£2.35 children aged 5–10) or dinner there in warmer weather.

Ticheville, 5 km (3.1 miles) south-east of Vimoutiers on D12 ☎ 02 33 36 95 84; *www.maisonduvert.com*).

3 rooms. Double €54–60 (£36–40), family room for four €80 (£54), extra bed €10 (£6.70). Cot free. Amenities: restaurant; guest living room with books, games and toys; gardens with animals; bike loan (adult bikes).

Around Alençon

EXPENSIVE

Just south of Alençon and a whisker over the Orne–Sarthe border, the **Château de Saint Paterne** (02 33 27 54 71; *www.chateau-saintpaterne.com*), where Henry IV honeymooned, is worth mentioning for its plush interconnecting family rooms (about €210/£140) and children's dinners (€10/£6.70) at 7.15pm – you can then whisk them up to the room and return armed with a 'babyphone' for a candlelit meal of recipes from the hostess's own cookbook (children can eat with you if they insist). There's also an outdoor pool, tennis courts, ping-pong and bikes for use in the 10-hectare park. Ask about 'Weekend familial' deals: for €810 (£540) you get two nights' accommodation for four, two adults' and two children's dinners, breakfasts, lunch in a nearby inn, a visit to a castle or mini-farm and an activity such as riding.

Manoir du Lys ★★★ FIND

Nature-lovers rejoice – in a clearing in the forest in the grounds of this half-timbered manor with its smart modern rooms lie seven newly built wooden pavilions especially for families, six of them on stilts and one at ground level for those in wheelchairs. Quite fashionable in décor, they generally have a double room with a kingsize bed or two twins and a living room with a sofabed, a huge bathroom, a private terrace and their own parking space; two have an additional single bed in the living room. All can easily fit an extra bed, which means they can accommodate five or six people in total. The grounds also have a children's play area, an indoor and outdoor pool, a tennis court, table tennis, billiards, mountain bike hire and easy access to walking trails.

The manor's stunning Michelin-starred **restaurant**, with its terrace beneath the apple trees for fine days, offers one of the best children's menus in Normandy – the *Petit Mousserons* for under-12s (€13/£8.70), with a cornet of fine ham or homesmoked salmon, then beef, veal or fish fillet with vegetables, sautée potatoes or pasta, then *crème brûlée* with Carambar (a French caramel) or chocolate mousse. Highchairs are available. For other children, half-portions of some of the dishes on the main menu can be offered – this menu includes the likes of Vire chitterling sausage with potato and Camembert waffle, steamed spring duckling with spring vegetables, and poached peach with spices. The *menus* include a tasting menu of mushrooms from the surrounding Fôret des Andaines, which even make their way into the desserts. After dinner, with the children down for the night, you might like to return to the piano bar for a *digestif* and perhaps a cigar from the *cave*. Breakfast (buffet or Continental €12/£8; under-12s €6/£4) is as good as you would expect from a place of this calibre, and if you can gather a group of eight or more, the chef will even create a 'picnic' for you on a table in the forest.

Route de Juvigny, La Croix Gautier, Bagnoles-de-l'Orne, 15 km (9⅓ miles) east of Domfront on D908 (℡ 02 33 37 80 69; www.manoir-du-lys.fr). 30 rooms. Double €65–195 (£43.50–131), pavilion for four €200–250 (£134–168). Extra bed €30 (£20), cot free. Amenities: restaurant; bar; indoor and outdoor pool; play area; tennis court; games; bike hire; babysitting service. In room: TV, telephone, minibar, hairdryer, Wi-Fi Internet access.

INEXPENSIVE

Another option just to the south of Alençon and over the Sarthe border at Champfleur, **La Garencière** (℡ 02 33 31 75 84; *http://monsite.wanadoo.fr/garenciere*) is a great bargain, with rustic B&B rooms for three, four or five (€48–49/£32–33), including one in a 'Petite Maison' in the old farm bakery, plus an indoor pool in use year-round. Children can make friends with the resident Jersey cow, Princesse, and the sheep, poultry, rabbits and cats, and there are optional evening meals (€19/£12.75) with country recipes such as Camembert tart, chicken in cream and homemade cakes.

FAMILY-FRIENDLY DINING

The Perche

EXPENSIVE

The **Domaine de Villeray** at Condeau (p. 122) has excellent food.

INEXPENSIVE–MODERATE

Just over the Orne–Sarthe border, in Mamers, **La Fringale** (4 rue du 115e Régiment d'Infanterie, ℡ 02 43 97 23 97) is an excellent crêperie with Provençal, Breton seaside and countryside-themed rooms, a pretty inner courtyard and a play space for children. As well as galettes and crêpes, it serves salads, grilled meats, omelettes, bruschettas and ice creams.

Grénier à Sel This useful option combines a ground-floor brasserie with an upstairs restaurant serving more elaborate dishes, meaning you can eat according to your mood and/or pocket. The brasserie is the obvious choice for those with children – it has a little play area plus a basic *menu enfant* (€7.50/£5) with standards such as *steak haché* and *jambon blanc* with chips, followed by ice cream, though the main menu may tempt them more, with its *hors-d'oeuvre* buffet, grills and salads. Various good-value *menus* include an Express *formule* for just €8 (£5.35), with a buffet platter and dish of the day or dish of the day and dessert. Or try the restaurant: this doesn't have a children's menu, but they may enjoy the home-smoked salmon, farm beef or even the black pudding, for which Mortagne is famous.

9 rue Montcacune, Mortagne-au-Perche (℡ 02 33 25 51 98). Main courses €7–14 (£4.70–9.40) (brasserie), €10–22 (£6.70–14.75) (restaurant). Open noon–2pm daily, 7–9.30pm Thur–Sat. Highchairs available.

Hôtel Le Montligeon This sweetly rustic dining room in a small provincial hotel is a welcoming spot where you can enjoy a choice of menus featuring Norman and specifically Percheron dishes made from good local produce. The under-12s menu, *La Vilette* (€7/£4.70), features a glass of apple juice, sausage or grilled tomato as a starter, then ham with potato gratin or salmon with fresh pasta, and an ice cream. Menus for over-12s start at €13.50 and go up to €34; dishes include snails with duck, melon soup with local ham and *confit* of duck with mushrooms. There's also a vegetarian menu based on seasonal produce, including a tasty vegetable tart, and a great-value daily-changing lunch menu (€8.50/£5.70). In good weather you can sit out on a leafy terrace for meals, or for an ice cream in the afternoon.

The seven hotel rooms include two with two double beds each; they're plain but very cheap €53–55 (£35.50–37) given that they have en-suite bath- or shower rooms and TVs,

and views over the village square with its fountain and church. Guests have exclusive use of the billiards table in the downstairs bar. You're right on the edge of the Réno Valdieu forest here.

Le Bourg, La Chapelle-Montligeon, 12 km (7½ miles) south-east of Mortagne-au-Perche off D10 (℡ 02 33 83 81 19; www.hotelmontligeon. com). Menus €8.50–34 (£5.70–22.80). Open July and August Tue–Sat noon–2pm and 7–9.30pm, Sun noon–2pm, rest of year Wed–Sat noon–2pm and 7–9.30pm. Highchairs available.

Around Argentan

EXPENSIVE

The wonderful **Pavillon de Gouffern** (p. 125) has a children's menu.

MODERATE–EXPENSIVE

La Camembertière ★★ The welcome here is genuinely warm, the building modest (it looks like a roadside shack), and the emphasis, as the name attests, is on cheese dishes, especially those made with Camembert, which originated just up the road (p. 121). Nevertheless, this is a gastronomic restaurant serving rich and sophisticated local cuisine. Among the choices are Camembert tart and skate wing with Camembert, but the highlights aren't necessarily the cheese dishes – try the savoury *assiette de pays* (€12/£8), with farmyard guinea hen in a pommeau (p. 233) reduction with whipped cream, plus a glass of cider or *poiré* (p. 228). There's a large and – if you don't speak French – rather bewildering array of menus; surprisingly, all of them are adapted for children, with corresponding prices (€8–25/£5.35–16.75). For smaller children unused to strong flavours, the chef has introduced a new €6 (£4) *Bout de Choux* menu with roast chicken and tagliatelle in a creamy sauce, plus an ice cream or other homemade dessert. Best of all, if you arrive early evening when nobody's about, the obliging staff will probably usher you to a table even if the restaurant isn't technically open yet.

Les Champeaux, 15 km (9⅓ miles) north of Argentan on D916 (📞 02 33 39 31 87). Main courses €10–21 (£6.70–14). Open Thur–Tue noon– 2pm and 7–9.30pm. Highchairs available.

MODERATE

The **Maison du Vert** in Ticheville (p. 126) is a rare oasis of vegetarian and vegan cuisine using lots of organic ingredients, with children's meals cooked to order.

Alençon & Around

EXPENSIVE

The Michelin-starred restaurant at the **Manoir de Lys** (p. 127) offers some of the best children's meals in Normandy, plus family suites on stilts in the forest. Junior foodies will also like the **Auberge Saint Paul** (📞 02 43 97 82 76, **www.auberge-saint-paul. com**) just over the Orne–Sarthe border at La Fresnaye-sur-Chédouet, with its 'mini' and 'maxi' children's menus (€9.50/ £6.40 and €12/£8) featuring Loué free-range chicken breast cooked in cream or fish of the day with chips, ice cream and a drink, plus, in the more expensive menu, a starter platter of cold meats or smoked salmon. Alternatively, there are half-price half-portions of certain dishes for *petits gastronomes* under 14. Popular main courses include duck with farm cider, sea bream with goats' cheese and veal kidneys with old-style mustard.

INEXPENSIVE–MODERATE

Brasserie des Ducs A handy Parisian-style brasserie and bar right in the centre of Alençon, this place is open all through the day every day for a wide range of dishes, from seafood and grilled meats to salads, sandwiches and pizzas, including a number of Alsace specialities. The *Petit Duc* under-12s menu varies daily according to what the chef picks up at the market but is always good value at €8 (£5.35) for a simple starter, main course and dessert.

19 place Poulet Malassis, Alençon (📞 02 33 26 37 49). Main courses €7–15 (£4.70–10). Open daily 10am–11.30pm. Highchairs available.

6 Calvados

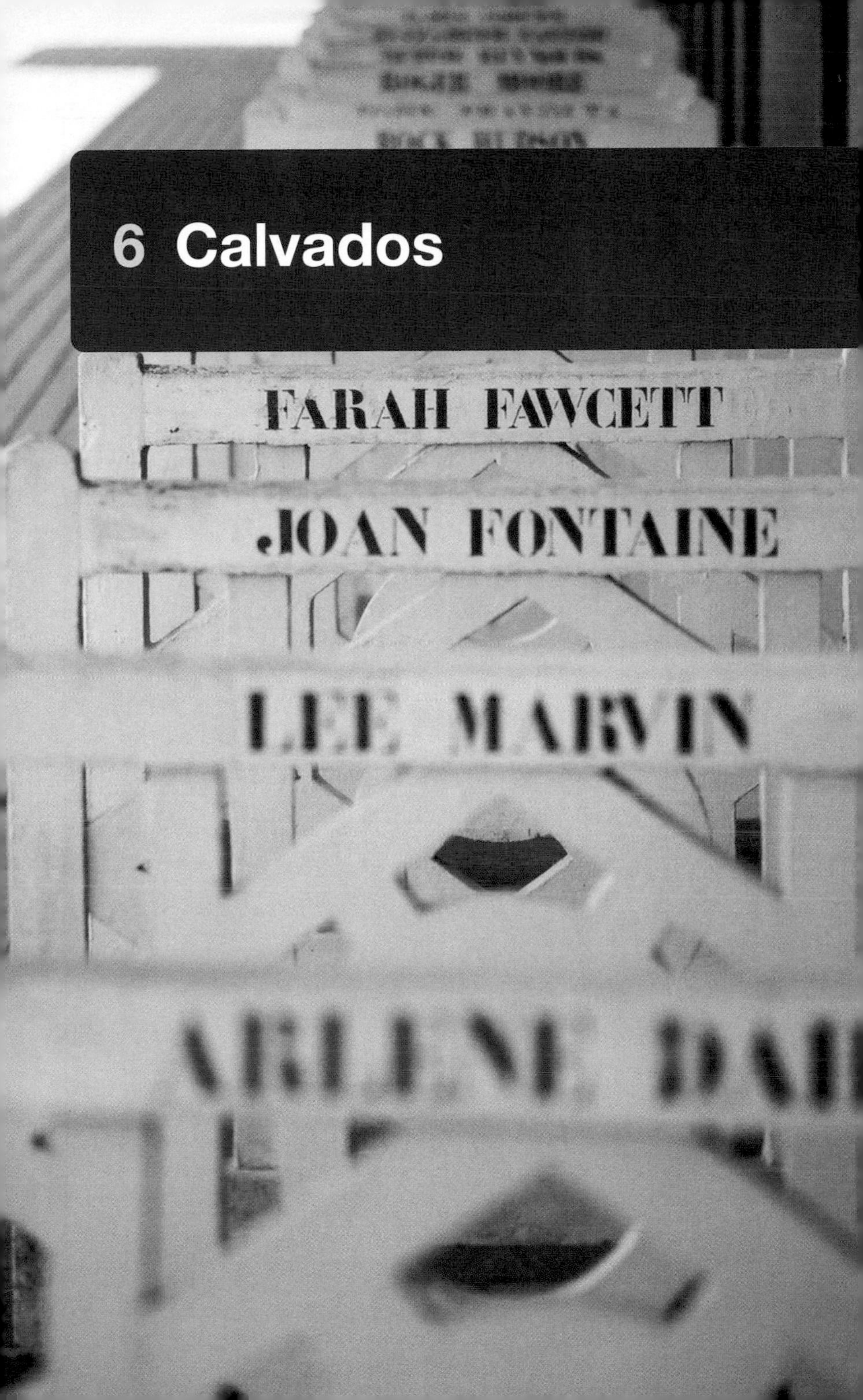

Calvados

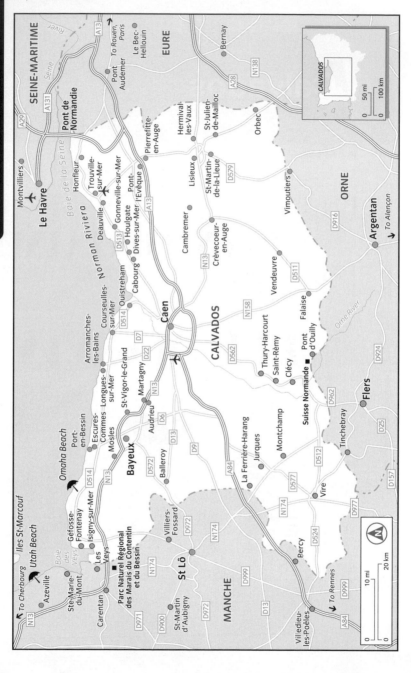

Calvados draws the crowds with its string of chichi seaside **resorts and picturesque ports** (dubbed the Norman Riviera), its D-Day landing beaches and its internationally famous Bayeux Tapestry, a sort of proto comic strip recounting William the Conqueror's Norman Conquest antics. The heart of northern France, it's accessible from all directions and by every mode of transport, and it's one area of northern France you could explore without a car, provided you stick to the coast. Inland, however, are a host of quirky châteaux and museums that it would be a shame to miss, as well as great outdoor sporting facilities, especially in the Suisse Normande with its peaks and gorges.

For foodies old and young, this is also Normandy's gourmet heart – a paradise of apple-based drinks, tarts, turnovers and other desserts made with the products of its orchards, of unctuous sauces created from the dairy produce provided by the region's cows, and of wonderful seafood. It's true that restaurants and accommodation here can be expensive, but there are bargains to be had, and you'll be more than satisfied whatever your budget.

Essentials

Getting There

By Plane At the time of writing, Caen-Carpiquet airport had no flights from the UK or Paris (or rather, it offered flights between Caen and Manchester but they were via Lyon 700 km south of Caen!). For the latest information, check **www.caen.aeroport.fr.**

In October 2006, Ryanair (p. 29) launched thrice-weekly budget flights between Deauville Saint-Gatien airport (**www.pays-auge.cci.fr/aeroportdeauville**), 10 km east of Deauville and London Stansted; see the airline's website for schedules and prices.

Alternatively, there are flights from the British south coast to Cherbourg in the Manche (p. 174) and Le Havre in the Seine Maritime (p. 54).

By Ferry Caen-Ouistreham port 14 km north-east of Caen itself is serviced by Brittany Ferries (p. 31) from Portsmouth up to four times a day, with 'classic cruises' taking 5 hrs 45 mins (7 hrs at night) and high-speed ferries (mid-March to mid-November) 3 hrs 45 mins. Vessels used are the *Mont-St-Michel*, with cinemas, an Internet café, a disco-club and video games area for teenagers and a children's entertainment programme; the *Normandie*, with its children's entertainment programme and games room; and the *Normandie Express*, with a playroom and video games room.

By Train There are no high-speed TGV services in the *département*; from Paris St Lazare normal trains run daily to Caen (2 hrs, sometimes with a change at Lisieux, 90 mins from Paris), Bayeux (2 hrs 15 mins, sometimes with a change at Caen) and Deauville–Trouville (2 hrs). For SNCF information, see p. 39.

VISITOR INFORMATION

The useful CDF website, *www.calvados-tourisme.com*, lists the contact details and websites of all the *département*'s tourist offices and *syndicats d'initiative*; click on 'Info Pratiques', or 'Useful Information' in the English version.

Orientation

Caen is at the centre of a spider's web of major roads that make Calvados one of the easiest *départements* to move around or to cross: the N13 down from Cherbourg in the Manche, via Bayeux, taking you on to Paris 240 km away via Lisieux; the A13 toll motorway also taking

you as far as Paris, via Rouen in the Seine Maritime; the N158 taking you down past Falaise and almost to Alençon in the Orne; and the A84 toll motorway taking you down to Rennes in Brittany (190 km). But if you're not in a hurry, the winding coastal roads linking the towns of the Norman Riviera and the D-Day landing beaches are often very scenic.

Getting Around

If you fly into Deauville or Le Havre (in the Seine Maritime) and don't plan to go much further than the Norman Riviera and the landing beaches, you can rely on Bus Verts de Calvados (📞 *0810 214214*): its number 20 plies the Caen–Deauville–Honfleur–Le Havre route all year, and it has a summer 'D-Day Line'.

If you need to hire a car, Easycar (p. 38) has pickup points at Caen-Ouistreham port, Caen-Carpiquet airport, Deauville station, Lisieux and Falaise.

Horse-drawn Carriages

Child-Friendly Events & Entertainment

Equi'Days A longstanding event that gets bigger every year, this equestrian festival involves more than 2500 horses in events held all around Calvados over two weeks in October. These include jumping competitions, horse shows, endurance races, carriage-driving, musical processions, stud farm tours and stalls by horse rescue charities. The highlight for many is the *Course des Stars*, where French media celebrities take part in a trotting race at Cabourg.

*Mid-October. Various locations (℡ 02 31 27 90 30; **www.equidays.com**). Admission free (most events).*

Festival des Jeux ★ Bayeux's annual weekend-long festival of games transforms much of its centre into one big play space that you can wander through, ogling the street performers and taking part in anything that catches your eye – there are stalls and kiosks, indoor and outdoor, with giant wooden games, board and card games, physical games, multimedia games and more, plus bouncy castles and a little wooden village for children. Incredibly, it's all completely free!

*Mid-May. Bayeux (℡ 02 31 92 85 899; **www.mairie-bayeux.fr**). Admission free.*

Fête de l'Enfant ★ Each summer this inland town gives over its centre to children for an afternoon, with free quizzes, storytelling, craft-making, games and more on a theme such as ecology. There's also face-painting, astronomy shows, table tennis, 'babyfoot' and board and card games, and inflatables, including a water one (bring swimming togs and a towel) and a Mississippi steamer. The local swimming complex, Le Nautile, takes up the baton a few days later, with inflatables and a surf simulator. It's a great occasion to mix with locals.

*Mid-August. Place de la République, Lisieux (℡ 02 31 48 40 86; **www.lisieux-tourisme.com**). Admission free.*

Fêtes Médiévales de Bayeux

★★ Another two-day festival in Bayeux, this one – which celebrated its 20th anniversary in 2006 – recalls the town's history with a medieval market and craft demonstrations, a reconstruction of a medieval building site, a costumed parade, a masked ball, and stilt-walkers, jesters, minstrels and jugglers animating the well-preserved medieval streets. You can also

Children at a Bayeux Festival

sample drinks and dishes made to recipes from the Middle Ages at stalls and in restaurants.

1st weekend July. Bayeux (cathedral and surrounding streets), (02 31 51 28 28 (tourist office); www.bayeux-tourism.com). Admission free.

Grande Fête Renaissance ★

Halfway between Caen and the sea, the Château de Fontaine-Henry, built in the 14th–16th centuries and, with its steeply pitched roofs, more reminiscent of Loire châteaux than of other local architecture, is the venue for this summer Renaissance festival, which includes tours by costumed guides, a crafts village, storytelling and shows for children, exhibitions and a medieval meal followed by music, dancing and general merrymaking until 7pm. Every Friday night in July and August there are also costumed nocturnal tours of the castle accompanied by Renaissance music, but these are a bit late for most children (10.30pm). Other family-oriented events held here throughout the year include teddy-bear fairs combined with Easter Egg hunts or with children's shows and old-fashioned games in summer, and a Franco-Scottish festival with a bagpipe contest, dancing, tug of war and other displays of strength and craft stalls.

Mid-August. Château de Fontaine-Henry, 15 km (9⅓ miles) north-west of Caen off D22 (06 89 84 85 57; www.chateau-de-fontaine-henry.com). Admission: €8 (£5.35) adults, €5 (£3.35) children aged 6–16.

Houlgate Plein Vent ★★ This spring festival of 'sliding' and windborne sports is one of the region's biggest events. It attracts hordes of spectators to Houlgate's beach to watch hundreds of amateur kite-surfers, landboarders, paragliders and so on in action on the sea or the sand, and to see giant kites flying high above them, including a synchronised display and a floodlit night flight. In fact, in the last couple of years it's got so popular, it's spread to other public spaces around the town, which host kite-making workshops, exhibitions, an 'Espace Kids' with bouncy castles, a climbing wall and a trampoline, and stalls.

Late April. Houlgate, 5 km (3 miles) east of Cabourg on D513 (02 31 24 34 79; www.villa-houlgate.fr). Admission free.

WHAT TO SEE & DO

Children's Top 10 Attractions

❶ Playing on **Cabourg's** giant beach as trotting horses train by the shore; p. 137.

❷ Window-shopping or spending a day at the races in chic **Deauville**; p. 138.

❸ Entering the surreal world of composer Erik Satie at the **Maisons Satie**; p. 149.

❹ Seeing the Norman Conquest come to life on the **Bayeux Tapestry**; p. 154.

❺ Learning about global war and peace at the **Mémorial de Caen**; p. 150.

❻ Visiting the **Château de Vendeuvre** with its talking mechanical figures, collection of kennels, miniature furniture, fantastical fountains and mazes; p. 152.

❼ Taking a jaunt through Normandy's action-packed history at the **Festyland** theme park; p. 156.

❽ Finding out about animal welfare at **La Ferme–Nature**; p. 141.

❾ Coming face to face with rare white lions at the **Zoo de Jurques**; p. 144.

❿ Splurging on a room at the **Château d'Audrieu** with its resident deer, children's treehouse and amazing food; p. 164.

Beaches & Resorts

Norman Riviera ★★★ The coast between Ouistreham and the Pont de Normandie became fashionable with visitors from the French capital in the 1840s, and even today it can become unbearably crowded at weekends, when the already inflated prices shoot up. That said, for a dose of French seaside chic, this really is like a little piece of the South of France relocated to the Channel coast (though you won't hear any French people referring to it as the 'Riviera Normande').

Moving west to east: lovely **Cabourg** makes for a gentle introduction to this coastline,

with one of Normandy's most child-friendly beaches – flat, wide and 4 km (2½ miles) long. Come out of season and you may have it to yourselves, save the odd dog-walker or pair of French trotting horses training here, pulling their riders in chariots. It's overlooked by the stunning **Grand Hôtel** (p. 161), where Proust derived inspiration for some of *A la Recherche du Temps Perdu*. The promenade in front of it, named after him, has boards with quotes from the novel, and there's a **toyshop** named after it (p. 158). The beach has three supervised beach clubs (Easter to September) covering ages 2–11 (including swimming lessons), and there's a teens' club in July and August, plus watersports for all ages. **Avenue de la Mer** leading from the flower-filled square in front of the Grand has grills, pizzerias, crêperies and cafés galore, and there's a *petit train* in high season.

Next comes **Houlgate**, which only really comes alive in high summer, when there are sandcastle, shrimping and fancy-dress competitions and a club for children aged 4–12. On its eastern beach, **Oasis Plage** (Easter to September) has a trampoline, a

Trotting Horses, Cabourg Beach

Deauville Beach

slide, bouncy castles and a snack terrace where you can eat waffles, crêpes and ice cream.

This brings you to **Deauville**, the coast's most famous, chichi and expensive town, largely by virtue of it hosting an annual American Film Festival (September) attracting Hollywood greats; you can see their names painted on the beach huts. It's also known for attracting rich elderly Parisians with their poodles, who get their own canine beauty parlours, but well-to-do families flock here too – for the grand hotels (p. 161), shopping (p. 158), *petit train*, children's clubs for ages 3–18 (July, August and a few other holidays), watersports, racecourses (La Touques, hosting the international Polo Cup every August, and Clairefontaine, p. 141). The deli of the Café de Paris on place Mornay is great for stocking up on nibbles for the huge beach. But more than anywhere else, Deauville is best out of season, before the hordes descend.

Adjoining **Trouville-sur-Mer** is more 'real', with fishermen selling their catch on the quay, a daily fish market and a good general market (Wed and Sun morning). Its winding lanes with their shops and cafés and its fine beach inspired the painter Monet, while writer Flaubert met his first love here aged 15. Families come for the children's clubs (Easter, July and August), Baby Parc (☎ *02 31 98 17 78*)

Petit Train, Deauville

for ages 1–14, with trampolines, ball pools and a baby area, pony rides, sandcastle, drawing and dressing-up contests, treasure hunts and donkey races (mid-August), canoeing, horse-and-carriage rides and mini coastal cruises; the tourist website details all. There's also a small aquarium (*02 31 88 46 04*) and a seafront swimming complex (*02 31 14 48 10*) with an open-air pool.

Last but by no means least, **Honfleur** is a prawn-fishing town focused around a picturesque inner harbour with buildings of varying heights and colours and an old-fashioned carousel. Its buggy-unfriendly cobbled streets attract their fair share of tourists, but it's a lovely place to explore after visiting its eccentric **Maisons Satie** (p. 149), with a *petit train*, lots of shops, cafés and restaurants (p. 168) and a weekly organic market (Wed morning on place Ste Catherine).

Tourist offices: **Cabourg**, *Jardins du Casino* (*02 31 91 20 00;*

www.cabourg.net/); **Houlgate**, *10 boulevard des Belges* (*02 31 24 34 79; www.ville-houlgate.fr);* **Deauville**, *place de la Mairie* (*02 31 14 40 00; www.deauville.org/);* **Trouville-sur-Mer**, *32 quai Fernand Moureaux* (*02 31 14 60 70; www.trouvillesurmer.org);* **Honfleur**, *quai Lepaulmier* (*02 31 89 23 30; www.ot-honfleur.fr).*

Other Natural Wonders & Spectacular Views

Souterroscope des Ardoisères ★
Abandoned and forgotten for most of the 20th century, these four huge underground caverns were once occupied by a slate mine, and in the tunnels and spaces carved out by the miners, beside subterranean lakes, you can now watch a sound, light and image show about the mineral and animal life of the caves, cave exploration and the mine. It all culminates in the dazzling *Arc en Terre*, an underground rainbow. The site is fully accessible to disabled visitors, and there's a very good

Suisse Normande

restaurant with a children's menu, a crêperie, a covered picnic area, a mini-golf course and a shop selling geodes (hollow rocks lined with crystals), craft items and more. You're also right by a children's play area.

Caumont-L'Eventé, 35 km (21¾ miles) west of Caen on D712 (☎ 02 31 71 15 15; www.souterroscope.com). April to June and September Mon–Fri 10am–5pm, Sat and Sun 10am–7pm, July and August daily 10am–7pm, October to March Tue–Fri 10am–4pm, Sat and Sun 10am–6pm. Admission: €10 (£6.70) adults, €5 (£3.35) children aged 4–11.

Suisse Normande ★ It's far from Alpine, but the 'Norman Switzerland', named for the way the Orne river has carved peaks and gorges south of Caen, is one of the region's loveliest landscapes. Its biggest attraction, **La Roche d'Oëtre**, is in the *département* of the Orne (Chapter 5), but its main towns are Thury-Harcourt, picturesque Clécy and charming Pont d'Ouilly, offering canoeing, pedaloing and swimming in the Orne, and even open-air dancing (*guingette*) on the riverbank on summer Sundays. The forests and valleys naturally attract lovers of the outdoors, who come for the great climbing, mountain-biking, horse-riding, walking and more; details of all are available from the helpful tourist offices or on the website below.

Tourist offices: Thury-Harcourt, place Saint Sauveur (☎ 02 31 79 70 45); Clécy, place du Tripot (☎ 02 31 69 79 95); www.suisse-normande.com.

Aquaria & Animal Parks

There's a small aquarium with a reptile section at **Trouville-sur-Mer** (p. 138).

Chèvrerie Martin ★ The welcome couldn't be warmer at this dairy farm with its 40 friendly Alpine goats and their breeder, who loves showing children round, taking them over the walkway looking down over the enclosures and showing them how to pet, feed and milk the contented creatures. There's a short documentary, in French or English, on the stages of cheese production here, and you can try different types; the whole visit takes about 90 mins. There's a picnic space if you want to linger, and a signposted nature walk with accompanying quiz sheets on local trees and the food chain. The farm hosts a big market once a year and has great summer bivouacs for children (€12/£8), with a night in a tent, a farm visit, the chance to milk and care for the goats and cheese tastings.

La Saffraie, Montchamp, 10 km (6.2 miles) north-east of Vire on D56 (☎ 02 31 68 41 16). Open daily 10.30am–6pm; booking required. Admission: €3.20 (£2.15).

Pig at La Ferme-Nature

Domaine de St-Hippolyte ★

This working farm around an impressive 16th century manor with dovecotes has displays on apple cultivation in an ancient cider press, cheese-making (including demonstrations of mechanised milking) and meat production. You can meet a barnful of Norman cows and calves, a Norman cob and a Cotentin donkey and follow signposted river and orchard walks, and the grounds are dotted with information boards (in French) on local traditions. A visit will take 1–2 hrs. The shop sells farm produce – cider, cheese, jam and more – but you can try before you buy in the tasting room.

St-Martin-de-la-Lieue, 4 km (2½ miles) south of Lisieux on D579 (☎ 02 31 31 30 68). Open daily May to September 10am–6pm. Admission: €5.50 (£3.70) adults, €4.50 (£3) children over 5.

La Ferme-Nature ★★★

This 'nature farm' deep in the countyside is part of La Dame Blanche rescue centre for injured/distressed wild animals, which means your entry fee (and donations) go to a very worthy cause. It makes for a fun and educational couple of hours in which you see – and meet, inside their enclosures, in some instances – more than 60 species of domestic animal, some rare. Charmingly, the birdhouses are mini-versions of their places of origin – hence, local varieties live in half-timbered Norman cottages, Brahmas in pagodas,

Deauville Racecourse

the Egyptian geese in a pyramid, the Dutch birds in a windmill, and so on. There are also some rampant goats who will ambush you for the bread sold at reception (mixed food bags €1/£0.67), dwarf Ouessant sheep, a huge black Berkshire pig, a lake with swans, bees in a transparent hive, a 'nursery' with chicks in incubators, a frog pond and baby rabbits. The circuit is dotted with seed machines so you have a constant supply of feed, and there are interesting displays (with text in French only) about animal welfare campaigns and initiatives, such as fitting power cables with curly devices to stop birds crashing into them.

St-Julien-de-Mailloc, Orbec, 5 km (3 miles) south of Lisieux on D519 (☎ 02 31 63 91 70; http://dame-blanche.chez-alice.fr). Open daily April to September 10am–7pm, October and February to April 10am–5pm. Admission: €5.50 (£3.70) adults, €3 (£2) children aged 3–12.

Hippodrome de Deauville Clairefontaine ★★★ VALUE

More family-friendly than the more famous, and more elite, La Touques racecourse nearby, this is a great place to watch trotting races, flat racing and steeplechases. On race days

(July, August and October), there are guided tours of the racetrack and short lessons in trotting and carriage-driving in the morning, and in the afternoon, themed events, pony and donkey rides, a track with mini Renault cars, play areas and a crèche, face-painting, popcorn and candyfloss stalls, surprise gifts for children and an under-12s supper – all for a couple of quid! There are two restaurants on site, a snack bar and a picnic area.

Route de Clairefontaine, Touréville, Deauville (📞 02 31 14 69 00; www. hippodrome-deauville-claire fontaine.com). Open July, August and October; call for days and times. Admission: €3 (£2), under-18s free.

Maison de l'Eau Until recently the Musée Mer et Desert ('Sea and Desert Museum'), the 'House of Water' is now managed by a scientific organisation whose primary interest lies in the ecology of ponds. It has retained its collections of shells and cacti from around the world but is gradually installing a number of tanks and pools where visitors can encounter freshwater life from around Europe, including many species of plankton. There are also annual summer exhibitions on the likes of lifesaving at sea or sharks. Leave about an hour for a visit.

10 rue du Général Leclerc, Villerville, 4 km (2½ miles) east of Deauville on D518 (📞 02 31 81 13 81). Open daily Easter to May, September and October 2–6pm, June to August 2–7pm. Admission: €4 (£2.70) adults, €3 (£2) children aged 4–15.

Maison de la Mer Though small, Courseulles' aquarium of mainly local species is not without its attractions – a touchpool with small sharks from the Channel as well as the more usual rays, a 15 m tunnel through one of the tanks and about 1000 shells from around the world, including a 100 kg giant clam. There are also displays on local fishing and a video. Ask about outings: fishing on foot at low tide, beach and dune discovery sessions and guided tours of the fishing port and oyster beds. And don't miss Courseulles' daily open-air fish market.

Place du 6 Juin, Courseulles-sur-Mer, 20 km (12½ miles) north of Caen on D79 (📞 02 31 37 92 58; www. lamaisondelamer.com). Open February to April and September daily 10am–noon and 2–6pm, May and June daily 9.30am–12.30pm and 2–7pm, July and August daily 9.30am–7pm, October, November and December Sat and Sun 2–6pm, school holidays 10am–noon and 2–6pm (call to check in winter). Admission: €6.30 (£4.20) adults, €4.70 (£3.15) children aged 5–12.

Musée d'Initiation à la Nature ★ Small but perfectly formed – and free to boot – this 'museum' was conceived to allow young children to get close to and learn about Norman plants and animals. In the grounds of William the Conqueror's Abbaye aux Hommes, parts of which are now the Hôtel de Ville (city hall), it has five exhibition rooms and a thematic garden with lots of local animal life, including marshland mammals, town-dwelling birds and coastal ducks. There's also a Norman garden with local trees, bushes, plants and rocks. Each summer sees a new themed exhibition with various interactive displays and games.

Grounds of Hôtel de Ville, Caen (℡ 02 31 30 43 27). Open 2–6pm Easter to early November Mon–Fri, rest of year Wed. Admission free.

Naturospace France's largest tropical butterfly house is home to more than 1000 free-flying *papillons*, including 50 species from South America, Asia, Africa and the Pacific, which were transported here as chrysalids. The equatorial forest that has been recreated for them contains canna, orchids, nutmegs, hibiscus, banana trees, bougainvilleas and a variety of rare species; French-language panels explain the links between the various plants and the butterflies. Part of the fun is spotting the eggs, chrysalids and caterpillars lurking amidst the foliage.

Boulevard Charles V, Honfleur (℡ 02 31 81 77 00; www. naturospace.com). Open daily late January to March and October to early December 10am–1pm and 2–5.30pm, April to June and September 10am–1pm and 2–7pm, July and August 10am–7pm. Admission: €7.25 (£4.85) adults, €2–5.30 (£1.34–3.55) children.

Parc des Bisons This park features, as the name suggests, bison (from Europe and the American plains), but there are yaks, Asian buffaloes, Highland cattle, zebus (humped dwarf cows), African Ankole-Watusi cattle, Scottish, sika and axis deer, elk and racoons too. It's open for educational guided tours in French, with no booking required. In August you can pre-book a rustic lunch featuring, if you can stomach it, bison meat, and there's a Native American style 'village' for picnics. You can also, year round, buy meat farmed here and pâtés made from it.

Maisoncelles la Jourdan, 7 km (4⅓ miles) south of Vire on D175 (℡ 02 31 67 72 80; http://perso.wanadoo.fr/ bison.tatanka/). Open for guided tours late April to June and September to early November Sun and public holidays 3.30pm, July and August daily 2.30pm and 4.30pm. Admission: €4.50 (£3) adults, €3.50 (£2.35) children aged 3–11.

Parc Zoologique de Cerza ★ The main attraction of this fairly large zoo in eastern Calvados is the Safari Train that trundles around the perimeter for 25 minutes to an African soundtrack, with commentary in French. There can be longish gaps between seeing any animals, but that's partly because the individual enclosures are large – no bad thing. Don't miss this trip, because it's the only way you get to see some of the animals. There are also two walking circuits – the red one lasts about an hour and takes you past the large African animal species; the 90-minute yellow one takes in the tigers (including some rare white ones), bison, wolves, bears, monkeys and deer. Ideally you should do both, but the red one is more manageable for those with little children and/or buggies. It also takes you though the mini-farm, where children can get close to dwarf goats, Vietnamese pigs and more.

There's a good shop and two restaurants – the Pagoda for full meals, the Baobab for self-service snacks; both have views over the rhinos. There's a picnic space outside, by the car park. Since 2006 you've also been able to stay at the zoo, or rather just outside it, in the **Cerza Safari Lodge** – wooden chalets on stilts, with double and twin bedrooms, a living room with sofabed and a kitchenette (€290–450/£194–300 for 3–4 days). Unless you get one of the front ones, the views aren't that great, but you do get free unlimited zoo entry for two people throughout your stay (a pass for extra people is €13.50/£9, children aged 4–9 €7/£4.70).

Hermival-les-Vaux, 5 km (3 miles) from Lisieux on D10 (0800 504 004/02 31 62 15 76; www.cerza. com). Open daily February, March, October and November 10am–5pm, April, May, June and September 9.30am–6.30pm, July and August 9.30am–7pm (last admission 4pm all year). Admission: €13.50 (£9) adults, €7 (£4.70) children aged 4–9.

Zoo de Jurques ★ This small-ish zoo near Caen has a big draw – two of only 32 white lions in the whole world, Timba and Nyala, who were born here in 2002. According to African legend, if a white lion looks at you, you will enjoy great happiness, so try to attract their

attention. Otherwise, there are Siberian tigers, giraffes, zebras and more, plus a mini-farm where children can pet donkeys and goats, and a playground beside a shady terrace from which mums and dads can keep watch. The regular events include snake-handling sessions in the vivarium, falconry displays by the owner of Les Bois des Aigles in the Eure (p. 94) and big-cat feeding. There's a restaurant and snack bar, plus a picnic area just outside by the car park.

Jurques, 25 km (15½ miles) south-west of Caen on D577 (02 31 77 80 58; www.zoojurques.com). Open daily early February to early April and late September to early November 1.30–6pm, last 3 weeks April and first 3 weeks September 10am–6pm, May to August 10am–7pm. Admission: €10.5–12 (£7–8) adults, €5.50–6.50 (£3.70–4.35) children aged 3–11.

Nature Reserves, Parks & Gardens

Jardin des Plantes and Jardin Botanique ★ Caen's beautiful public gardens have great play-grounds for different ages that make them a (free) family favourite. But don't let children miss the plant life (more than 800 species), especially in the lush hothouses and orangery, including a banana tree, coffee plant, vanilla orchid, cacti and famous giant waterlily from South America; free discovery sheets for them are available at reception (or in the hothouses at weekends). There's also a huge population of ladybirds – a natural way of controlling pests – and some stunning *mosaïcultures* – flowerbeds forming a butterfly and other shapes.

The city is also home to the Colline des Oiseaux ('Bird Hill', avenue de l'Amiral Mountbatten, ☎ 02 31 94 14 23), with themed gardens, a maze, wooden playgrounds and huts, mini-golf, animals (including llamas), a miniature model of Normandy and a crêpe stall. Avoid it on summer weekends, though.

5 place Blot, Caen (☎ 02 31 30 48 30). Open February and March Mon–Fri 8am–6pm, Sat, Sun and public holidays 10am–6pm; April and May Mon–Fri 8am–7.30pm, Sat, Sun and public holidays 10am–7.30pm; June to August Mon–Fri 8am–8pm, Sat, Sun and public holidays 10am–8pm; September and October Mon–Fri 8am–7pm, Sat, Sun and public holidays 10am–7pm; November to January Mon–Fri 8am–5.20pm, Sat, Sun and public holidays 10am–5.30pm. Admission free.

Labyrinthe de Bayeux ★ Past themes of this five-hectare corn maze include Norman produce and animals, and Time, with the labyrinth itself often taking on a relevant shape (a clock, an apple). You get a map and fun booklet, and there are games, riddles, giant puzzles and artwork along the way. Fairytales and music are commissioned too, making this a great outing, especially during the nocturnal events. The site has a picnic area, snack bar and shop with local produce.

Ferme de la Fresnée, Mosles, 8 km (5 miles) west of Bayeux on N13 (☎ 02 31 21 04 31; www.labyrinthe-bayeux.com). Open mid-July to August Fri–Wed 10.30am–7pm, Thur 10.30am–11pm; September Mon–Fri 2–6pm, Sat and Sun noon–6pm. Admission: €7 (£4.70), €6 (£4) children aged 4–12.

Historic Buildings & Monuments

Château de Crèvecoeur ★

One of few local fortresses still intact, 11th century Crèvecoeur ('breakheart') runs some great family events – Easter egg festivals with egg hunts and children's workshops; summer *Médiévales* with jousting and other shows and displays, old crafts and a medieval market; bird discovery walks; candlelit evening visits with music and games; and folklore festivals with dancing and stalls selling local products. Year-round there are exhibitions in its half-timbered farm outbuildings and chapel – music in the Middle Ages, the daily life and history of the castle, local architecture and oil exploration (the brothers who restored the place invented a piece of machinery that's used around the world).

Château Guillaume le Conquérant

Young Blood

Also known by the French as William the Bastard, William the Conqueror had to grow up fast: he succeeded his father Robert as Duke of Normandy aged eight and later described how he was 'schooled in war since childhood' – almost literally, since one of his tutors was murdered by a pretender to the throne, as were some of his guardians. By the age of 19 he was foiling rebellion and invasion plots, including an attempt on his own life. As a result of this upbringing, he turned out very cruel – when citizens of the besieged town of Alençon in the Orne taunted him about his illegitimacy, he had their hands and feet chopped off.

On the death of Edward the Confessor in 1066, William claimed the throne of England, saying his childless cousin had named him heir. When the dead king's brother-in-law was crowned instead, William invaded England, winning the Battle of Hastings, and, in what became known as the Norman Conquest, suppressing English revolts. The Bayeux Tapestry (p. 154) commemorates this victory, which led to Norman becoming the language of the English ruling classes for nearly 300 years.

William remained King of England until his death in 1087, when he was buried in ignominious circumstances in Caen – his stone sarcophagus was too small, and when he was forced into it 'the swollen bowels burst, and an intolerable stench assailed the nostrils of the bystanders and the whole crowd,' according to the *Historia Ecclesiastica* of monk Orderic Vitalis. Worse was to come: in the Wars of Religion, a mob of Huguenot reformationists destroyed William's tomb and scattered his remains, leaving only a thighbone; this in turn was destroyed in the Revolution. William's burial place is now marked with a simple marble slab in the church of St Etienne attached to his Abbaye-aux-Hommes in Caen.

Crèvecoeur-en-Auge, 30 km (18.6 miles) south-east of Caen on N13 (02 31 63 02 45; www.chateau-de-crevecoeur.com). Open April to June and September daily 11am–6pm, July and August daily 11am–7pm; October Sun 2–6pm. Admission: €5 (£3.35) adults, €4 (£2.70) children aged 10–18.

Château Guillaume le Conquérant ★ William the Conqueror (above) was born on this site in 1027 or 1028, but the castle that stood then has almost entirely disappeared – what you see today is a remarkably intact 12th and 13th century structure with two square keeps built by William and his successor after the 1066 conquest of England. Part of it now hosts an exhibition that begins with a model of the town and a video introducing the castle and its history; you then pick up an audio-guide (available in

English) with narration and music that works in conjunction with state-of-the art lighting effects and images projected onto the bare walls in the modern yet atmospheric interior. Note that the castle, which only opened to the public in the late 1990s, is subject to ongoing restoration work – in 2006 a six-year project to restore the ramparts began.

A **Fête des Jeux** ★★ is hosted here in mid-August, with games for young and old, including giant chess and checkers, pick-up sticks and darts, plus a market with local produce and crafts, and music and horse shows.

Place Guillaume le Conquérant, Falaise (℡ 31 41 61 44; www. *chateau-guillaume-leconquerant.* *fr). Open daily early February to June and September to December 10am–6pm; July and August 10am–7pm; last admission 1 hr before closing. Admission: €6 (£4) adults, €3 (£2) children aged 6–16.*

The Top Museums

Automates Avenue ★ Just the ticket for lovers of the offbeat or historical ephemera, this museum aims to recreate the sense of wonder children (and many adults) felt in front of Parisian department store windows in 1920–1950, with their animated scenes featuring mechanical puppets. Here, in reconstructions of Parisian streets, 300 automata go through their motions in 11 shop fronts – they include *La Naissance des Poupées*, with

Father Christmas making dolls in his workshop (put on in the window of the Galeries Lafayette in 1950), and *La Tour du France Cycliste*, with cyclists knocked off their bikes by a farm cart (displayed at the Grands Magasins du Louvre in 1936). There are quiz sheets for children aged 6–10 and a 10-minute video; a visit takes about 45 minutes. The shop sells old-fashioned toys, collectors' items, books about automata and old postcards of Paris. Upstairs is a viewing galley over the street scene and a Parisian-style café.

Boulevard de la Libération, Falaise (℡ 02 31 90 02 43; www.automates-avenue.fr). Open daily April to September Mon–Sat 10am–12.30pm and 1.30–6pm, Sun 2–6pm; October to early January, February and March Sat and holidays 10am–12.30pm and 1.30–6pm, Sun 2–6pm. Admission: €5 (£3.35) adults, €4 (£2.70) children.

Chemin de Fer Miniature The picturesque town of Clécy in the Suisse Normande (p. 140) is home to this model railway, Europe's largest, with more than 400 m (¼ mile) of tracks, 220 locomotives and 350 wagons, and a model town with 1250 road vehicles, 650 houses, a fort, an airport and a campsite, all enlivened by *son-et-lumière* effects. The building it's housed in is surrounded by a little park with a miniature train ride (€1.20/£0.80) and a snack bar serving crêpes and homemade cider, and there's a shop selling train-related souvenirs and local produce.

Thérèse Martin

Clécy, 35 km (21¾ miles) south-west of Caen on D562 (*02 31 69 07 13;* ***www.chemin-fer-miniature-clecy. com***). *Open early March Sun 2–5.30pm; Easter holidays daily 2–5.30pm; Easter Saturday to June daily 10am–noon and 2–6pm; July and August daily 10am–noon and 2–6.30pm; September Tue–Sun 10am–noon and 2–6pm; October Sun 2–5pm. Admission: €5 (£3.35) adults, €3 (£2) children.*

Diorama Thérèse Martin
Cheesier than the Camembert museum in nearby Vimoutiers (p. 118), this little waxwork museum – newly relocated to the basilica – is for religious pilgrims or lovers of kitsch, though the story it recounts, that of a local girl who made up her mind to become a saint in infancy and asked to become a nun at the age of nine, is not without interest to children. One of the life-size tableaux shows Thérèse with the Pope at the age of just 14: amazingly, she had secured an audience with him so she could persuade him to let her enter the

convent, and she got her way. Audio-guides (in French, English, Dutch, German, Spanish and Italian) combine with a *son-et-lumière* show to tell Thérèse's life history from childhood to her early death, aged 24, from tuberculosis. Tours begin every half an hour and last 25 minutes. Don't miss the stunning basilica **crypt**, entirely covered in marble and mosaics with scenes from Thérèse's life.

If you come in summer, it's worth knowing that the town holds a huge **market** every Wednesday from 3.30pm (early July to August, place François Mitterrand, (*02 31 61 66 00*), with crafts, food and family entertainment, including supper and a free evening concert.

Basilique de Sainte-Thérèse, Lisieux (*02 31 48 55 08). Open April to October 9.30am–noon and 1.30–6.30pm, Sun and public holidays 2–6pm. Admission: €3 (£2) adults, €1 (£0.67) children.*

Les Fosses de l'Enfer ★
Despite the gimmicky name ('The Pits of Hell'), this is a serious-minded geology museum – otherwise known as the *Maison des Ressources Géologiques de Normandie* – telling the story of Earth from its origins 650 million years ago to the 1970s, when the iron mine that occupied this site closed. Younger children love the iron dinosaur models and the miniature mining town with its viaduct and little cars, buses and trucks, but there's plenty else to enthrall including a multimedia show and a documentary about the

miners, interactive displays on animal and plant evolution and Norman geology (with lots of fossils) and waxwork tableaux bringing to life key moments in the history and philosophy of science. Worksheets are available to help parents explain things to children. Beyond the museum, you can go on discovery walks looking at the natural and geological heritage of the valley, and there's a picnic area.

Saint-Rémy, 30 km (18.6 miles) south-west of Caen on D562 (℡ 02 31 69 67 77; www.musee-fosses-denfer.com). Open April and October Wed–Mon 2–5.30pm; May, June and September 2–6pm; July and August 10am–12.30pm and 2.30–6pm. Admission: €4.60 (£3.07), €2.30 (£1.54) children aged 6–18.

Maison de la Baleine The 'house of the whale' – another of the one-offs that Normandy seems to specialise in – came into being when a 40-tonne, 19-metre whale beached here in 1885. Since then its skeleton has been displayed in the town park, making for a truly odd sight amidst the trees and flowerbeds. There's an accompanying exhibition on both this whale, with photos and documents from the time, and whales in general – their biology, conservation and so on – and a shop with whale-related souvenirs and books and postcards.

Parc Municipal, rue de la Mer, Luc-sur-Mer, 12 km (7½ miles) north of Caen on D7 (℡ 02 31 97 55 93). Open April, May and September Sat, Sun and public/school holidays 2.30–6pm; June daily 2.30–6pm; July and August daily 10am–noon and 2–7pm. Admission free.

Maisons Satie ★★★
Composer Erik Satie, born in this half-timbered house in Honfleur in 1866, was known for his eccentricity: he collected umbrellas and ate only white food, and his 180-note *Vexations* was directed to be repeated 840 times – when recorded in 1963, it took a relay team of 10 pianists more

Mémorial de Caen

NON-VIOLENCE

War & Peace

Like its neighbour the Manche (p. 173), Calvados has lots of museums on the D-Day landings and Battle of Normandy. The Mémorial de Caen ★★ (avenue Eisenhower, ℓ 02 31 06 06 45, *www.memorial-caen.fr*) has displays on Normandy and France as a whole during the 'dark years', but puts this in the context of conflict around the world since 1918 – hence the display of debris from the World Trade Center, donated by the mayor of New York. There are also exhibitions on Cold War weapons, bombed cities, Nobel Peace Prize winners, modern-day peace initiatives and more. Plenty of interactive technology gets children involved, and there's a large park to stretch your legs in, but if you prefer to have some time alone, there's a great free crèche for under-11s. Under-10s get free entry; otherwise it's €14–16 (£9.40–10.70) for 10–18s, €16.80–17.50 (£11.20–11.70) for adults.

At Courseulles-sur-Mer north of Caen, Juno Beach Centre (ℓ 02 31 37 32 17, *www.junobeach.org*), the only museum about the Canadian role in the landings, has hands-on displays and two fictional characters, Peter and Madeleine, to introduce younger visitors to the history of Canada from the 1930s, the Battle of Normandy and contemporary Canada.

Just west, at Arromanches-les-Bains, the Musée du Débarquement (ℓ 02 31 22 34 21, *www.normandy1944.com*) tells of the 'Mulberry', a floating harbour used here to land troops and supplies – you can see concrete vestiges of it just offshore. In the same town, Arromanches 360 ★★ (ℓ 02 31 22 30 30, *www.arromanches360.com*) is one of only three circular cinemas in France (the others are at Disneyland Paris and

than 18 hours to perform. This museum in his honour is suitably madcap, with music by Satie, *son-et-lumière* effects, images, videos and oddball objects combining to produce a series of surreal stage sets evoking Satie and his times. There are invisible ticking clocks, shadows flitting across walls, lots of umbrellas, a giant pear with metal wings (one of Satie's compositions, which you hear playing, was entitled 'Three Pear-shaped Pieces'), a 2-metre-tall talking mechanical monkey

and a 'laboratory of emotions' with a carousel ride featuring nonsense instruments. The audio-guides (in French or English), operated by infrared signals, also feature commentary inspired by Satie's writings against a soundtrack of daily noises – rain falling, whispers and so on. It can all get rather spooky, especially if you come at a quiet time and are the only ones here. You can also see works by some of Satie's famous contemporaries, many of whom he collaborated

Futuroscope). Its 30-minute film, *The Price of Freedom*, combines archive footage shot by war correspondents from tanks, ships and helicopters with modern-day images taken at the same locations, relayed onto nine screens and accompanied by music and sound effects (there's no commentary). Spectators generally watch standing up, but do ask for a chair if you need one.

High on the cliffs a short way to the west, Longues-sur-Mer has the most famous of Hitler's 'Atlantic Wall' gun batteries, and the only one retaining its original 150 mm guns, which could shoot a distance of up to 19.5 km (just over 12 miles). You can visit the site at any time to explore the bunkers and observation towers freely.

Among other war sights here are the Musée America–Gold Beach (Ver-sur-Mer, ✆ 02 31 22 58 58), recalling both D-Day planning and the history of transatlantic flight – the first transatlantic mail flight landed by Ver's lighthouse in 1927; the Musee des Epaves Sous-marines du Débarquement (Port-en-Bessin, ✆ 02 31 21 17 06), with items recovered from the landings, from tanks and ships' guns to soldiers' possessions; and two museums at Omaha Beach, the Musée Mémorial d'Omaha Beach (✆ 02 31 21 97 44) and Musée D-Day Omaha (✆ 02 31 21 71 80). Back near Ouistreham, at Ranville, the Mémorial Pegasus (✆ 02 31 78 19 14) houses a canal swing bridge that was the first bridge to be liberated on continental France. It is also home to a replica Horsa glider unveiled by Prince Charles in 2004; hundreds of these were used on D-Day.

For landing beach tours, see p. 155.

with, including Picasso, Braque and Cocteau, and there's a shop with related products.

If you're here for a while and have musical children, Honfleur has an Erik Satie music school (✆ 02 31 89 40 73) with courses in 'musical awakening' for 5–6-year-olds and music training for children aged seven and over. *67 boulevard Charles V, Honfleur (✆ 02 31 89 11 11). Open Wed–Mon May to September 10am–7pm; October to December and mid-February to April 11am–6pm.*

Admission. €5.10 (£3.40) adults, €3.60 (£2.40) children aged 3–16.

Musée de l'Automobile et des Costumes du Monde

Packing a triple whammy, this museum in the Renaissance Château de Betteville now has a collection of 80 traditional costumes from more than 35 countries and 5000-plus toys and models that may appeal to those left unmoved by the exhibition of about 100 prestigious vehicles dating from 1900 to 1950. The latter, which can be admired – rather surreally – to the strains of an old mechanical organ, include horse-drawn carriages, bikes and motorbikes as well as the likes of Cadillacs and Buicks, some peopled by costumed waxworks. The château also has a crêperie and tearoom, and opposite it is a 60-hectare lake with a leisure centre (p. 156).

Pont-l'Evêque (📞 02 31 65 05 02). Open daily April to June and September 10am–12.30pm and 1.30–7pm; July and August 10am–7pm; October to mid-November 2–6pm. Admission: €5 (£3.35) adults, €3 (£2) children aged 3–12.

Musée des Ballons This exhibition on hot-air ballooning came to be after US publisher Malcolm Forbes, who set six ballooning world records, bought the Louis XVIII castle in which it is set. If you've taken your children on balloon trips over the local coastline (p. 198), they'll be all the more interested in this little museum in a converted stable, with its miniature balloons, paintings, documents and historic artifacts, including a little tableau recreating the first balloon flight (for 10 km or 6.2 miles), by physician Pilâtre de Rozier in Paris in 1783. There's a little shop with wooden toys, plus tours of the château's period rooms and a new tearoom.

Château de Balleroy, 40 km (24.8 miles) west of Caen on D13 (📞 02 31 21 60 61; www.chateau-balleroy.com). Open mid-March to mid-October daily 10am–6pm; rest of year Mon–Fri 10am–noon and 2–5pm. Admission: €4.30 (£2.88) (€6.90/£4.60 with castle) adults, €3.80 (£2.55) (€5.35/£3.58 with castle) children aged 7–16.

Musée et Jardin du Château de Vendeuvre ★★★ It's hard to know where to begin at this castle built in 1750, with its offbeat collections – of life-sized mechanical figures bringing to life scenes from daily life in centuries gone by (some of them even talk); of miniature furniture, books,

Kitchens, Château de Vendeuvre

clocks, family portraits and more; and of dogs' and cats' kennels and baskets, some made of silk. Some items are separated off, others are integrated into the various rooms of the castle, which is still inhabited by the Count of Vendeuvre. In every corner lurks something to intrigue or amuse, and the sense of being in a magical kingdom continues outside. As well as formal gardens, there's a 'surprise' water garden with delightful water mechanisms, including the *Cascade des Tortues* with four stone tortoises spitting water into a fountain; a 'nymph's grotto' with walls encrusted with 200,000 seashells; and two mazes, one a 'wild' trail through the woods, dotted with Burmese and Japanese tea pavilions and other oddities.

Vendeuvre, 10 km (6.2 miles) northeast of Falaise on D511 (02 31 40 93 83; www.vendeuvre.com). Open May to September daily 11am–6pm, October Sun and holidays 2–6pm. Admission: €6.50–8.50 (£4.35–5.70) adults, €4.90–6.50 (£3.28–4.35) children.

Musée de Normandie ★

Normandy's regional museum is a storehouse of its archaeological and ethnological treasures, from Viking weaponry to cider-making equipment and local costumes. It's one of those places that's so diverse, you need to plan what you're going to concentrate on. Happily, French-language booklets, free at reception, have been produced for families, including one on animal themes throughout the collections and an observation game. There are also periodic events, such as themed nocturnal visits with music and a science festival (October) with workshops. The museum is housed in the former lodge of the governor of Caen's castle; the latter was built by William the Conqueror (p. 146) and is now largely ruined but has good city views and pleasant lawns. Here, too, you can make use of family observation sheets from the museum reception and take part in treasure hunts, and there's a book fair (mid-May) with storytelling and shows.

The castle grounds also contain the **Musée des Beaux Arts** (02 31 30 47 70, *www.ville-caen. fr/mba*), Caen's fine arts museum, housing works from the 15th to 20th centuries, including a view of Deauville beach by Eugène Boudin, born in Honfleur. It runs 90 min–2 hr family creative workshops twice a month (Sun, free), family discovery visits (September to June, €6/£4 for four) and, in the summer holidays, *Samedis libérés* ('freed Saturdays') with a 1-hour guided visit of the museum for parents and a 2-hour workshop for children aged 7–10 (€8/£5.35 one adult and one child, then €2/£1.34 per adult and €6/£4 per child). You need to pre-book for all (02 31 30 47 73). **Château, Caen** (02 31 30 47 60; *www. musee-de-normandie.caen.fr*). Open Wed–Mon 9.30am–6pm (daily June to September). Admission free; temporary exhibitions €3 (£2) adults, under-18s free.

Bayeux Tapestry

Arts & Crafts Sites

For family activities at Caen's
Musée des Beaux Arts,
see p. 153.

Bayeux Tapestry ★★ Like
the Mont-St-Michel, the world-
famous *Tapisserie de Bayeux*
may already be familiar to some
children from its pop culture
references – parts of it were used
as a basis for the opening credits
of *Bedknobs and Broomsticks*
(1971) and in the credits for
Robin Hood: Prince of Thieves
(1991). Not actually a tapestry
but nine embroidered panels
joined to form a cloth nearly
70 m (229 ft) long, it's a bit like
an old-fashioned comic strip
telling the story of the Battle
of Hastings and the Norman
Conquest (p. 146). It's generally
believed to have been commissioned by William the
Conqueror's half-brother, Bishop
Odo de Conteville of Bayeux,
given that it was rediscovered in
Bayeux cathedral in the late 17th
century. Much to French cha-
grin, as it's a national treasure,
it's likely to have been made in
England, where Odo spent a
good deal of time.

The tapestry is in its very own
museum, behind glass in a dark-
ened room with special lighting
to conserve it. Although it helps
to know about the events
depicted, largely chronologically,
there are lots of charming little
details that children can appreciate without getting overloaded
with historical facts. Point out to
them, for instance, the difference
between the Norman figures,
recognisable by the shaved backs
of their heads, and the musta-
chioed Anglo-Saxons; Halley's
comet, which in the Middle Ages
was seen as a harbinger of doom;
the brightly coloured cavorting
horses and other creatures, from
dogs to dragons; and the Norman
locations, including the bay of
the Mont-St-Michel (p. 187). A
visit, including the introductory
exhibition detailing the historical

background in various languages, takes up to two hours; free audio-guides are available in 11 languages.

Centre Guillaume le Conquérant, rue de Nesmond, Bayeux (℡ 02 31 51 25 50; www.bayeux-tourism.com). Open daily mid-March to April and October 9am–6.30pm; rest of year (excl 2nd week of January) 9.30am–12.30pm and 2–6pm. Admission: €7.60 (£5.10) adults, €3 (£2) children aged 10–18.

Conservatoire de la Dentelle

One of the last places still producing figurative bobbin lace in Normandy, Bayeux's conservatory has three lace-makers who work in collaboration with such global fashion names as Dior, Lacroix and Hermès, as well as creating commissions for the public and gifts for the on-site shop (where prices start at about €30/£20). You can see examples of their intricate work here in the workshop, with its motifs such as leaves and shells, and displays on the history of lace and lace-making techniques, and – best of all – watch the women at work. If you're inspired by what you see, one-day courses are available, or you can get lace-making kits in the shop.

Maison Adam et Eve, 6 rue du Bienvenu, Bayeux (℡ 02 31 92 73 80). Open Mon–Sat 10am–noon and 2–6pm. Admission free.

Child-Friendly Tours

For helicopter/plane **flights over the landing beaches** from Le Havre, see p. 76.

Many people who come to this area wonder if it's possible to take children on the very popular **landing beach tours**, in which case the experience of leading firm **Battlebus** (℡ 02 31 22 28 82, *www.battlebus.fr/*) is instructive – in 2006 they launched specialist family tours but found it was difficult to provide entertaining tours for younger children over a full day. Instead they recommend that people with under-12s do their own mini-tour, perhaps just visiting one of the museums and one landing beach over a few hours. Otherwise, children aged 12 and over can come on their standard tours, but be aware that they last 8–9 hours and involve lots of standing and listening and a fair amount of walking. An alternative is to book a 'step-on' guide who travels with you in your own vehicle, at a flat rate of €250/day (£167.50) (a one-day standard tour is about €80pp/£53.60). Alternatively, **Gold Beach Evasion** also runs tours in an old army Jeep, and **Le Grand Hard** offers tours by horse and cart. For more battlefield tour companies, see *http://battlefieldsww2.50megs.com*.

For Active Families

See also '**Beaches, Resorts & Islands**', p. 180–182. For **watersport operators** across the *département*, see *www.calvados-nautisme.com* (with an English translation), which has a clickable map.

For activities in the Suisse Normande, see p. 140.

Festyland ★★ Normandy's biggest theme park (not that that's saying much), Festyland offers a light-hearted romp through the region's history with more than 30 prehistoric, Viking, William the Conqueror and pirate-themed rides and attractions, and some modern ones for good measure. You can conquer William's castle, ride a mini Paris–Granville train, watch horseback shows and jousting tournaments and take a simulated flight over the Grand Canyon in the 180° cinema. For older children and parents there are several rollercoasters, for little ones some gentler bumper boats, a carousel, old-fashioned cars, a goat park and more. There are a couple of snack stops, a shop and baby-changing facilities.

The Caen suburb of Bretteville-sur-Odon is also home, since 2006, to **Ouga Ouga** (avenue de la Voie au Coq, ☏ 02 31 30 26 00), a themed indoor play centre for children aged 1–12. The centre has giant slides, trampolines, climbing walls, mini-karting, 'babyfoot', a multimedia space, Saturday-night discos and more, and a bar/restaurant so parents can keep watch on proceedings from a safe distance.

Bretteville-sur-Odon, Caen (☏ 02 31 75 04 04; www.festyland.com). Open July and August daily 10.30am–7pm; call for complicated opening days and times for the rest of year. Admission: €12 (£8) adults, €10 (£6.70) children under 12, children shorter than 95 cm (about 3 feet, 1 inch) free.

Gold Beach Evasion ★ This agency with some English-speaking staff organises an array of family activities on the Calvados coast: specialities include five-day sailing courses for 5–7-year-olds; parent-and-child horse rides and equine activities; and family landboarding sessions on the beach (ages eight and up), all run by experts. There's also mountain bike hire, karting, diving, wakeboarding, windsurfing, sea kayaking and more, plus **landing beach tours** in a WWII army Jeep (€75/£50 half-day; children €68/£45.50). They're unlikely to be of interest to under-8s but there's no minimum age, and they can be as short as 1–2 hrs.

2 avenue Maurice Schumann, Asnelles, 18 km (11 miles) north-west of Caen on D65 (☏ 02 31 22 75 80; www.goldbeachevasion.com). Open all year. Prices vary according to activity: a 2-hr 30-min horse ride for a parent and child is €45 (£30), a 2-hr family landboarding session €37pp (£24.80).

Normandie Challenge ★ Ten minutes south of Deauville, this huge leisure park offers a beach of its own – on the edge of its 60-hectare lake, with lifeguards in July and August – plus walks alongside a protected river and numerous activities. The latter include sea-scootering and sea-karting, paragliding, canoeing (on the lake or river), pedaloes, pony rides and horse rides beside the river or in the forest, tennis, football and volleyball, *pétanque* and mini-golf; check the website for activities that it is wise to book in advance. There's also a restaurant/bar where you can enjoy local produce, including grilled fish, or get something to take away (sandwiches, chips and so on), and a four-star campsite with pitches that overlook the river or lake.

Pont-l'Evêque lake (☎ 02 31 65 29 21; www.normandie-challenge.com). Open Sat and Sun Easter to June, September and October; daily July and August; times vary by activity, call for details. Admission: leisure base free; prices vary according to activity.

Viaduc de la Souleuvre ★★

Designed by Gustav Eiffel in 1889, this viaduct is part of the bungee-jumping empire of New Zealand recordbreaker A.J. Hackett. The railway bridge collapsed long ago – you now cross a suspension footbridge to leap from the jumpdeck protruding from the top of one of the 61-metre (200 ft) stone columns. Jumpers have to be 13 or over. There's also the unique 'scable', a 'flying fox' swing that travels 400 m (1312 ft) across the valley at 100 km/h (62 mph), for which you have to be at least 1.3 m (4 ft 3 in) tall, and a treetop adventure course for those 1.4 m (4 ft 7 in) and taller. Advance booking is required for all. See the website for skydiving, rafting, paragliding, climbing, canoeing and horse-riding facilities around the viaduct.

La Ferrière-Harang, 15 km (9¼ miles) north of Vire off D56 (☎ 02 31 66 31 66; www.ajhackett.fr). Open March to mid-June and mid-September to November Sat and Sun; mid-June to August daily; call for times. Prices: bungee jump €75 (£50), €46 (£30.80) for 2nd jump same day; scable tandem €25pp (£16.75), single €35 (£23.50); treetop course €20 (£13.40), under-13s €16 (£10.70).

A la Recherche du Temps Perdu Toyshop, Cabourg

Where It's Never Too Hot to Shop

Deauville is more than just a pretty beach – on its chic streets such classy names as Louis Vuitton, Hermès and Printemps (p. 78) give you the measure of this sometimes snooty town. The main shopping street, rue Eugene Colas (which turns into rue Désire Le Hoc), is home to, among others, Comptoir des Cotonniers (℡ 02 31 88 89 31), with pretty, feminine clothes for women and young girls; Les P'tits Z'anges (℡ 02 31 87 48 46), a trendy designer children's wear shop with a pink plastic chandelier, stocking Dolce & Gabbana, Lily Gaufrette, Diesel and more; Sept Coeurs pour Alicia (℡ 02 31 87 46 30), full of classy white and pink knitted babygros, soft toys and photo albums; and Petit Pelons (℡ 02 31 14 45 70), for quality children's shoes. On nearby place Morny, meanwhile, you'll find a branch of the Petit Bâteau children's wear specialist (℡ 02 31 98 49 42), and on avenue Lucien Barrière Fille & Garçon (℡ 02 31 14 41 14) is a children's designerwear emporium stocking Burberry, DKNY, Kenzo and more.

Shopping

There's a Printemps department store (p. 78) in Caen (28 rue St Jean, ℡ 02 31 15 65 50).

A la Recherche du Temps Perdu (Côté Enfant) ★ The link between this chichi little toy shop and the Proust novel it takes its name from isn't obvious, except that it's set in the town that inspired the novel. Perhaps it's the deliberately old-fashioned stock – wooden toys and games, pretty pastel metal buckets (not cheap, at €36/£24) and other items for the beach two steps away. There's also delectable

Isigny Caramels

baby- and toddlerwear, including stripy tops, swimming trunks and sou'westers. A couple of doors away, the main shop bearing the same name has some soft toys, but this is more mums' territory, with oh-so-tasteful crockery, picture frames, toiletries, bedsocks and the like, and a great sewing department.

2 avenue Jean Mermoz, Cabourg (℡ 02 31 91 98 48). Open Fri, Sat and Sun 10.30am–1pm and 2.30–7pm (on other days excl Tue ask at main shop); daily in school holidays.

Caramels Isigny Lovers of old-fashioned teeth-sticking caramels will swoon in this factory shop with its 70 or so varieties of *caramel tendre*, along with other products made on site – hard caramels, fudge (a concession to British visitors, in vanilla, vanilla/honey, chocolate and chocolate/honey flavours), caramel sauce, popular on crêpes, caramel spread and popcorn with caramel, plus butter biscuits. On weekday mornings you can see the sweet stuff being made in the workshop (mid-April to mid-September), with a free tasting after the 45-minute tour.

In the same town, you can also tour (in July and August) the **Isigny Sainte-Mère** factory (℡ 02 31 51 33 88), which produces prize-winning *crème fraîche*, butter and Pont-l'Evêque and Camembert cheeses, and then buy some in its on-site shop.

ZA Isypole, Isigny-sur-Mer, 30 km (18.6 miles) west of Bayeux on N13 (℡ 02 31 51 66 50; www.caramels-isigny.com). Open mid-February

to September Mon–Fri 8.30am–6.30pm, Sat 9.30am–12.30pm and 2.30–6.30pm; rest of year Mon–Fri 8.30am–5.30pm.

Marché à l'Ancienne ★ Every Sunday morning in high summer, and a couple of other times a year, sleepy little Cambremer, best known for its cider, comes alive with a local produce and crafts market. It makes for a great family browse, with stallholders dressed in traditional Norman costume, open-air folk music and dancing, and horse-and-cart rides for children, plus various animals to pet.

There's a similar costumed *marché campagnard à l'ancienne* every Sunday from June to September in nearby **Pont-l'Evêque**, plus a weekly market (Monday) that's especially good for cheese (the town has one named after it).

Place de l'église, Cambremer, 12 km (7½ miles) west of Lisieux off D50 (℡ 02 31 63 08 87 (tourist office)). Open Sun 10am July and August, plus Easter Sunday, 1st May and Whit Sunday.

FAMILY-FRIENDLY ACCOMMODATION

The Norman Riviera

VERY EXPENSIVE

Normandy Barrière ★★ This grand seaside hotel has long been a classic among weekending Parisians with children, with its nursery, children's club and even a restaurant especially for children. It's set in a whimsical half-timbered Anglo-Norman style 'manor' amidst Deauville's couture shops (p. 158), facing the sea but a little way back from it, decorated with eccentric touches, including, on the steep rooftops, carved animals and a squirrel weathervane. Inside it's all very traditional, which is perfect if that's what you're looking for – those used to modern décor might find some of the wallpaper and fabrics rather florid. It's also a little impersonal in feel, with its seemingly endless, monstrously wide corridors that bring to mind the Outlook Hotel in *The Shining*. The seven family suites comprise a double and a twin bedroom, the first with a bathroom, the second with a toilet. Children get games consoles, plus little bathrobes and fruit-scented toiletry packs. However, the bathrooms themselves are rather sterile and the loo paper of the cheap variety –

little details that matter when you're paying these sorts of prices. On the other hand, staff go out of their way to provide anything you might lack, such as an adaptor plug. But then this is the kind of place where room service offers dishes for pets (€9/£6 for meat and veg, since you ask).

The free nursery, for children up to four, also feels a bit sterile (the French have stricter hygiene rules than Brits where childcare facilities, pools and so on are concerned). However, staff are warm and speak sufficient, if not great, English (English and Italian guests use the nursery a lot in high season, along with the French, but few Americans). There's also a children's club for 4–12s (€15/day, that's £10) with games, big-screen cartoons, activities, beach outings and afternoon tea, and a video games room. *La Fermette* restaurant is a colourful space where children

Normandy Barriére Hotel

can socialise at mini-tables surrounded by cut-outs of farm animals. It's a great idea but, this being France, it only opens for dinner at 6.30pm, which may be late for some tots (in the UK this sort of facility would open at 4 or 5pm). Three-course meals there are €22 (£14.75), as is the children's menu in the main restaurant (below). All children's facilities are open at weekends, plus daily in Parisian, British and Belgian school holidays. Other facilities include an indoor swimming pool with games, waterwings and so on – it's not huge so can get quite busy – a fitness suite, and two tennis courts.

The group that owns the Normandy has turned Deauville into something of a private resort – on a hilltop nearby you'll find the **Hôtel du Golf Barrière**, which also has a children's club for 4–12s, plus a golf course, and there's also the Royal Barrière a couple of blocks away. Check the website (below) for *Fugue Familles* (family breaks) at the Normandy and the Golf. Your electronic room card allows you to bill to your account any facilities within the 'resort' or with partner firms, which include a nearby riding centre, adventure sports centre and thalassotherapy centre. You also have a choice of 11 Barrière restaurants around town, including two beach bars. The Normandy's own restaurant, **La Belle Epoque**, offers light regional cuisine; in summertime you can dine in the pretty inner courtyard with its apple trees and wisteria. Buffet or Continental breakfasts (€24/£16 or €12/£8 children aged 4–12) can be enjoyed here too, or in your room.

38 rue Jean Mermoz, Deauville (☎ 02 31 98 66 22; www.lucienbarriere. com). 291 rooms. Double €288–525 (£193–350), family suite for four €600–863 (£400–578). Extra bed €55 (£36.85). Cot free. Amenities: restaurant; children's restaurant (selected days); bar; 24-hr room service; concierge; indoor pool; fitness suite; tennis courts; sporting amenities including access to golf course; nursery and children's club (selected times); games room; babysitting; laundry/dry cleaning; casino. In room: satellite/cable TV, pay movies, games console, Internet access, minibar, safe, hairdryer.

MODERATE–VERY EXPENSIVE

Le Grand Hôtel ★ You can't stay in Proust's old room (the manager bagged that for his office) but you do get something of the feel of life in more sedate times at this stately Belle Epoque establishment – the very image of a Victorian French seaside hotel. If you must, the *Chambre Marcel Proust* has been furnished according to the novelist's descriptions of the room he used to stay in; otherwise, you have a number of options, all very spacious and the majority heavy on the chintz. If you want sea views, there are family rooms for 3–4, interconnecting doubles/twins and the lavish Art Deco *Suite Coquatrix* with a double room, salon with sofabed and dressing room. Less expensive rooms with views over the casino and flower-filled town square include 3–4-person rooms and the *Suite Victoria* with a sofabed and the possibility of extra beds to fit up to 5/6. In fact, the family rooms without a sea view make this a surprisingly affordable option.

Eating options are as refined as you might expect: breakfast (€16/£10.70; €8/£5.35 children aged 3–12) features the *madeleines* that sent Proust on his trail of childhood remembrances, the piano bar serves posh snacks and aperitifs, and there's a very plush restaurant, *Le Balbec*, with rooms overlooking the square or beach. On Sundays and public holidays this is the place for extravagant buffet brunches (€50/£33.50 for adults but just €4/£2.70 for under-12s) of salads, cold meats, iced seafood, hot and cold fish and meat dishes, cheeses, desserts and drinks. Otherwise, come for lunch or dinner (sometimes accompanied by swing jazz) featuring the likes of roast langoustine tails on warm mango with young herbs, grilled Norman beef with red-onion jam and tapenade *jus*, and chocolate ganache with balsamic orange marmalade. Think €26 (£17.50) for a main course. For children it's €16 (£10.70) for a starter, main and dessert – various dishes can be simplified and adapted to children's tastes – and there are highchairs.

Promenade Marcel Proust, Cabourg (02 31 91 01 79; www.cabourg-web.com/grandhotel). 70 rooms. Double €196–315 (£131–210), family room for three/four €185–300

(£124–200), interconnecting rooms €216–295 (£144–197) each. Cot free. Amenities: restaurant; bar; salons; 24-hr room service; concierge; laundry/dry cleaning; bike hire; casino. In room: satellite/cable TV, pay movies, telephone, Wi-Fi Internet access, minibar, radio, air-conditioning, hairdryer.

Les Maisons de Léa ★★ The sister hotel of Vent d'Ouest in Le Havre (p. 60) is a similarly stylish proposition, set in a former salt warehouse and three adjoining 16th century buildings in lovely Honfleur (p. 139). The *maisons* are themed double rooms and suites – children adore the farmyard décor, including life-sized wooden chickens, of *Campagne*; parents might prefer the chic marine décor of *Capitaine*. They include five triples and two suites; one suite has a double bedroom and a living room with a sofabed, the other is basically two interconnecting bedrooms with a bathroom each, with a double bed in one and a sofabed in the other. There's also a gorgeous half-timbered fisherman's cottage in a cobbled alley a few steps from the hotel, with a kitchen, dining room and loo on the ground floor, living room with a sleeping corner (a sofa opening out into twin beds) on the first, and double bedroom and bathroom on the second floor. Unlike many apartments, it's available by the night as well as the week, although this makes the price sky high. It allows you to be independent yet enjoy the hotel facilities at your whim – you can, for instance, choose to breakfast (€12/£8, under-12s free) at the hotel or have it brought to the cottage, and you have access to the hotel tearoom serving homemade cakes, its library and its pretty terrace. The owners have also recently created a children's corner with games, puzzles and colouring books, and there are highchairs in both the cottage and the hotel.

Place Ste-Catherine, Honfleur (☎ 02 31 14 49 49; www.lesmaisons delea.com). 30 rooms. Double €99–155 (£66–104), cottage for four €295 (£198) (€1400 wk/£938). Extra bed €20 (£13.40). Cot free. Amenities: tearoom; library; terrace. In room: TV, kitchen (cottage).

MODERATE

L'Argentine ★ If your budget won't stretch to a room at the Grand (p. 161), this is the next best thing – you can admire Proust's hotel of choice and the garden square in front of it from your room or suite in this hand-some Victorian villa, or from its pretty terrace. It offers large doubles and triple B&B rooms that can fit an extra bed, or two suites for families, with one double and one twin room and a little sitting area. The décor has a kind of faded, old-fashioned charm that befits the location, and all rooms bear Proustian names. Alternatively, there's a duplex apartment with a sepa-rate entrance, living room, kitch-enette/dining space and shower room; there's a sofabed in the salon and a double room upstairs. The flat has its own TV

and DVD player, but you can also use the main hotel *salon* with its big-screen TV. Breakfast hours here are unusually long (8.30–11am), and you can have it in your room for a small supplement. In the afternoon (2–7pm) the breakfast room with its cosy fireplace becomes a tearoom open to the public, serving homemade crêpes, ice cream, brownies and custard, *madeleines*, fruit cake and more, plus teas, Normandy cider and *bière blonde*.

3 Jardins du Casino, Cabourg (☎ 02 31 91 14 25; www.argentine-cabourg.com). 6 rooms. Double €55–145 (£37–97), family suite for four €112–165 (£75–110), flat for four €150 (£100) (ask about weekly rates). Extra bed €20 (£13.40). Cot free. Amenities: salon with TV; tearoom. In room: TV, DVD player (flat), minibar (some), jacuzzi (some), kitchenette (flat).

INEXPENSIVE

Camping Les Falaises The big attraction of this four-star site between Houlgate and Deauville is its direct access, via wooden steps, to the beach beneath the dark cliffs of **Les Vaches Noires** – a listed Jurassic-era site that, unfortunately, doesn't look in the least like cows but is a rich source of fossils. You may be lucky and find some on the beach, but since the mid-1990s access to the cliffs themselves has been forbidden – if you ask at the tourist office of nearby Villers-sur-Mer (☎ 02 31 87 01 18), however, a staff member will arrange for you to see their fossil collection and take a one-hour tour with a guide. As to the campsite, as well as great sea views it has a pleasant circular outdoor pool, a play area, a giant chessboard, volleyball, basketball, football and *boules* areas, a games room, a rustic terrace for Continental breakfast or, later in the day, ice cream and cocktails, a restaurant with traditional cuisine, fast food and takeaway meals, a bar, a grocery, a small launderette and baby facilities. Campers get the choice of basic or 'luxury' plots (with water, waste disposal and electricity; extra €2.10/£1.40), and there are six-person mobile homes that get booked up well in advance.

Gonneville-sur-Mer, 7 km (4⅓ miles) east of Cabourg on D513 (☎ 02 31 24 81 09; www.lesfalaises.com). Tent/caravan pitch + car €5.30–5.50 (£3.55–3.70), then €4.50–5.10pp (£3–3.40) adults, €3.30–3.40 (£2.20–2.30) under-7s; mobile home for up to six €300–490 wk (£200–328) (2-night stays available out of high season). Amenities: outdoor pool; play area; games; restaurant; snack bar; bar; shop; launderette; baby facilities.

Motel Monet ★★ On such a high-priced stretch of coast, this basic but sweet motel-style option is a lifesaver for families on a budget. Set in one-storey buildings around a pretty front courtyard/car park in a green setting overlooking the Pont de Normandie (p. 137) and rooftops of Honfleur but only a five-minute walk from the latter's lovely port (p. 139), it has plain and compact but perfectly acceptable guest rooms with

showers and front terraces where you can breakfast (€6.50/£4.35 or €4/£2.70 children) in good weather (otherwise, it's brought to your room); they feature freshly baked pastries. The one family room with a double and two single beds is in a separate little building, together with a twin room with which it can interconnect – helpful when a family of four is travelling with grandparents. There are also triples to which a cot can be added free of charge, and the very friendly owners will heat babies' bottles and even give well-behaved children little gifts.

Charrière du Puits, Honfleur (☎ 02 31 89 00 90; www.motelmonet.fr). 10 rooms. Double €58–72 (£38.85–48), family room €78–92 (£52–61.50). Cot free. In room: TV, telephone, hairdryer.

Caen, Bayeux & Around

Château d'Audrieu ★★★
Where some château hotels can seem either fusty or frosty to those with children, this 18th century listed monument between Caen and Bayeux welcomes them with open arms. Its 60-acre grounds with huge old oaks, cedars and other trees and resident deer contain a little wonderland of a children's play area, with a log cabin, a tree house perched in a beech, and a slide and swings. You can also borrow bikes/mountain bikes to explore the 3 km (1.8 miles) of pathways and the woods, and there's an outdoor

Château de Martragny

pool surrounded by loungers. Accommodation comes in various guises, from snug attic rooms to vast suites, hence the wide price range. Though they have Louis XV and XVI furniture and quite traditional décor, they feel light and modern, and the marble bathrooms are superb. All but the attic rooms are available with an extra bed or double sofabed, to a maximum of three extra beds in the stunning Art Deco suite.

Prices in the restaurant, candlelit by night, will make your eyes water – think €27–49 (£18–32.85) for a starter alone! But there's no denying that this is astonishing food – try crabcake with strawberries, fresh onion yogurt and cucumber *jus*, local seabass with mango *jus*, almonds and new potatoes, or poached apricots with olive oil, saffron pistachio macaroon and sesame cream. Children get a

reduced-portion main course and a dessert for €15 (£10), and there's a highchair. Make sure to book well ahead – there must be some rich folk in this neck of the woods, as it gets very busy. Breakfasts (Continental or buffet, €17/23 – or £11.40/ 15.40; prices for children depend on age, but it's free for very young children) feature top-quality local breads, pastries, hams and sausages, and excellent afternoon teas are served in the drawing rooms.

Audrieu, 12 km (7½ miles) west of Caen off N13 (☎ 02 31 80 21 52; **www.chateaudaudrieu.com**). *29 rooms. Double €120–410 (£80–275), suites €320–440 (£214–295). Extra bed free for under-15s, then €35 (£23.50). Cot free. Amenities: restaurant; bar; reading room; drawing rooms; outdoor pool (usually June to September); playground; cycling paths; bike loan; concierge; babysitting. In room: satellite TV, telephone, hairdryer, jacuzzi (some).*

Château de Martragny ★ If you've read other chapters of this guide, you may have noted my soft spot for campsites in the grounds of historic châteaux – it takes some of the masochism of the experience away, and also reminds you that you're actually in France. This 17th century castle with its tree-lined driveway, ornamental lake and walled garden is a perfect example – you may pitch your tent or caravan on the other side of those walls, but they bestow a more civilised feel on the surroundings. Indeed, the bar, snack bar, games rooms, grocery and launderette are all in the castle outbuildings, built in pretty local Caen stone. This is a four-star site, so you also get a good outdoor pool (with a direct view of the castle), play areas and bike hire, plus extras such as fishing and painting.

Martragny, 8 km (5 miles) east of Bayeux on N13 (☎ 02 31 80 21 40; www.chateau-martragny.com). Tent pitch + car €9–10.50 (£6–7), caravan + car/motorhome € 9.50–11 (£6.35–7.40), then €4.50–5 (£3–3.35) per adult, €2.50–3 (£1.68–2) per child under seven. Amenities: outdoor pool; bar; snack bar; play areas; games and activities; bike hire; shop; laundry. Closed mid-September to April.

Ferme Manoir de la Rivière ★ Right up by the Manche border, on the Baie des Veys with its population of seals, this farm offers a four-person gîte within its impressive manor house, on its ground floor but with a separate entrance. Inside there's a double and a twin room, a living/dining room with a TV, and a separate kitchen with a washing machine and dishwasher. Quite smartly furnished, it opens onto the pretty garden with its children's play area; beyond it is the farm with friendly dogs and cows. If you don't want to stay a whole week (or weekend outside school holidays), there are also three quite smart B&B rooms on the first floor, with en-suite shower rooms. They're basically doubles and triples, but an extra bed can be added if required, without it becoming too much of a squash. There's a homely vaulted room with a massive fireplace in which to enjoy the plentiful Continental breakfasts, and in the evenings, with advance reservation, you can get dinner for a minimum of four (€23/£15.40 or €15/ £10 children).

Géfosse-Fontenay, 30 km (18.6 miles) west of Bayeux off D514 (☎ 02 31 22 64 45; www.chez.com/manoir delariviere). 4 rooms. B&B double €57 (£38), room for four €97 (£65), gîte €300–420 wk (£200–280). Cot €10 (£6.70). Amenities: garden with play area; animals; evening meal with advance booking (excl Sun). In room (gîte): TV, kitchen.

Logis les Remparts ★ The 5pm check-in and 10.30am check-out at this B&B in the centre of medieval Bayeux get my goat, but the whimsical loveliness of the rooms and the prices make it irresistible. There are just three rooms – two with a

Honfleur Port

double and a single bed, one a suite with interconnecting rooms containing a rather remarkable double bed (think Louis Quinze meets 1950s kitsch) and three singles. All have en-suite shower rooms, and prices for each vary according to how many beds are occupied. The owner has cider and calvados orchards 10 km (6¼ miles) outside Bayeux; in the cellar of this house you can sample a glass of his cider or apple juice, plus homemade desserts such as *tergoule* (p. 223) and crêpes with apple jelly. The latter also feature at breakfast, which is served in a cosy room with a booster and highchair, together with croissants, homemade cake and cereals.

4 rue Bourbesneur, Bayeux (℡ 02 31 92 50 40; www.lecornu.fr). 3 rooms. Double/twin €52–62 (£34.80–41.50), suite for four €100 (£67). Amenities: tastings.

Relais des 3 Pommes ★ VALUE

If you're looking for a cheap place to rest your heads on the way to or from the ferry at Caen or Cherbourg, this modern motel in rural surroundings five minutes from the centre of Bayeux has basic rooms, including one triple and two quads, with tables and chairs on a verandah overlooking a little garden square. You can park right in front of them, taking the horror out of unloading and meaning you don't have to schlepp up and down stairs at all hours when you realise you've forgotten nappies or other essentials. Another handy feature is the self-service restaurant with its very cheap children's menu (€3.50/£2.35 for *steak haché*, breaded fish or chicken nuggets, ice cream or a yogurt and an orange juice or fizzy drink) and its play area and selection of children's books. The €7.50 (£5) main menu includes bread, a starter, a main course (*steak haché*, chitterling sausage, roast chicken or dish of the day, and dessert). There's also a 'proper' restaurant and a café with newspapers, a billiards table and a terrace; the buffet breakfast here is a bargain €5 (£3.35).

Boulevard Winston Churchill, St-Vigor-le-Grand, just off Bayeux ring road north-east of town (02 31 21 59 10; www.relaisdes3pommes. com). 35 rooms. Double €48–50 (£32–33.50), family room for four €59–61 (£39.50–40.85). Amenities: restaurants; play area; café.

FAMILY-FRIENDLY DINING

The Norman Riviera

EXPENSIVE

Auberge des Deux Tonneaux
★ If you fancy a break from the coast, this place is only 10 minutes inland yet feels very rural – it's in a protected village, in a half-timbered house with a thatched roof and a big garden with tables under the cherry trees. You can eat from two *menus* of traditional local cuisine, or there's a *carte* with robust country fare such as haddock salad with lentils, lobster terrine with garden herbs, Caen-style tripe, and black pudding – you're unlikely to feel at home if you're a veggie. That goes for the good children's menu too (€11/£7.40), which features sausages or steak with mash or sautée potatoes, ice cream and apple juice. Note the

comparatively early evening opening time.

Pierrefitte-en-Auge, 15 km (9⅓ miles) from Deauville off D579 (02 31 64 09 31). Main courses €13.90–17.80 (£9.30–11.90). Open daily noon–3pm and 6–10pm. Highchairs available.

Auberge de la Lieutenance
★★ Tucked away on a pedestrianised square round the corner from Honfleur's port, this restaurant in a pretty half-timbered building (okay, okay, so just about all buildings here are pretty and half-timbered...) serves some of the best seafood on the coast. It's a great place to come for lunch on a Saturday, after browsing the traditional market held in the square, and feast on local oysters, brochette of scallops and prawns with creamy lime sauce and carrot purée with chives, and chocolate and hazelnut fondant with pistachio custard. There's also a very good €23 (£15.40) menu, and a deeply decadent seafood platter for two (€85/£56.95). The children's menu may seem pricey but is good value given the choice and quality – for €11 (£7.40) under-9s get smoked salmon or salami, then chicken breast with cream and mashed potato or poached salmon with butter or cream and rice, followed by ice cream, sorbet or *fromage blanc* (p. 234).

12 place Ste-Catherine, Honfleur (02 31 89 07 52). Main courses €18–30 (£12–20). Open July and August daily noon–2.30pm and 7–10pm; rest of year Tue–Sat noon–2.30pm and 7–10pm, Sun noon–2.30pm. Highchairs available.

MODERATE–EXPENSIVE

La Petite Chine ★ A delightful, if overpriced, place for breakfast, brunch, lunch or afternoon tea – apparently it's a favourite with Yves Saint Laurent – this combined shop, tearoom and restaurant is squeezed into a higgledy-piggledy house near the port. The ground-floor restaurant serves light fare such as vegetable soup, tarts and *tartines* (open sandwiches) and pasta dishes; for tea you might enjoy comforting *clafoutis* (a fluffy, custard-like dessert from southwestern France), brownie with cream or *fromage blanc* (p. 234) with cinnamon, honey and almonds. On your way out, browse the shelves of teapots and related trinkets, stock up on fine teas, jams and pastries, and treat the children to a tooth-jangling old-fashioned sweet stick in flavours such as apricot, ginger and liquorice.

14–16 rue du Dauphin, Honfleur (☎ 02 31 89 36 52). Afternoon tea around €6–7 (£4–4.70), main courses in restaurant €12–19 (£8–12.75). Open daily 10am–6pm.

MODERATE

Il Parasole Though it doesn't have highchairs, this cheery little place round the corner from the Normandy Barrière hotel (p. 159) extends the usual Italian welcome to children, with solicitous, speedy service and fair prices for the location. There's a basic children's menu of *steak haché* and *frites* or pizza margherita, then ice cream, but they may prefer to choose from the wide-ranging main menu – in which case one pizza and one pasta dish can be enough for two little children and a scavenger parent too. The choice of pizzas runs to nearly 30, including an unusual salmon *soufflé* with cheese and *crème fraîche*, and there are plenty of pasta options too. Good alternatives include beef or salmon *carpaccio* dishes, *bresaola* (dried beef), interesting salads and sandwiches and meat and fish dishes, with daily specials available. Everything can be provided as a takeaway. There's also a branch in Trouville (2 place Fernand Moureaux, ☎ 02 31 87 33 87).

6 rue Hoche, Deauville (☎ 02 31 88 64 64, www.ilparasole.com). Main courses €7.50–19.90 (£5–13.30). Open daily July and August noon–midnight; rest of year noon–3pm and 7pm–midnight.

INEXPENSIVE–MODERATE

Dupont avec un Thé ★★ This award-winning patisserie with its operatic soundtrack is great for relaxed family breakfasts – unless you're ravenous, two *super complets* (€10.20/£6.80) with pastries, baguette, *fromage frais* and red fruits, butter and jam, juice and coffee, tea or hot chocolate should be enough. There is also a range of snacky savoury fare – sandwiches, salads and hot *tourtes* with salad, including *croque monsieur*, mini pizza and salmon and spinach pie. But above all, this is a place for chocoholics, who will be torn between the *Gouter Tout Chocolat* (chocolate cake, a chocolate sweet and a chocolate caramel, plus old-fashioned hot chocolate; €10.20/£6.80), or the dark chocolate fondue for two (€19/£12.75), with seasonal fruits, homemade biscuits and chocolate macaroons. If Cabourg has made you come over all Proustian, from 3pm Les Heures du Proust (€5.80/£3.90) comprises two *madeleines* and Brazilian or Caribbean hot chocolate or a cup of tea. There are more than 40 types of tea, plus non-alcoholic cocktails, aperitifs and wines. On a fine day, stock up with sweet and savoury tarts and divine breads for the beach, or a homemade ice cream from the cart; if you're homeward bound, the gorgeously wrapped biscuits and chocolates make great pressies. There are other branches of Dupont in nearby **Dives-sur-Mer, Trouville-sur-Mer** and **Deauville**.

6 avenue de la Mer, Cabourg (℡ 02 31 24 60 32). Sandwiches and salads €4.80–11 (£3.20–7.40). Open daily 9am–7pm.

Les Tonneaux du Père Magloire ★ Tacky but fun, this restaurant serves rustic local fare at tables set inside vast old Calvados barrels that have been chopped in half, with waiters dressed in peasant gear. Reserve ahead, though, or you may have to settle for a regular table; it may also be a good idea to check ahead that they don't have a hen night or some such booked – it's that sort of place. The specialities here are cheese fondues (including, naturally,

Pont-l'Evêque), cider fondue with fish or meat, and dessert fondues (caramel, chocolate or milk jam); for €7.90 (£5.30) children get a mini cheese fondue, chicken breast or ham with homemade mash, then ice cream, chocolate cake or *tergoule* (p. 223), plus fruit juice or syrup and water. There's a shop on site, selling Norman produce.

Route de Trouville, Pont-l'Evêque (℡ 02 31 64 65 20). Main courses €7–14 (£4.70–9.40). Open daily noon–2.30pm and 7–10pm. Highchairs available.

INEXPENSIVE

Marny Crêpe ★ Looking like something out of a time warp, this food counter on Deauville's main shopping street – recognisable by the life-sized model of an old lady on the pavement out front – still has its original wall tiles. Decorated with ancient posters, it's a great place to stop for a crêpe or sandwich to munch while window shopping in this chic town (p. 158), to buy the elements of a beach picnic or even to get an evening snack if you had a full lunch. As well as crêpes there are old-style waffles, tarts *à la grande-mère* (perhaps *she*'s the mysterious figure outside), baguettes, paninis, club sandwiches and pastries. It's also an old-fashioned sweet shop, selling all kinds of delectable bon bons, and a place to get your ice cream fix – Ben & Jerry's is among the brands.

Rue Desiré Le Hoc, Deauville, no telephone. Sandwiches €3–5 (£2–3.35). Open Thur–Tue 10am–midnight.

Caen, Bayeux & Around

EXPENSIVE

There's a gastronomic restaurant at the **Château d'Audrieu** (p. 164).

Le Boeuf Ferré ★ Near the castle, this restaurant in a 15th century building with exposed beams but slightly fusty décor prides itself on its French beef and other meats, including specialities from the Périgord (the Dordogne) – try the duck with acacia honey and raspberry vinegar. But if you only eat fish, there's plenty of seafood prepared in traditional Norman ways, including scallop and crayfish stew, monkfish and turbot. It's not cheap, but there's a superb-value €18 (£12) three-course *Menu Plaisir* with four options for each course, including rabbit terrine with shallot jam, salmon in a herb crust, and Norman apple crisp with *coulis*. The children's menu (€10.50/€12.50, or £7/8.40) for 2/3 courses) is adventurous – salad, country terrine or mini mussel flan, then grilled steak with lavender butter, salmon steak in a creamy sauce or fish fillet with aniseed, then sorbet, *crème brûlée* or vanilla profiteroles with warm chocolate sauce – but let the charming staff know if you want to adapt a dish for a fussy child. Booking ahead is a good idea.

10 rue des Croisiers, Caen (☎ 02 31 85 36 40). Main courses €9–18 (£6–12). Open Mon–Sat noon–2pm and 7–10pm, Sun noon–2pm excl July and August. Highchairs available.

La Chenevière ★★ This 18th century château at the end of a tree-lined drive has a lovely dining room with picture windows overlooking its park and woods. It's the perfect spot for refined but original fare such as couscous cake with blue lobster and spicy honey dressing, pan-fried Dover sole with vanilla Bourbon and baby artichokes, local lobster with salted Isigny butter, morel risotto and warm lobster claw salad, followed by the likes of warm bitter-chocolate cake with salted-caramel ice cream or strawberry carpaccio with olive-oil ice cream. A typical children's menu might be soup of the day or smoked salmon, then roast chicken with potato gratin in *sauce normande* (p. 222) or fish of the day with basmati rice, followed by a homemade dessert, for €15 (£10). There's also a vegetarian *menu* – a boon in meat-heavy Normandy. It might inspire you to take a cooking course here, led by renowned *chef-patron* Claude Esprabens and including a guided tour of Port-en-Bessin's quays and fish market (famous for a kind of scallop found only here), a gastronomic dinner and accommodation. The château's 29 **rooms and suites** combine old-fashioned luxury with modern chic, including flatscreen TVs. All can fit three with an extra bed, and there are suites for up to four, with a double room and two extra beds placed in the sitting room (€350–450/£234–300). Very good breakfasts are

€19/£12.75, or €9/£6 for children aged 10 and under. There are also tennis courts, a croquet lawn, a pool with a children's area, and massage rooms.

Escures-Commes, Port-en-Bessin, 7 km (4⅓ miles) north of Bayeux on D6 (℡ 02 31 51 25 25; www.lacheneviere.fr). Main courses €40–€50 (£26.80–33.50). Open Mon–Wed 7–9.30pm, Wed–Sun noon–1.30pm and 7–9.30pm. Highchairs available.

MODERATE

Le Pommier ★ This popular restaurant in the medieval heart of Bayeux has three convivial dining rooms where you can enjoy typical Norman dishes, many of them featuring organic ingredients (for the health-conscious there's even a vegetarian *formule*). Highlights are fish and crab terrine with garlic sauce, chicken in lemon and cider sauce, pears cooked in wine and hibiscus flower with spiced ice cream, and chocolate cake with bilberry ice cream. Children, who are made to feel very welcome by the friendly staff, get a relatively unexciting menu of steak, ham or fillet of fish, followed by ice cream, for €7.50 (£5). Advance booking is advised.

38–40 rue des Cuisiniers, Bayeux (℡ 02 31 21 52 10). Main courses €11–17 (£7.40–11.40). Open March to October daily noon–2.30pm and 7–9.30pm; November

to mid-December and mid-January Thur–Mon noon–2pm and 7–9.30pm. Highchairs available.

INEXPENSIVE

Dolly's, The English Shop ★★ It's quite unlike me to recommend a British place abroad, but Dolly's is at the opposite end of the spectrum from Irish theme pubs or homogenised burger joints – and if you've been here a while and are in need of a slap-up cooked English breakfast or brunch, this quirky deli, tearoom and fish'n'chip shop is the place to come. The afternoon teas are popular, too – with a choice of good scones, crumbles, brownies and cheesecake – and there are a handful of comfortingly familiar mains such as shepherd's pie, toad in the hole and sometimes even the likes of chicken korma (well, curry is said to be Britain's national dish...). Veggies get a few options too. Staff are charm personified, and there are squashy armchairs and sofas to sprawl on. Don't worry about it being the preserve of tourists – it has quite a following among Anglophile locals.

16–18 avenue de la Libération, Caen (℡ 02 31 94 03 29). Main courses €5–12 (£3.35–8). Open Tue and Wed (plus Sun June to September) 9.30am–7.30pm, Thur–Sat 9.30am–9pm.

7 Manche

Speeding off the ferries and down through the long, thin Cotentin peninsula that is largely synonymous with the Manche *département*, or whizzing through its southernmost portion on the way between Calvados and Brittany, visitors tend to bypass the not-inconsiderable charms of this largely rural area with its green rolling hills and pretty granite villages. Its seaside, though home to some gems, is mostly overlooked too, and even its main attraction, the world-famous Mont-St-Michel in its awe-inspiring bay, is often thought to be in Brittany. In fact, many Bretons still challenge Norman ownership of the mount, claiming that the latter is only the result of the River Couesnon, the historic border between Brittany and Normandy, having changed course.

Aside from a dozen or so war museums commemorating events on the Cotentin's northern and eastern coasts on and around D-Day – one or two with much to recommend them to younger visitors – Manche is full of welcoming farms, animal parks and natural treasures that make it another great place for an active holiday, inland or by the sea. Good family accommodation is surprisingly scarce, and those looking for luxury will need to go elsewhere, but this is a fine spot for families who enjoy the open air, unpretentious lodging and down-to-earth local cuisine featuring famous *pré-salé* lamb, delicious seafood and much more.

ESSENTIALS

Getting There

By Plane In summer 2006 **Flybe** (p. 29) ran low-cost thrice-weekly 40-min flights between **Southampton** and **Cherbourg** airport 11 km (6.8 miles) east of the city; at the time of writing they were expected to continue in 2007. There are also twice-daily flights between Cherbourg and **Paris-Orly** with **Twin Jet** ((0892 707 337, *www.twinjet.net*), and the same firm runs services to the Channel Island of **Jersey**. For schedules, see *www.aeroport-cherbourg.com*. Otherwise, the airports of **Rennes** and **Dinard** in Brittany are within easy reach of the southern Manche; see the

companion guide to this book, *Brittany With Your Family*.

By Ferry Cherbourg is served by **Brittany Ferries** (p. 31) from **Poole**, with up to three 'classic cruises' (4 hrs 30 mins/6 hrs 30 mins overnight) a day and one daily high-speed crossing (2 hrs 15 mins). The first are aboard the *Barfleur*, which has a games room, children's entertainment and accommodation with cots; the second uses the *Normandie Vitesse*, with its play area. The firm also runs up to two daily 3-hr sailings from **Portsmouth** (mid-March to mid-November), on the *Normandie Express* with its playroom. **Condor Ferries** (p. 31) sails between Portsmouth and Cherbourg too, but only on

MANCHE

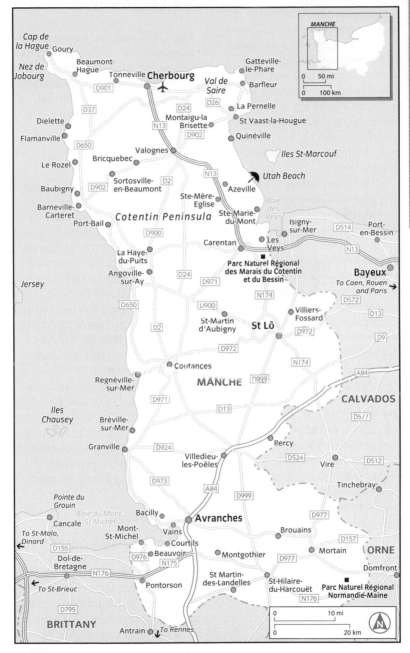

MANCHE

0   50 mi
0   100 km

Cap de la Hague
Goury
Nez de Jobourg
Beaumont-Hague
Tonneville
Cherbourg
Val de Saire
Gatteville-le-Phare
Barfleur
D901
D24
D26
La Pernelle
St Vaast-la-Hougue
Dielette
Montaigu-la-Brisette
D37
N13
D902
Quinéville
Flamanville
D650
Valognes
Iles St-Marcouf
Le Rozel
Bricquebec
N13
Utah Beach
Baubigny
Sortosville-en-Beaumont
D2
Azeville
D902
Ste-Mère-Eglise
Barneville-Carteret
Cotentin Peninsula
Ste-Marie-du-Mont
Baie des Veys
Isigny-sur-Mer
D514
Port-en-Bessin
Port-Bail
D900
Carentan
Les Veys
N13
La Haye-du-Puits
Parc Naturel Régional des Marais du Cotentin et du Bessin
Bayeux
Jersey
Angoville-sur-Ay
D24
D971
To Caen, Rouen and Paris
D650
D900
N174
D572
St-Martin d'Aubigny
St Lô
Villiers-Fossard
D13
D2
D972
D9
D972
Coutances
N174
A84
Regnéville-sur-Mer
MANCHE
N999
CALVADOS
D971
D13
D577
Iles Chausey
Bréville-sur-Mer
Granville
D924
Percy
Villedieu-les-Poêles
D524
Vire
D512
D973
Tinchebray
A84
Pointe du Grouin
Baie du Mont-St-Michel
Bacilly
D999
Avranches
D977
Cancale
Mont-St-Michel
Vains
Brouains
D157
To St-Malo, Dinard
D155
Courtils
Montgothier
Mortain
ORNE
Dol-de-Bretagne
Beauvoir
D977
Domfront
N176
N175
St Martin-des-Landelles
St-Hilaire-du-Harcouët
Parc Naturel Régional Normandie-Maine
To St-Brieuc
Pontorson
N176
D795
BRITTANY
Antrain
To Rennes

0   10 mi
0   20 km

Sundays from late July to early September, taking 5 hrs 30 mins. **Irish Ferries** (☎ *08705 171717*, *www.irishferries.com*) and **Celtic Link** (☎ *01 82 30 136*, *www.celtic linkferries.com*) sail between **Rosslare** in Ireland and Cherbourg several times a week, taking 18 hrs 30 mins (overnight); the Irish Ferries' vessel, the *Normandy*, has playrooms and children's entertainment in high summer.

Otherwise, you are close to the ports of **Caen-Ouistreham** in Calvados (p. 133) and **St-Malo** in Brittany.

You can sail to and from the British **Channel Islands** and the Cotentin with **Manche Iles Express** (*www.manche-iles-express.com*); its high-speed catamarans run between **Granville** and Jersey, **Barneville-Carteret** and Jersey or Guernsey, and **Dielette** and Guernsey or Alderney, taking 45 mins–1 hr.

By Train There are no TGV services within the Manche, but normal trains from **Paris St Lazare** to **Cherbourg** take only 3 hrs. Trains from Paris St Lazare to **St Lô** also take nearly 3 hrs, since you need to change at Caen. Or you can get to **Avranches** from **Paris-Montparnasse** in just over 4 hrs, changing at Dol-de-Bretagne in Brittany and backtracking slightly. For SNCF details, see p. 39.

VISITOR INFORMATION

The CDT website, *www.manche tourisme.com*, can be useful, but for tourist office contact details go to *www.normandy-tourism.org* and click on 'Useful addresses' then 'County (Départemental) Tourist Boards'.

Orientation

The **N13** (a continuation of the A13 up from Paris) takes you into the Manche from Caen and up as far as the *département*'s main town, **Cherbourg**, skirting the coast. The other main road through the narrow Cotentin peninsula is the **N174**, which branches off the N13 just south of Carentan and takes you down past **St Lô** to join the toll **A84** motorway between Caen and **Avranches** (and on to Rennes in Brittany). Beware that both the N13 and the N174 can get horrendously busy with **lorry traffic** to and from the ferries at Cherbourg, and factor in extra time for journeys, especially if you're catching a ferry yourself.

Getting Around

Exploring this quite rural area is a challenge without your own wheels, though tourist offices will provide advice and bus and train schedules. In the unlikely event that you don't bring your own vehicle or hire one outside the Manche, **Easycar** (p. 38) allows you to **hire cars** through its website for pickup at **Cherbourg** airport, ferry port and city centre, and in **Avranches**. **Europcar** (p. 38) also services Cherbourg airport and train station, plus **St Lô** (41 rue Alsace Lorraine, ☎ 02 33 05 56 57).

Child-Friendly Events & Entertainment

Barneville-Carteret (p. 180) is a good place to celebrate Bastille Day (14th July), with street performances, a concert and a fireworks display over the sea. For the **Normandie Horse Show**, see p. 184.

Carnaval ★ Granville's famous four-day Mardi Gras carnival is thought to date back to 1872 and was originally mainly an opportunity for local fishermen to blow off some steam before embarking on eight-week sailings to Newfoundland. These days it's more family oriented, with a parade of children in fancy dress and masks accompanied by brightly decorated floats, a children's ball, a funfair, marching bands, open-air concerts, exhibitions on nautical themes, a floodlit night procession and, on the last evening, the mock trial and burning of the carnival effigy on the beach and a confetti fight by the town hall.

On and around Shrove Tuesday, early May. Granville (☎ 02 33 91 30 03 (tourist office)). Admission free.

Les Féeriques de Montgothier

★ One of the biggest *son-et-lumière* shows in northern France, this extravaganza against the backdrop of a medieval castle involves 750 volunteers, 35 horses, 12 carriages, 35 dogs and 4000 spectators. On colossal open-air stage sets reflected in the castle's moat, a succession of 'tableaux' bring to life, over two hours, local legends and history, including the fairy Sélune, the life of William the Conqueror from childhood, the Hundred Years' War and World War II, with a soundtrack in English and German as well as French. Being reliant on darkness for its effects, it doesn't start until nightfall, but the site is open from 7pm and you can have dinner here (€11/£7.40, child €7/£4.70). Advance reservations are recommended, as this is a tourist favourite.

Mid-July to August, usually Sat. Montgothier, 12 km (7½ miles) south-east of Avranches on D47 (☎ 02 33 60

Les Féeriques de Montgothier

60 70; *www.feeriques.com*). Tickets: €18 (£12) adults (€16/£10.70 in advance), €7 (£4.70) children aged 5–12.

Festi' Ferme ★★ **FIND** This festival brings together a dozen or so farms around Manche for a two-week programme of activities and events, including 'bee walks' and honey tasting, Easter egg hunts, old-fashioned Norman games, animal-drawing competitions, storytelling evenings, evening concerts, guided farmyard tours and garden visits. At most places you get free tastings and the chance to buy local produce. The website has detailed listings of events and locations (in French), plus a map so that you can see what's happening near you.

Second half April. Various locations (📞 *02 33 06 48 89; http://festiferme manche.free.fr*). *Admission: events and activities vary but average about €5 (£3.35) for adults, €3 (£2) for children.*

Festival du Livre de Jeunesse et de BD Cherbourg's festival of children's literature and *bande dessinée* (comic strips) involves national publishers and local schools but is also open to the general public for two of its four days. Held within La Cité de la Mer (p. 189) and structured along a different theme each year – ecology, for instance, or food – it offers, in addition to the opportunity to meet children's authors and illustrators and to buy books, a supervised activity corner for younger children. This involves drawing, alphabet

Canoes, Mont-St-Michel

games, terracotta pot-making, gardening, face-painting workshops and more. If your older children speak good French and are *really* into books, who knows what future might open up to them if they attend one of the talks on book production, from writing to publishing.

Early June. La Cité de la Mer, Cherbourg (📞 *02 33 10 08 80; www. festivaldulivre.com*). *Admission: €3 (£2) adults, children free.*

La Rando Baie du Mont-St-Michel ★★★ **FIND** You can walk, cycle, ride and canoe in or around the bay of the Mont-St-Michel all year (p. 197), but this weekend-long family event also features stilt walkers, Breton music and dance, a twilight walk with actors in medieval costumes, a *fest noz* (nocturnal Breton festival of Celtic music and circle dances), rollerblading by the beach, horse-and-carriage rides and more. Some events are held over the Breton border in the Ille-et-Vilaine. Sunday is the best day to come – the free 'festive village' from 10am to 6pm has displays on local ecology, a photo exhibition, local produce and craft stalls, plus children's workshops and events – kite-making, face-painting, canoeing, story-telling, a climbing wall and so on – and a ball for 3–10-year-olds.

Mid-May. Baie du Mont-St-Michel (02 33 89 64 00 (Maison de la Baie, Genêts); http://randobaie.free.fr/). Admission free to 'village'; activity prices average €8 (£5.35).

Les Triolettes ★ This folklore group travels all over Europe and even as far as Canada to put on its shows comprising traditional Norman singing, dancing and humorous sketches, but you might be lucky and catch them in action in their home town of Villedieu-les-Poêles in the southern Manche. The singers, dancers and musicians sport authentic and often rare local costumes, including old *coiffes*. It does help if you understand French, especially for the sketches, but you will be hard-pressed to understand the Norman *patois* used for most of the songs, which are about local produce (apples, cider and so on) or the sea. Even so, you can't fail to appreciate the authentic charm of such performances as *Mon père à tué le loup* ('My father killed the wolf'), a fishermen's dance from Saint Léonard de Vains.

All year; call/see website for dates. Villedieu-les-Poêles; locations vary but include the town's place de la Mairie (02 33 48 11 59; http://perso.orange.fr/lestriolettes/). Ticket prices vary.

WHAT TO SEE & DO

Children's Top 10 Attractions

❶ Exploring the breathtaking bay of the **Mont-St-Michel** on foot or horseback or by bike, canoe, fishing boat or hot-air balloon; p. 197 and p. 198.

❷ Taking an amphibious boat to the former plague island of **Tatihou**; p. 181.

❸ Looking for birds, bats, seals and more in the **Parc Naturel Régional des Marais du Cotentin et du Bessin**; p. 186.

❹ Seeing how local children lived during World War II at the **Mémorial de la Liberté Retrouvée**; p. 193.

❺ Climbing the **Phare de Gatteville**, Europe's second-tallest lighthouse; p. 189.

❻ Taking part in guided walks or boat trips under the stars at **Ludiver**; p. 192.

❼ Climbing aboard the subma-rine *Le Redoutable* and driving a mock submarine at **La Cité de la Mer**; p. 189.

❽ Petting some of the 300 or so tortoises who live at **Alligator Bay**; p. 183.

❾ Watching church bells being made at the **Fonderie des Cloches**; p. 195.

❿ Filling your basket with Norman goodies at the **Maison Gosselin**; p. 201.

Beaches, Resorts & Islands

Barneville-Carteret ★ Situated on the west Manche coast opposite the Channel Islands (you can sail to Jersey from here; p. 174), this embraces an historic town (**Barneville-bourg**) with an ancient church (check out the inside columns decorated with fantastical carvings of people, animals and plants) and a good weekly **market** (Saturday morning); a fishing port and marina (**Carteret**) with lots of shops and restaurants; and a family beach resort (**Barneville-plage**) with watersports facilities. The latter has a **children's beach club** and lifeguards in July and August; there's also a small beach with summer lifeguards at Carteret, and to the north a wilder beach, **Plage de la Vieille Eglise**, with dunes stretching north as far as Le Rozel, popular for sand-yachting and speed-sailing. Other high-summer activities include rock pool trails organised by the tourist office, regattas and *pétanque* training and competitions. This is also a great place to celebrate Bastille Day (p. 177), and there's a *train touristique*

Barneville-Carteret coastline

running south along the coast to Port-Bail (p. 199).

Tourist offices: 10 rue des Ecoles and place Flandres Dunkerque (℡ 02 33 04 90 58; www.barneville-carteret.fr).

Iles Chausey ★ Once the preserve of pirates and smugglers, these barren islands and islets – there are claimed to be one for every day of the year, making up the biggest archipelago in Europe – lie 12 km (7½ miles) from Granville at the southern end of the Cotentin peninsula. These days they're home only to lots of seabirds and the inhabitants of the 50 or so houses on the only island that can be visited – La Grande Ile – which is hardly 'large' at barely 1.5 km (0.9 miles) in length. You can join them, in 20 **self-catering apartments,** at La Ferme de Chausey (February to December, ℡ 02 33 90 90 53, €244–544/wk, that's £163–365, for a four-person studio); there are also four **gîtes** in an old presbytery (year round; call tourist office, p. 176) and a 10-room **hotel**, Hôtel du Fort et des Iles (Easter to late November, ℡ 02 33 50 25 02; double with half-board €60/£40) that gets booked up aeons in advance, and that houses one of the island's two restaurants. The bakery operates from Easter to late November, and there are no chemists, cars or even bikes. In fact, there's little to do besides lazing on the six fine sand beaches, watching for dolphins or trying to spot animal and human shapes in the contorted granite rocks that emerge

Iles Chausey

at low tide. Footpaths lead past landmarks such as the 39 m (128 ft) lighthouse, a fortress that was restored by Louis Renault of the car empire and a fort built by Napoléon III and used as a prison for Germans in World War I and a Nazi garrison in World War II, and that now houses fishing families. **Sea canoes** can be hired, and Vedettes de Granville (below) run 70-minute **boat tours** of the archipelago.

Tourist office: cours Jonville, Granville (mainland) (☎ 02 33 91 30 03; www. ville-granville.fr, www.ileschausey. com). Sailings Vedettes de Granville (☎ 02 33 50 31 81) year round (call for times), return trip €19 (£12.75) adults, €11.70 (£7.80) children aged 3–14; Emeraude Lines (☎ 02 23 18 01 80) also sail from St-Malo in Brittany.

Ile de Tatihou ★★ This uninhabited island 2 km (1.2 miles) off the eastern coast of the Cotentin was inaccessible to the public until 1992. Today you can either walk to it over the oyster beds at low tide or cross the narrow strait by amphibious boat (a boat with wheels – a great hit with children). Either way, book ahead – only 500 visitors are allowed a day, to preserve the animal and plant life, which includes lots of migrating birds (there's a reserve with free guided tours and an observatory). The island has a fascinating past: in 1720 it was used to quarantine sailors with the plague; 150 years later the Muséum d'Histoire Naturelle took over the quarantine hospital for a marine research lab. In the 1920s the island became a holiday and 'hygiene-training' centre for children, replaced in

Ile de Tatihou

1948 by a rehab centre for young offenders. These days there's a **Musée Maritime** in a tower-fortress, with items from shipwrecks, archaeological and ethnological artifacts, and displays on coastal flora and fauna and ecology; **botanical and maritime gardens**; and some historical buildings, including powder magazines.

An annual **festival of maritime music** takes place here in August, and there are periodic **workshops** on Bronze Age metalworking, pottery and prehistoric tool-making (there was a Viking presence on the island), some specifically for children aged 6–14 and 8–12; you need to bring a picnic and supper. You can also stay the night on the island, in a basic **hotel** within the old barracks, with eight twin rooms, one double, 19 singles and six triples

with their own bathrooms, with prices starting at €38pp/night (£25.50) for half-board accommodation with meals in the island's one **restaurant**.

Accueil Tatihou, quai Vauban, St Vaast-la-Hougue (mainland) (02 33 23 19 92; www.tatihou.com). Open daily April to September 10am–6pm; July and August 10am–7pm (reception 9.30am–12.30pm and 1.15–5.30pm, museum 10am–5.30pm); boat departures every 30 mins at high tide, every hour at low tide. Admission: return boat trip €4.60 (£3.10) adults, €1.50 (£1) children aged 4–11; return boat-trip and museum €7.60 (£5.10) adults, €3.05 (£2.05) children aged 4–11.

Other Natural Wonders & Spectacular Views

For the **Baie du Mont-St-Michel**, see p. 197.

A Tainted Coast

It's not all rosy at the 'Nose of Jobourg': while you get idyllic views to the west, to the east lies a nuclear waste treatment plant at Beaumont-Hague. Further south, meanwhile, Flamanville, which is already home to a power station with two nuclear reactors, has been earmarked as the site at which France will add the first of its third generation of reactors by 2012.

Parents may remember the sinking of the *Rainbow Warrior* by the French foreign intelligence services during a disabling operation in New Zealand in 1985. Five years earlier, the Greenpeace boat had attempted to stop a ship bringing spent nuclear fuel to the Beaumont-Hague plant. Today, more than a quarter of a century later, both Greenpeace and local environmental groups believe the plant to be one of the world's largest sources of nuclear radioactivity, contaminating the north-east Atlantic Ocean, the North Sea and the Barents Sea as well as streams in the Cap de la Hague area, and increasing the risk of children living near the plant and in Alderney developing leukaemia. To support **Greenpeace**, see ***www.greenpeace.org/international/***.

Nez de Jobourg ★ The second most-visited sight in Manche, the Nez de Jobourg – which sounds like 'Nose of Jobourg' but actually derives its name from the Scandinavian *naes*, meaning cape – is a promontory poking out into the Channel from the northernmost tip of the Cotentin peninsula. As well as holding the crown for having the highest cliffs in Europe, the Hautes Falaises reaching up to 128 m (420 ft), it offers wonderful views out as far as the Channel island of Alderney on clear days. There's also an old customs officers' path leading down to the tiny port of Goury with its lighthouse, taking you past caves and abundant plant- and birdlife (the Nez is a bird reserve), though you need to be wary of the sometimes violent winds on this exposed coastline.

*Tourist office (Beaumont-Hague): rue Jallot (℡ 02 33 52 74 94; **www. lahague.org**).*

Aquaria & Animal Parks

There's a good aquarium in **La Cité de la Mer** in Cherbourg (p. 189).

Alligator Bay ★ Formerly the Reptilarium, this attraction a few minutes from the Mont-St-Michel was renamed in mid-2006 in honour of its new tropical hot-house containing Europe's biggest group of alligators, crocodiles and caimans (around 200). For many visitors, however – especially children – the highlight remains the 'farm' of 300 tortoises, where you can climb into one of the enclosures and pet the shy creatures, including giant specimens from the Seychelles. There's also plenty of snakes, chameleons and so on. Things can get a little smelly indoors, but older children enjoy the system of little ladders, bridges and 'trappers' cabins' set up to allow viewpoints into some

Alligator Bay

of the vivariums, and there are iguana, giant lizard- and crocodile-feeding sessions (daily April to September). There's a picnic space, plus a good shop; a visit takes about 1 hr–90 mins.

Beauvoir, 3 km (1.8 miles) south of Mont-St-Michel on D976 (☎ 02 33 68 11 18; www.alligator-bay.com). Open April to September daily 10am–7pm; October to December, February and March daily 2–6pm; January Sat, Sun and school holidays 2–6pm. Admission: €11 (£7.40) adults, €9 (£6) children aged 13–18, €7 (£4.70) children aged 4–12.

Aquarium du Roc It may be small and low-tech in an age of high-falutin' sealife centres, but Granville's aquarium goes beyond its remit. As well as 25 tanks with both local and tropical fish and a sealion pool, it has a *Palais Minéral* with geological specimens, some of them dating back several million years and one of them, an amethyst, weighing more than 100 kg; the dreamlike *Féérie des Coquillages* with lots of interesting shells; and a *Jardin des Papillons* with butterflies and various insects. Reckon on about 90 mins to look around all three. There are free guided tours of the aquarium and butterfly museum by request.

1 boulevard de Vaufleury, Granville (☎ 02 33 50 19 83; www.aquarium-du-roc.com). Open daily mid-April to mid-September 10am–7pm; rest of year 10am–12.30pm and 2–7pm. Admission: €7 (£4.70) adults, €3.50 (£2.35) children aged 4–14.

Ferme-Musée du Cotentin
This museum in an old farm and its outbuildings has antique farm machines and tools, former stables, a cider press, dairy and conservation orchards to explore and a whole host of animals, including Cotentin donkeys, Cotentin and Roussin de la Hague sheep, Blanc de Hotot rabbits, Cotentin hens and Duclair ducks. Sporadic events include local produce markets, a sheep festival and local breed competitions. If you want to stay, there are four sweetly rustic **B&B rooms** (€50/£33.50 for four, including museum visit).

Chemin de Beauvais, Ste Mère-Eglise, 12 km (7½ miles) north of Carentan on N13 (☎ 02 33 95 40 20). Open daily April, May and school holidays (excl Christmas) 2–6pm; June and September 11am–6pm; July and August 11am–7pm; last admission 1 hr before closing. Admission: €4 (£2.70) adults, €1.60 (£1.10) children aged 7–15.

Haras National de St Lô One of 30 national stud farms set up by Napoléon I in 1804, St Lô is a good bet for horsey families, especially on the *Jeudis du Haras* (Thur 3pm, late July to early September) – horse-and-carriage shows in its grand 19th century courtyards. Over five days in August, it also hosts the **Normandie Horse Show** (*www.normandie-horse-show.com*), with showjumping, carriage-pulling and more. Otherwise you can look around the stables full of Normandy cobs and French saddle horses, though bear in mind that in spring and early summer most go out to do their duties in local firms. There are also changing exhibitions in a former stable, some of them designed especially for children.

Avenue du Maréchal Juin, St Lô (℡ 02 33 55 29 09 (tourist office); www. haras-nationaux.fr). Open June and September daily 2–6pm, with guided visit 4.30pm; July and August by guided visit only, daily 11am, 2.30pm, 3.30pm and 4.30pm; no guided visits on Jeudis du Haras. Admission: €4.50 (£3) adults, €2.50 (£1.68) children aged 12–16; Jeudis du Haras €4 (£2.70) adults, under-12s free.

Parc Zoologique St Martin

This modest little zoo within a 15-hectare wooded park has four large ponds teeming with birdlife and a variety of animal species both familiar and exotic, from wolves and Ouessant sheep to dwarf zebus (the humped sacred cow of India) and Bennett's wallabies. Before or after looking around, little children can enjoy Shetland pony rides (2pm, or all afternoon in July and August), and there's also a snack bar, a picnic spot and a shop.

Hameau Masson, Montaigu-la-Brisette, 8 km (5 miles) north of Valognes off D902 (℡ 02 33 40 40 98;

www.zoomontaigu.com). Open September to April Sun and public holidays 2–5pm; May Sat, Sun and public holidays 2–6pm; June Mon–Fri 11am–5pm and Sat, Sun and public holidays 2–6pm; July and August Mon–Fri 11am–7pm and Sat, Sun and public holidays 2–6pm. Admission: €5.50 (£3.70) adults, €4 (£2.70) children.

Zoo de Champrépus ★

Manche's biggest animal attraction is still small enough to be manageable for those with little children. It divides into two rough sections, with a bridge leading from near the entrance over the main road into the mini-farm with its goats, unfeasibly hairy Baudet-Poitou donkeys, cows, Vietnamese potbellied pigs and sheep; you can go into the goat and sheep enclosures, but don't be surprised if the sheep chase you for your bags of popcorn. Back in the main part of the zoo, there are camels, giraffes, zebras and more, viewable from pretty plant-lined pathways (the zoo layout is based on a series of themed gardens). Some of the enclosures do look a

Dwarf Zebus

bit cramped, but the creation of the new African Plain zone in 2006 will hopefully have started easing the pressure. Highlights are the lemur and otter feeding sessions several times a day (April to August); you can even enter the lemurs' reserve. To make the most of your visit, ask for one of the free (French-language) quiz sheets to use in conjunction with the information boards around the zoo. At the end there's a brilliant play area with bouncy castles for different age groups, a ball pool and animal-themed playground rides. There's also a friendly café with crêpes, salads, sandwiches, and so on, a large shady picnic area, souvenir shop and baby-changing facility.

INSIDER TIP

Look out for vouchers giving discounts at Festyland in Calvados (p. 156) when you buy your zoo ticket.

Between Villedieu-les-Poêles and Granville, 6 km (3.7 miles) from A84 (exit 37) (02 33 61 30 74; www.zoo-champrepus.com/). Open daily April to June and September 10am–6pm; July and August 10am–7pm; October 1.30–6pm; February and March call for days and times. Admission: €11.50 (£7.70) adults, €6.50 (£4.35) children aged 3–12.

Nature Reserves, Parks & Gardens

Southern Manche includes a small section of the Parc Naturel Regional Normandie-Maine (p. 115).

Jardin Public It's not every public park that has sea lions, especially ones that you can come and see being fed (Tue–Sun 10am and 4.15pm). They're just a few of the inhabitants of the children's zoo here; there is also an aviary, sheep, goats, swans and ducks. Though small, the walled park has a river, grotto, fountains, paths, ancient trees and lovely lawns for picnicking, plus a playground by a bandstand.

Avenue de Paris, Cherbourg (02 33 20 43 40). Open daily on average 8.30am–5.30pm, with small seasonal variations. Admission free.

Parc Naturel Régional des Marais du Cotentin et du Bessin ★★★ One of the newest of France's 44 regional natural parks, created in 1991, this marshland covers 145,000 hectares roughly centred on Carentan and the Baie des Veys, with a tongue extending into Calvados as far as Trévières. The best place to get a handle on it is the Maison d'Acceuil at St Côme-du-Mont: this is the starting point for a 1 km (0.62 mile) 'interpretation footpath' with information boards leading to bird observatories. You can also hire 2–3-person barges to reach these, or take a guided boat trip. Inside the *Maison* is a 'discovery space' with displays on nature and culture in the area, and there are lots of wonderful family-oriented events, including *Crépuscule d'Eté* evening guided walks with storytelling or bat hunts, and outings to spot seals. The park is crisscrossed by walking trails, including *Voies Vertes* on old railway lines or towpaths (you can also cycle and ride on many of these), plus *Véloroutes* earmarked for family bike rides. A map of the best ones, *Les plus belles balades*, is available at the *Maison d'Acceuil* and local tourist offices for €12.80 (£8.60), or you can get free pamphlets for individual routes. The *Maison* and tourist offices will also inform you about bike and binocular hire, horse-and-carriage rides and boat trips in the Baie des Veys.

Maison d'Accueil, Les Ponts d'Ouve and Espace de Découverte des Marais du Cotentin et du Bessin, St Côme-du-Mont (☎ 02 33 71 65 30; www.parc-cotentin-bessin.fr). Maison d'Accueil open Easter to September daily 9.30am–7pm; mid-October to mid-December and early January to Easter Tue–Sun 9.30am–1pm and 2–5.30pm. Admission free; interpretation paths/bird reserve €3.10 (£2.10) (guided tour €4.60/£3.10), children under 7 free.

Historic Buildings & Monuments

Mont-Saint-Michel ★

OVERRATED The big news at the Mont-St-Michel is that it's going to become an island. In June 2006, French PM Dominique de Villepin announced a €150-million (£100 million) hydraulic dam project to help remove the silt accumulated around this rocky islet 2 km (1¼ miles) off the French coast, topped by a dramatic Benedictine abbey and steepled Romanesque church. The current causeway – which replaced a natural land bridge covered at high tide – will be dismantled and a bridge and shuttle service put in place. The work should be complete by 2012, but the site will remain accessible throughout.

A Roman stronghold, the mount first became home to a monastery in the 8th century, after, according to legend, the

Cotentin and Bessin Marshlands Regional Park

Picnic here at Mont-St-Michel

archangel Michael told the Bishop of Avranches to build a church here (reinforcing his message by burning a hole in the bishop's skull with his finger; you can see the skull in Avranches' church; p. 196). A site of pilgrimage for many centuries, its influence waned with the Reformation, and after the Revolution it served as a prison until a campaign led to it being declared a historic monument in 1874. A little over a century later, it became a UNESCO World Heritage Site. Children may recognise it from a scene in *Mickey, Donald, Goofy: The Three Musketeers* (2004), and it also inspired the design of Minas Tirith in *The Lord of the Rings: The Return of the King* (2003).

This is one of the strangest places you'll ever visit – though one of the world's most-photographed structures, it looks truly mysterious from outside, with the walk or drive along the causeway (there's a car park at the foot of the mount) only increasing the anticipation. Inside, it's a buzzing hive of tourists, even out of high season (it's the most-visited French site outside Paris), and you will probably feel deflated. The cobbled alleys would be atmospheric were they not lined with tacky souvenir shops and tourist-trap restaurants occupying the quaint half-timbered houses. Try not to bring a buggy: at some point, faced with the seemingly unending series of steep steps, most people abandon them and carry their babies and toddlers. If your child is small enough, a 'baby backpack' (p. 23) is a good idea; toddlers will get tired and you will have little choice but to carry them. On a safety note, there are lots of gaps in the upper **ramparts** that a tot could conceivably squeeze through, so keep a firm rein on them. For all that, the views out over the glistening sandflats, usually dotted with ant-like walkers, are truly incredible, as is the vista back over the Mont's higgledy-piggledy rooftops.

Otherwise, the best bit for children is the **Archéoscope**, a multimedia space with a *son-et-lumière* show about the mount's history, construction and legends (in French, but with great footage from a helicopter). You can also visit the **abbey** itself, including the spooky crypts; the **Musée Maritime** with model boats and the current displays on local tides, ecology and the current desilting work; and the **Musée Historique (Musee Grévin)**,

Inside the Walls, Mont-St-Michel

with waxwork prisoners, reconstructed *oubliettes* (prison cells set in dungeon floors), a 19th century periscope that lets you look at the bay, torture instruments, weapons and more. There are also services held by the handful of monks and nuns who still live here (including Mass Tue–Sun 12.15pm).

For **guided walks in the bay**, with its tides that the writer Victor Hugo described as 'swift as a galloping horse' (they come in at a speed of a metre a second, with roughly 14 m between high and low water marks), see p. 197. **Never walk in the bay without a guide:** the quicksand still swallows people up every year as it once did medieval pilgrims.

Tourist office: left of main entrance (☎ 02 33 60 14 30; www.ot-mont saintmichel.com). Admission free; car park €4 (£2.70); abbey: €8 (£5.35) adults, €5 (£3.35) ages 18–25, under-18s free; 1 museum: €4 (£2.70) adults, €5 (£3.35) school-age children; 4 museums: €15 (£10) adults, €9 (£6) school-age children.

Mont open all the time; abbey and museums open May to August daily 9am–7pm; September to April 9.30am–6pm, last admission 1 hr before closing (Musée Maritime closed January; other museums closed mid-November to January excl Christmas holidays).

Phare de Gatteville ★ Not the most picturesque of lighthouses, Gatteville on the northern coast of the Cotentin has the distinction of being the second highest in all Europe, at 75 m (246 ft). If you are sturdy of leg and lung, you can ascend its 365 steps to reach a viewing platform that affords awe-inspiring views over the Channel, the northern Cotentin marshes and the Calvados coastline. There's also a small exhibition room at the base of the lighthouse, where you learn that it was built in 1829–1834 to help sailors navigate through the hazardous Raz de Barfleur, and consists of around 11,000 pieces of granite.

Gatteville-le-Phare, 30 km (18.6 miles) west of Cherbourg on D901 (☎ 02 33 23 17 97). Open daily February, 1st half November and 2nd half December 10am–noon and 2–4pm; March and October 10am–noon and 2–5pm; April and September 10am–noon and 2–6pm; May to October 10am–noon and 2–7pm (closed in storms/winds over 50 km/h). Admission: €2 (£1.34) adults, children under 13 free.

The Top Museums

La Cité de la Mer ★★★
Though it consists in part of a very good aquarium, Cherbourg's main family attraction – situated

Life by a Thread

One of the Cotentin peninsula's most famous (and oddball) sights is the effigy of an American paratrooper dangling from the steeple of the church at Ste Mère-Eglise, the first village in Normandy to be liberated by the Americans on D-Day. The mannequin represents Private John Steele, who got snagged on the tower by his parachute and, despite being deafened by the church bells, played dead until the Germans noticed him and took him prisoner; his story is told in the film *The Longest Day*. The church walls are still pocked by bullet holes, and inside is a poignant display about colleagues of Steele's who didn't make it – most were shot and hung dead in the trees around the square – including a stained-glass window featuring the Virgin Mary with paratroopers in the background. As light relief, there are also some wonderful animal carvings.

The town also has a **Museé Airborne (℡ *02 33 41 41 35, www.airborne-museum.org*)** about operations in the area, including a glider you can climb into. About 10 km (6.2 miles) north of Ste Mère, meanwhile, you can take guided tours of the **Batterie d'Azeville (℡ *02 33 40 63 05*,** April to October), some giant Nazi bunkers used to fire at ships landing at Utah Beach, including lots of underground passageways.

Ste Mére-Eglise Church

in the city's former transatlantic terminal – has something quite unique: a decommissioned submarine, the 128 m (420 ft) *Le Redoutable*. France's first missile-firing nuclear submarine, it was launched by General de Gaulle in 1967 during the Cold War, after construction that took nearly 10 years and involved 4500 people. It returned to Cherbourg in 1991, having sailed the equivalent of three times the distance between the Earth and the Moon. With the help of audio guides in French, English, Dutch or German, narrated by a fictional captain, you can visit all parts of the craft, including the

engine rooms, missile section, control room and living quarters. After the 35-minute tour, you follow a 45-minute 'submarine trail' with displays on the history of submarines, from hairbrained early projects to cutting-edge technology, plus a simulated control station where you can play at navigating a submarine yourself. Under-6s aren't allowed aboard the submarine for safety reasons, and general access may be restricted at very busy periods; if so, the overall admission price is reduced.

Before all this, there's the **ocean exhibition**, which looks at life on the seabed and at the history of underwater exploration, from early attempts in diving suits to modern oceanography. There's lots to hold your attention here (leave about an hour and a half), including a section on the underwater archaeology carried out off Cherbourg in 1984 after the French Navy's discovery of the wreck of the CSS *Alabama*, sunk during the American Civil War. There's also sections about diving techniques and seabed exploration, with machines and robotic cameras that can go deep into ocean trenches and ravines. The focal point is the 'abyssal aquarium', Europe's tallest cylindrical tank (12 m/39 ft deep); you follow a spiral walkway around it from top to bottom, seeing different fish and oceanic life at each depth. There are also temporary exhibitions, and in the great hall, as well as a pivoting cannon from the *Alabama* and an impressive old bathyscape, a multimedia library, snack bar, shop, tourist information point and post office. The building also houses a good brasserie-style restaurant (p. 208).

Gare Maritime Transatlantique, Cherbourg (☏ 02 33 20 26 26; www.lacitedelamer.com). Open daily May, June and September 9.30am–6pm; July and August 9.30am–7pm; end January/early February to April and October to December 10am–6pm, but closed on many Mondays (call to check). Admission: €12.50–14 (£8.40–9.40) adults, €9–10 (£6–6.70) children aged 6–17.

Ecomusée du Moulin de la Sée, Maison de l'Eau et de la Rivière

Ecomusée du Moulin de la Sée, Maison de l'Eau et de la Rivière Set in a beautiful valley, this restored paper mill with its working wheel contains displays on old paper-making techniques (including demonstrations) and on the Sée river and its banks, with large tanks full of salmon, trout, minnows and chub and an exhibition about salmon migration. You can follow up your tour by taking a 'discovery trail' in search of the valley's trees, birds and mammals, and it's possible to stay and eat here, in the Auberge du Moulin, which offers *formules découvertes* (breakfast, lunch and tours of the mill and other local historical sites).

*Brouains, 25 km (15½ miles) east of Avranches on D911 (**http://perso.orange.fr/moulin-de-la-see**). Open March to June, September and October Mon–Fri 9am–12.30pm and 2–6pm, Sat, Sun and public holidays 2–6pm; July and August Mon–Fri 7am–7pm, Sat, Sun and school holidays 11am–7pm. Admission: €5 (£3.35) adults, €3 (£2) children aged 7–16.*

La Ferme Musicale ★ FIND

The 'musical farm' combines a museum of instruments, summer music workshops and a bunch of friendly animals – horse, pigs, hens, sheep and Cotentin donkeys. The museum traces the history of wind instrument manufacture from the Renaissance on, with opportunities to touch and play. The half-day and day-long workshops in French, open to the public in July and August (booking required), are flexible but may include guided museum visits, talks about the origins of various instruments and the chance to sing, touch and play accordions, African drums and more, and use interactive terminals.

Angoville-sur-Ay, 25 km (15½ miles) north of Coutances on D900 (02 33 07 41 72; www.lafermemusicale. com). Open Mon–Sat 9am–noon and 1.30–6pm excl public holidays; workshops July and August Mon–Sat 2.30–7pm excl public holidays. Admission: €5 (£3.35) adults, €3 (£2) children aged 6–12.

Ludiver, l'Observatoire Planétarium du Cap de la Hague ★★

Situated at the Cotentin's northern tip, away from polluting light sources, this weather station has a mission to reveal to the public the mysteries and beauty of the Universe. Interactive displays, 3-D installations, *son-et-lumière* technology and videos introduce the Milky Way, the Sun, the stars, meteorology and satellites; if you happen to come on a fine day, you'll be able to see the surface of the Sun projected onto a screen via a special telescope. But it's not all about looking outwards: there's an Earth Room with a huge model of our planet cut into two hemispheres, so you can journey to the centre of it *à la* Jules Verne. The adjoining planetarium has shows on most days, but best of all is the fantastic range of events. These include term-time and school-holiday workshops for children – age ranges differ, but 3–18-year-olds are generally catered for, and activities might

include making an astronomical puzzle, decorating and launching a powder rocket, or investigating the logistics of space flight through experiments. Or all the family might come for the regular observation nights; the free 'Starry Nights', with museum visits, mini-shows in the planetarium, storytelling, face-painting, puzzles, games, and powder rocket displays; the 6-km (3.7-mile) Randos Astros walks on nearby footpaths (bring a torch); or evening boat trips beneath the stars.

Rue de la Libération, Tonneville, 5 km (3.1 miles) west of Cherbourg off D901 (02 33 78 13 80; www.ludiver. com). Open September to June Mon–Fri 9am–12.30pm and 2–5.30pm, Sun and public holidays 2–6pm; July and August daily 10am–7pm; planetarium shows September to June Mon–Fri at 3pm, Sun and school and public holidays 3–4.30pm; July and August daily 11.30am, 3.30pm and 4.30pm. Admission: museum €3.50 (£2.35) adults, €2 (£1.34) children aged 7–18; museum and planetarium €7 (£4.70) adults, €5 (£3.35) children aged 7–18.

Musée Christian Dior ★ No budding clothes horse should miss this museum in the suitably pink childhood home of the inspirational designer, whose clothes were worn by such fashion icons as Eva Peron, Jackie Kennedy and the Duchess of Windsor. As well as hosting a new exhibition each year, on themes such as Dior's childhood influences, it has a permanent collection with couture gowns and accessories by Dior and

War Stories

Depending on the age of your children, you'll probably want to visit at least one of Manche's numerous war museums; one of the most child-friendly is Quinéville's ★★ **Mémorial de la Liberté Retrouvée** ('Memorial of Freedom Regained'; ☎ *02 33 95 95 95*, *www.memorial-quineville.com*), which opened right beside Utah Beach in 2005 on the site of a smaller museum. Full of space and light, it differs from most war museums in that it looks more at daily existence under Occupation than at specific battles, with a special section on what life was like for women and children, with mannequins, everyday objects, including toys, and a reconstructed street. You learn, for instance, how older sons and daughters often had to go out to work at a very young age to support their family after losing their dads in the fighting. All items have display boards in French and English, and there's a 20-minute film (with English subtitles) with footage from the landings at Utah Beach to the liberation of Cherbourg. You can go inside a real *blockhaus* with views over the beach and its anti-tank wall.

Other war museums here are the **Musée de la Libération** (Cherbourg, ☎ *02 33 53 03 58*), **Musée de la Percée d'Avranches** (Avranches, ☎ *02 33 68 35 83*), **Musée de la Liberté** (Carentan, ☎ *02 33 42 33 54*), **Musée des Prisonniers de Guerre Evadés** (Barfleur), **Musée de la Libération de St Lô** (St Lô, ☎ *02 33 55 19 65*), **Musée du Débarquement d'Utah Beach** (Ste Marie-du-Mont, ☎ *02 33 71 53 35*), **Musée Airborne** (p. 190) and **Exposition 'Résistance PTT'** (Percy, ☎ *02 33 61 26 39*).

War Museum, Utah Beach

some of those who designed for him (Yves Saint Laurent and John Galliano among them), sketches and prototypes, photos, old *Vogues* and other magazines, and some of Dior's belongings, including scissors. The clifftop garden, restored to its 1920s style, has a recently expanded scented garden where you can sniff the plants and flowers used in Dior perfumes, see photo exhibitions and follow a new 'image walk' created using 1930s stereoscopes (optical instruments giving pictures the appearance of solid forms). Together with the house, the garden is floodlit on high-summer evenings; it's also the site of a new tearoom with sea views and Belle Epoque-style furniture, so you don't have to visit the museum to enjoy a civilised moment here. The same is true of the shop, which, as well as Dior scarves, jewellery

and gifts, offers chic stationery for those with smaller wallets. Mums and teenage daughters who speak good French might like to book places on one of the perfumery workshops (Wednesday 3pm), during which you learn how to distinguish the components of a perfume and find out how they are extracted, as well as finding out about the evolution of perfume.

The town also has the Musée d'Art Moderne Richard Anacréon (place de l'Isthme, ☏ 02 33 51 02 94), with good collections on Colette and Jean Cocteau, and temporary exhibitions often accompanied by fun worksheets for children aged 7–13.

*Villa Les Rhumbs, Granville (☏ 02 33 61 48 21; **www.musee-dior-granville.com**). Open mid-May to late September daily 10am–6.30pm. Admission: €5 (£3.35) adults, €4 (£2.70) children, €15 (£10) family (4+).*

Garden, Musée Christian Dior

Musée Emmanuel Liais ★ A bit like the British Museum on a much smaller scale, Cherbourg's natural history and ethnography museum – set within a botanic garden with tropical hothouses – is wildly eclectic, meaning all members of the family should find something to get them thinking. It's styled as a series of 'curiosity cabinets' – 16th century collections of oddities. The ground floor has a wonderland of rocks, crystals, ammonites, corals and prehistoric fossils, preserved insects, Amazonian spiders and scorpions and stuffed reptiles, seabirds and mammals. On the first floor, the ethnography collections embrace pre-Colombian divinities, Eskimo kayaks and hunting tools, Neolithic Japanese pottery, African musical instruments, Oceanic puzzles and masks and – closer to home objects excavated on the Cotentin peninsula. The highlight for most children is the Egyptian room with its sarcophagus and mummy.

Rue Emmanuel Liais, Cherbourg (02 33 53 51 61). Open April to September Tue–Sat 10am–noon and 2–6pm, Sun and Mon 2–6pm; October to February Wed–Sun 2–6pm. Admission free.

Village Miniature des Années 30 This reconstruction of a 1930s village, on a 1:10 scale and with elements animated by electric motors, took around 29,000 hours to create in all its amazing detail. It's a delightful place to spend an hour or so, admiring the farm with its animals, shops and houses, chapel, coalmine, quarry and mill, fishing port with lighthouse, aerodrome with planes, hot-air balloon, blacksmith's, village fête in full swing and schoolroom. Look out for the resident ghost in the medieval castle.

There's a similar attraction 10 minutes away, at Villiers-Fossard, where a retired policeman has created a farm, La Ferme Miniature (02 33 57 06 41), to a scale of 1:20. It's only open on Sundays and public holidays between March and October, but is free to visit.

Base Touristique Centre Manche, St Martin-d'Aubigny, 22 km (13.6 miles) north-west of St Lô on D900 (02 33 46 74 98; www.villageminiature. fr.fm). Open April, May and mid-September to October Sun 2.30–6pm; June and 1st half September Sat and Sun; July and August daily. Admission: €3.60 (£2.40) adults, €2.10 (£1.40) children over 6.

Arts & Crafts Sites

Fonderie de Cloches ★ This working foundry, which continues a tradition that began in Villedieu-les-Poêles in the Middle Ages, and which is one of the world's last church bell specialists, makes for a unique visit. A ringing bell welcomes you into the garden; a guide then leads you into the 19th century workshop in which bells are still being made. After watching the artisans at work for about 20 minutes, perhaps making moulds from clay, goat hair and horse dung, filling them with molten copper or checking the sound using modern gadgetry, you can look at some ancient bells. The best bit is kept for last – in the outside yard, visitors can take turns playing a few of the bells. There's also a shop selling handheld bells, decorative bronzes, weathervanes, cooking pans and more.

Famous for its metal-beating, Villedieu is also home to a copper workshop, the **Atelier du Cuivre** (☎ *02 33 51 31 85, www.atelierducuivre.com*), and the **Maison de l'Etain** (☎ *02 33 51 05 08*), a pewter workshop and foundry; you can get combined tickets for these. There's also a copper-working and lace-making museum, **Musée de la Poeslerie et Maison de la Dentellière** (☎ *02 33 90 20 92*).

Rue du Pont Chignon, Villedieu-les-Poêles (☎ 02 33 61 00 56; www.cornille-havard.com). Open early February to mid-November Tue–Sat 10am–12.30pm and 2–5.30pm; mid-July to August daily 9am–6pm. Admission: €4.30 (£2.90) adults, €3.50 (£2.35) children under 12.

Scriptorial d'Avranches ★★

Avranches has housed the collection of just over 200 medieval manuscripts created by the Benedictine monks of the Mont-St-Michel (p. 187) and the abbey's 14,000-strong collection of books in its library since the monastery was dissolved in the French Revolution. In mid-2006, it finally gave them the home they deserve – a new building with state-of-the-art interactive displays and video projections that bring manuscript copying and illumination

Avranches

alive for today's audience. As well as religious and legal treatises, they include sumptuously illustrated works on botany. After looking at the pigments, parchments, quills and inks used, you are brought bang up to date with an exhibition on modern books, printing and computers. There are free leaflets and audio guides (€3/£2) in French, English, German and Spanish.

In the town's church of St Gervais, don't miss the gold-plated **skull of St Aubert**, town bishop, with a hole supposedly created by the archangel Michael's finger. You might also like to see, on place Daniel Huet, a funerary stone marking the site of the north door of the Cathédrale Saint-Andrée (destroyed in the Revolution), where English king Henry II knelt for a day in penance for the murder of the Archbishop of Canterbury, Thomas à Beckett, in 1172.

15 rue de Géôle, Avranches (☎ 02 33 79 57 00). Open May, June and September Tue–Sun 10am–6pm; July and August daily 10am–7pm; October to December and February to April Tue–Fri 10am–12.30pm and 2–5pm, Sat and Sun 10am–12.30pm and 2–6pm; last admission 1 hr

before closing. Admission: €7 (£4.70)
adults, €3 (£2) children aged 10–18,
€15 (£10) family.

Le Tourp ★ The Cap de la
Hague's resolutely modern 'cultural space' in a handsome old
manor is a great place to spend an
afternoon without paying a bean,
looking at photographs, videos
and multimedia displays evoking
the particular climate, landscapes,
culture and history of this northern tip of the Cotentin peninsula.
A multimedia game, for instance,
lets you learn about local fishing
techniques, and interactive terminals introduce you to land use on
this coast. The superb temporary
exhibitions, on the likes of animal
photography or pirates, are sometimes accompanied by events
such as sculpture weeks, where
you can watch artists at work.
The *médiathèque*, open to adults
and children, is a great free
resource with books, magazines,
DVDs and CD-Roms about
archaeology, geography, history,
the natural sciences and more,
plus Internet access for just
€1.50/hr (£1).

Omonville-la-Rogue, 25 km
(15½ miles) north-west of Cherbourg
on D45 (☎ 02 33 01 85 89; www.
letourp.com). Open daily 2–7pm.
Admission free.

Child-Friendly Tours

Découverte de la Baie du Mont-St-Michel ★★★

Exploring the sandflats of the bay
of the Mont-St-Michel is one
of the top outings in northern
France, but under no circumstances attempt to do so without

a professional guide – quicksand
and Europe's fastest-moving tides
still claim victims. Among the
companies that run walks and
horseback rides are **La Maison
du Guide** at Genêts: its family-
friendly offerings include 6-km
(3.7-mile) evening storytelling
and picnic walks, fishing on foot
and treasure hunts. Walks are
undertaken barefoot and wearing
shorts, warm clothing and a
waterproof jacket; for longer ones
you bring a picnic. Have sunscreen to hand too; even when it's
not that hot you can get burnt.

For an in-depth calendar and
the contact details of all companies running guided trips in the
bay, including private excursions,
see *www.mont-saint-michel-baie.*
com; this also has details of a
25-km (15½-mile) **Véloroute**
(cycling route) across the
marshes. Note that the Maison
de la Baie at **Le Vivier-sur-Mer**
in Brittany (☎ 02 99 48 84 38) also
runs bay walks, and there are
two further Maisons (interpretation centres) in the Manche, at
Vains (☎ 02 33 89 06 06) and
Courtils (☎ 02 33 89 66 00); the
latter has displays on the bay for
children featuring cartoon characters called Georges and Géo,
plus a bird observatory. **Genêts'**
Maison de la Baie is a tourist
information point and shop.

For the annual grand **Rando-
Baie** event, see p. 178.

La Maison du Guide, 1 rue Montoise,
Genêts, 8 km (5 miles) west of
Avranches on D911 (☎ 02 33 70 83
49). Open all year; call or see above
website for times. Rates vary accord-
ing to walk; expect to pay around
€16 (£10.70) (under-12s €8.50/

£5.70) for a 2-hour horse ride, €15 (£10) (under-12s €9/£6) for a 3-hour storytelling walk.

La Granvillaise ★★★ This
restored *bisquine* (traditional fishing boat) offers another perspective on the Baie du Mont-St-Michel, on its trips from the working port of Granville. A half-day excursion takes you around Granville's bay in about 4 hrs; a day trip lasts about 10 hrs and takes you way out into the bay of the Mont-St-Michel, often with stop-offs to swim, stroll and picnic in the Iles Chausey (p. 180) or explore Cancale in Brittany. Those who wish can help unfurl the sails and steer the boat, or you can just sit and admire the scenery – including, if you're lucky, dolphins swimming alongside. You need to bring food, and don't forget your camera, sunscreen, swimming gear, hats, a sweater and a waterproof jacket – the weather can change quickly here.

La Granvillaise

Longer trips are possible to St-Malo, Paimpol and other destinations in Brittany, the Channel Islands and even Britain (Portsmouth).

43 boulevard des Amiraux Granvillais, Granville (℡ 02 33 90 07 51; www. lagranvillaise.org). Sailings April to October; call for times. Tickets: half-day €35pp (£23.50), €75 (£50) family (2 adults + 1 child under-16) then €16 (£10.70) per extra child. Full-day €50pp (£33.50), €105 (£70) family (2+1) then €16 (£10.70) per extra child.

Normandie Montgolfière ★★
Another way of appreciating the splendour of the Baie du Mont-St-Michel and the Mount itself is to take a stunning 1-hour hot-air balloon flight over the sands. You need to leave 3–4 hrs for transfers to and from the take-off point, balloon preparation and so on. Balloons take up to four people, including children aged seven and up, and at the end the adults enjoy a complimentary glass of champagne to celebrate their trip – how very civilised. You can also fly over the **Parc Naturel Régional des Marais du Cotentin et du Bessin** (p. 186).

Sélune Montgolfières (℡ *02 33 60 50 00*, *www.selunair.fr.st/*) also offer balloon flights over the bay, for ages 12 and up (depending on height and weight), lasting 40 minutes.

Les Veys, 15 km (9⅓ miles) north of Carentan off D913 (flights over the Mont take off near Avranches) (℡ 02 33 42 49 08; www.normandie-montgolfiere.com). Open April to October daily when weather allows; flights early morning and evening. Price: €240–320pp (£160–215).

Train Touristique du Cotentin ★ This little 1930s train chuffs 9 km (5½ miles) along the coast between Barneville-Carteret (p. 180) and Port-Bail, through a landscape of dunes with views over to Jersey. On Tuesdays and Thursdays you can catch the train to the markets of Port-Bail and Carteret respectively, or on sporadic dates through the year there are themed trains (folklore, demonstrations of old trades, Father Christmas, etc.). There's French commentary and a bar on all, and picnic areas at both ends of the line. At Port-Bail you might look at the ruins of the Gallo-Roman baptistery and walk a little way south to see **Lindbergh-Plage**, where Charles Lindbergh crossed land on the first transatlantic flight, which took place in 1927.

Between Barneville Carteret and Port-Bail (☎ 02 33 04 70 08; www. traincotentin.com). Call for opening days and times. Tickets: €7 (£4.70) adults, €4 (£2.70) children aged 4–12 (themed trains €8/£5.35 adults and €4/£2.70 children).

For Active Families

See also 'Beaches, Resorts & Islands', p. 180. The extremely good tourist board website, *www. mancherandonnee.com*, contains masses of information on walking, riding and cycling paths within the *département*, including in the **Val de Saire** to the east of Cherbourg, with its tranquil winding lanes, picture-postcard villages, woods and waterfalls.

La Gourmette Saint Loise If you're here in summer and your children speak good French and love horses, this stable, run by volunteers, offers all kinds of courses for young riders, whether total beginners or very experienced. There are also horse and pony rides in the countryside around St Lô, along the banks of the Vire and sometimes even on the beaches and salt marshes north of Granville (part of the stable relocates in summer). Book ahead for the popular *Baby Jeux* days for children aged 4–6 and *Baby Poneys* lessons for children aged three and up on the stable's Shetland ponies Zébulon, Astuce, Préhistoire, Noé, Trésor, Abricot and Obélix.

Rue des Ecuyers, St Lô (☎ 02 33 57 27 06; http://gourmette.sl.perso. cegetel.net/). Open all year. Prices vary by course or activity; a 3-hour Baby Poneys session with walk, games and picnic is €25 (£16.75).

Musée Maritime/Fours à Chaux du Rey ★★ Set in a port that shipped chalk to Brittany, this museum based around four old chalk ovens runs excellent *Musée des Enfants* summer workshops for 7–12-year-olds. They can study fossils, visit the ovens and then make fossil moulds; visit the maritime museum to learn about wind in seafaring then make a windsock (used at airports and ports to show the strength and direction of the wind); or learn to make a variety of knots. Workshops last 3.5 hrs and include an early supper. Parents, meanwhile, might be taking part in an art workshop on frescoes, enamelling or wood sculpture (open to all but too advanced for younger children). You can also take guided visits of the museum and ovens and see demonstrations of chalk production, or attend summer *Rendez-Vous Spectacles*, with bring-your-own picnics on the grass followed by a show at nightfall, which may include circus, theatre, acrobatics and multimedia effects. Programmes are downloadable from **www.cg50.fr**.

14 route des Fours à Chaux, Regnéville-sur–Mer, 9 km (5½ miles) south-west of Coutances on D49 (☎ 02 33 46 82 18). Museum and ovens open daily 2–6 pm April, May and school holidays (excl Christmas): June and September 11am–6pm; July and August 11am–7pm; summer workshops and shows call for dates. Children's workshops €5.60 (£3.75), art workshops €15 (£10).

Parc d'Attractions et de Loisirs Ange Michel
Handy if you're on your way to or from the Mont-St-Michel and need to stretch your legs (if hard to find, down windy lanes), this park could do with a lick of paint. In its favour, it does cater to a wide age range, with its water park (June to August), karts for tots and older children, bumper boats, pony rides, a road train, animals and old farm implements, and pretty chalet with lake views and snack bar. Beware, though, that staff aren't exactly on the ball when it comes to proffering safety information or supervising rowdy unaccompanied children. And the merry-go-round with a button

you need to keep your finger on to operate made us feel we'd fallen into a time-warp...

*St Martin-des-Landelles, 25 km (15½ miles) south-east of Avranches off D30 (☎ 02 33 49 04 74; **www.ange-michel-attractions.com**). Open June to August daily 10.30am–7pm; 2nd half April and May Sat, Sun and public holidays 11am–6pm; September Sat and Sun 11am–6pm. Admission: €8.50–9.50 (£5.70–6.40) adults, €6.50–7.50 (£4.35–5) children aged 4–12.*

Le Village Enchanté
This leisure park mixes tacky but fun rides and amenities for children aged 2–10 with natural attractions over seven hectares. There are footpaths through a forest with streams and waterfalls and past reconstructions of historical buildings, an 'elves' wood' adventure trail with rope bridges and goats and other farm animals. The tacky stuff includes huge inflatables, superior playground equipment such as a castle with maze and slide, a Three Little Pigs rollercoaster, a mechanical theatre, a ball park, children's quad bikes and a miniature railway. All round, it wins out over the better-publicised **Parc Ange Michel** nearby (above), especially for younger children. It's also a good place for a picnic, though there's a snack bar with a terrace, plus B&B rooms and a communal gîte.

*Bellefontaine, 35 km (21¾ miles) east of Avranches on D33 (☎ 02 33 59 01 93; **www.village-enchante.fr**). Open daily March to October 10am–6.30pm. Admission: €7–9 (£4.70–6) adults, €5 (£3.35) children.*

Normandy Shell Biscuits

Shopping

Abbaye de Valonges This 17th century abbey may not seem the most obvious place for a shopping expedition, but it's famous for its *pâtes de fruits* – fruit jellies – handmade by some of the 33 nuns to an ancient recipe and sold in its on-site shop. Made with natural fruit flavours and free from colouring or preservatives, they come as they are or chocolate-covered – parents should look out for the grown-up mint ones swathed in plain chocolate. There are also Fair Trade products such as African-fruits jam made by a convent in Togo, local specialities such as Normandy milk jam and some religious items.

8 rue des Capucins, Valonges (02 33 21 62 87). Open Tue–Sat (plus Mon in July, August and December) 10.30am–12.30pm and 3.15–5.45pm, Sun 11.30am–1.20pm and 3.15–5.30pm.

La Maison du Biscuit ★★ The 'Biscuit House', one of the last producers of handmade biscuits in Normandy, filled with the aromas of hot chocolate and ground almonds and hazelnuts, is three attractions in one: a workshop offering a free tasting (including, on Sundays, the firm's famous brioche still warm from the oven), with a big-screen film about biscuit production and windows from which you can watch products being made; an English-style tearoom where you get a free sampler plate of house biscuits and cakes with your tea, coffee or hot chocolate (it's also a great place for breakfast or light meals); and a shop with more than 250 kinds of house cakes, biscuits and chocolates, plus 800–1000 local products.

Place Costard, Sortosville-en-Beaumont, 7 km (4⅓ miles) north-east of Barneville-Carteret on D902 (02 33 04 09 04; www.maisondubiscuit. fr). Open Tue–Sun 9am–12.30pm and 2–6.30pm; closed January and 1 week in mid-September.

Maison Gosselin ★★ This famous family-run grocery, established in 1889, attracts its fair share of tourists but remains a charming place for a browse, full of gastronomic delights and interesting gifts, including old-fashioned metal toys and wonderful soaps. Parents pile their trolleys high with Norman soups, cheeses, jams, canned fish, caviar, fresh fruit and veg, wines, ciders and other booze, and spices from French mustards to saffron and Jamaican pepper. Meanwhile, you'll be hard-pressed getting children away from the eye-boggling array of sweets, which includes caramels, lollipops, apple sugars, nougat, chocolate by the likes of Cluizel and Valrhona and chewing gums. Don't miss the bread fresh from the oak-burning oven. If you're staying in the vicinity, there's a delivery service, including to boats in the marina; at weekends the round is made in the shop's replica Ford T Van.

Rue de Verrüe, St Vaast-la-Hougue, 15 km (9⅓ miles) north-east of Valognes on D1 (℡ 02 33 54 40 06). Open July and August Mon 9am–12.30pm and 5–7.30pm, Tue–Sat 9am–12.30pm and 3–7.30pm, Sun 9am–12.30pm; rest of year Mon, Wed–Fri 8.30am–12.30pm and 3–7.30pm, Tue 9am–12.30pm and 3–7.30pm, Sat 8.45am–12.30pm and 3–7.30pm, Sun 9am–12.30pm.

FAMILY-FRIENDLY ACCOMMODATION

Northern Cotentin Peninsula

MODERATE

Le Grand Hard ★★ This horse-riding centre is based around a characterful old mansion with a billiards room, a drawing room and surprisingly swish accommodation in the form of nine double rooms and five duplexes for four people, each with its own entrance and terrace. Breakfasts (€9/£6, children aged 2–12 €7/£4.70) are a copious buffet affair, and you can have dinner by prior arrangement. As well as horse rides on the nearby beaches and marshes, you can explore the surroundings, including the World War II landing sites, by horse and cart, and hire bikes. Children, meanwhile, get access to the *Poney Club*, a petting farm and playground.

Ste-Marie-du-Mont, 12 km (7½ miles) north of Carentan on D913 (℡ 02 33 71 25 74; http://le-grand-hard. club.fr). 14 rooms. Double €70–80 (£47–54), duplex for four €115–130 (£77–87). Extra bed €15 (£10), cot €8 (£5.35). Amenities: horse-riding centre; horse-and-cart rides; children's farm; playground; billiards room; lounge; bike hire.

L'Hostellerie du Château ★

This comfortable option in part of the medieval castle of the pretty inland town of Bricquebec counts Queen Victoria and Field Marshall Montgomery among its past guests, but it's not as luxurious as that fact might imply. Still, you inevitably get a feeling of history – the accommodation, which includes three family rooms with two double beds and a shower or bath, is all different, with interesting architectural details such as arches or even little turrets, and antique furniture, and the restaurant is atmospherically situated in the old knights' hall with its vast fireplaces. The latter is very popular with locals for its good-value menus (translated into English) featuring the likes of cream of artichoke soup, fillet of sea bass with fennel and lemon confit, and two-chocolate charlotte with almond milk; don't miss the dessert of rhubarb soup with strawberries and basil. For €10 (£6.70), children get their choice of starter, main and dessert; there are highchairs, and the delightful staff are as solicitous to children as they are to parents. After a buffet breakfast (€9/£6 or under-10s €5/£3.35), you are free to explore the château with its largely intact ramparts and crypts, or if you're here on a Thursday, don't miss the town's large market. Note that this is only 20 minutes from the port of Cherbourg and, hence, handy for those going to or from the ferry.

4 cours du Château, Bricquebec, 15 km (9⅓ miles) north-east of Barneville-Carteret on D902 (☎ 02 33 52 24 49; www.lhostellerie-bricquebec.com). 18 rooms. Double €70–95 (£47–63.50), family room €115 (£77). Cot €12 (£8). Amenities: restaurant; grounds. In room: TV, minibar (some, inc family rooms).

INEXPENSIVE

Camping Bel Sito ★ The virtue of staying at a modest two-star family-run site such as this one by the resort of Barneville-Carteret (p. 180) is that you don't get the noise and rowdiness of some of the big-hitters. As well as benefiting from lovely views (over the protected dunes of Baubigny and some of the

Channel Islands), you get peace and quiet – there's a policy of no evening entertainment, which means you fall asleep with the sounds of nature in your ears. You stay in your tent or caravan, or well-equipped two-bedroom chalet overlooking the sea less than 1 km (0.62 miles) away, with access to table tennis, volleyball, a play area and a fishing pond. The sanitary blocks are more like those of a four-star site, and there's a launderette, a grocery and a bread store (July/August).

Baubigny, 5 km (3.1 miles) north of Barneville-Carteret off D650 (☎ 02 33 04 32 74; www.bel-sito.com). 85 places. Car + tent or caravan/ motorhome €7–9 (£4.70–6), then €5–5.50 (£3.35–3.70) per adult, €2.80–3 (£1.90–2) per child aged 2–7, €1–1.50 (£0.67–1) per child aged under 2. Chalet €310–550/wk (£207–368) (short stays available). Amenities: games; fishing. Closed mid-September to mid-April.

La Ferme St Nicholas ★ This idyllic rural spot a short way south-east of Port-Bail (p. 199), surrounded by munching cows and with its own population of farm animals (including horses, donkeys and goats), offers four B&B rooms in a half-timbered main farmhouse and a larger suite in a cottage in the two-hectare grounds with their lovely orchards. All are very plain but have countryside views. In the main house, one is a straight double, one a double with a sitting area with a single sofabed, one a twin with a single sofabed, and one a double with two single sofabeds; the last is the only one with a bath – others have showers. Then there's the suite, with a double room, twin room and double sofabed in the ground-floor living room, a bathroom with bath and a terrace. The Continental breakfasts are based on organic produce from local farms; the cakes, bread, jam and yogurt are homemade. Picnics can be made up for you too, and traditional evening meals are available with prior notice. A highchair and cot can be provided, and the hostess can even offer or arrange babysitting. Mountain bikes are loaned free of charge.

St Symphorien-le-Valois, 20 km (12½ miles) south-east of Barneville-Carteret on D903 (02 32 56 67 36; **www.lafermesaintnicolas.com**). *5 rooms. Double €55–65 (£37–43.50), room for four €95 (£63.50). Cot free. Amenities: grounds with animals; dinner by request; picnic hampers; Internet access; babysitting. In room: hairdryer, tea- and coffee-making equipment*

Southern Cotentin Peninsula

MODERATE

Villa Beaumonderie ★ VALUE
General Eisenhower's World War II HQ, this handsome villa north of Granville is now an intimate seaside hotel with luxurious amenities for its price range. It has a lovely pool with a retractable glass roof and bar, where you can enjoy *aperitifs* and *tapas* of an evening, tennis and squash courts, a stylish terrace with parasols and armchairs and

a restaurant serving some of the best food in the area – think scallops and citrus fruit with vanilla oil, beef carpaccio with basil oil and parmesan, lobster from the Iles Chausey just offshore (p. 180) and pecan brownies. Children get fish or steak with chips, or a reduced-price main course from the menu, and an ice-cream *coupe* or other dessert and drink for €10 (£6.70), and there's a highchair. Some of the 16 rooms and suites get gorgeous sea views and balconies (others face the street); two are duplexes with a ground-floor living room and double and twin bedrooms on the first floor. All are furnished in restful creams and beiges, and the bathrooms, provided with fluffy robes, are first rate, as is the Continental breakfast (€12pp/ £8; free under-8s).

20 route de Coutances, Bréville-sur-Mer, 3 km (1.8 miles) north of Granville off D971E (02 33 50 36 36; www. la-beaumonderie.com). 16 rooms. Double €85–165 (£57–110), duplex €140–180 (£94–120). Cot €8 (£5.35). Amenities: indoor/outdoor pool (April to September); restaurant; bar; salon; tennis court; squash court. In room: satellite TV, telephone, Internet connection.

INEXPENSIVE–MODERATE

Hôtel Le Grand Large ★ VALUE
It lacks more than a little in character and decorative flair, but this modern option overlooking the bay of the Mont-St-Michel is a flexible family seaside option. It has a choice of double rooms, 1–2-person studios and

3–4-person duplexes and apartments, most with sea views and a balcony, and all with baths. Rooms with kitchenettes are generally available by the week, but those staying four days can get one with a one-off supplement of €30 (£20). This means you can self-cater but still enjoy the services and amenities of the three-star hotel – which include a lounge and bar with books, sun terraces, a sauna and jacuzzi, a lift directly down to the beach, bike loan, breakfast in your room if desired (otherwise, it's a buffet for €8/£5.35, €4/£2.70 for children) and a launderette. Guests also enjoy direct access to the neighbouring thalassotherapy centre, and those in self-catering accommodation get free cots and highchairs.

*5 rue de la Falaise, Granville (℡ 02 33 91 19 19; **www.hotel-le-grand-large. com**). 51 rooms. Double €48–99 (£32–66), 3–4-person duplex €68– 113 (£45.50–75.50) (with kitchenette €476–791 week/£319–530), apartment €92–124 (£61.50–83) (with*

kitchenette €644–868 week/£431– 582). Cot free. Amenities: lounge/bar; sauna; jacuzzi; access to thalassotherapy centre; sun terraces; launderette; concierge; bike loan. In room: TV, telephone, Wi-Fi Internet access, hairdryer, safe, kitchenette (some).

INEXPENSIVE

Camping Lez Eaux ★ This peaceful site in the pretty 12-hectare grounds of a manor house has an excellent water park with lush plants, three giant slides, a paddling pool and outdoor and indoor swimming pools – the latter useful for days when the weather keeps you from the beaches a two-minute drive away. A four-star site, it also offers a children's playground, tennis and football facilities, volleyball, bike hire, a billiards and games room, a bar and takeaway food counter, a grocery and a launderette, plus low-key evening entertainments and fishing in the duck pond. The pitches for tents, caravans and motorhomes are more spacious than average, and there are

Camping Lez Eaux

five- and eight-person wooden chalets with terraces and eight-person mobile homes.

Note that this popular campsite can be booked through some of the camping tour operators (p. 27)

Lez Eaux, 4 km (2½ miles) south of Granville on D973 (02 33 51 66 09; www.lez-eaux.com). Pitch €13.50–41 (£9–27.50), then €8.50 (£5.70) over 7s, €6.50 (£4.35) children aged 2–6, €5 (£3.35) car; chalet €280–990/week (£188–660), mobile home €350–990/week (£234–660) (shorter stays possible). Amenities: water park; playground; games; sports facilities; bike hire; bar; takeaway counter; shop; launderette; shows.

Domaine de la Chauvinière ★

Stay in one of these adorable gites for 2/3, 3/4 or 5 people in charcterful 17th century buildings just 3 km (1.8 miles) inland of the bay of the Mont-St-Michel and you can enjoy your own one-hectare bird refuge filled with exotic plants, such as palm trees, bamboos and magnolias, and lovely statuary and fountains. They're filled with grand-looking antiques and interesting knick-knacks and have lovely restored stone walls that set them apart from the norm. The medium-sized gîte, adjoining an old cider press, has a double room with air-conditioning, a twin room and a washer-drier in the kitchen. The largest has a double room, a room with three single beds (two of them part of a bunk bed) plus room for a cot or another bed for an infant, a TV, a dishwasher, a washing machine and dryer, plus, outside, a ping-pong table and

hammock. All have a private terrace plus access to a swing, football pitch, sandpit and barbecue equipment, and you can hire television sets for the smaller gîtes that don't already have one, plus mountain bikes.

Bacilly, 7 km (4⅓ miles) west of Avranches on D31 (06 71 67 88 82; http://perso.orange.fr/domaine delachauviniere). 3 rooms. Gîte for three/four €219–439 (£146–294), gîte for five €399–599 (£266–401); weekend rates also available. Cot free. Amenities: garden; games; BBQ equipment; bike hire. Gîtes: TV (in 1; can be hired in others), private terrace, kitchen, dishwasher (in 1), washer/dryer (in some).

Around the Mont-St-Michel

For other choices around this stunning bay, see the companion guide to this book, *Brittany With Your Family*.

MODERATE

Hôtel Montgomery ★ Though now part of the Best Western chain, this ivy-clad hotel in a house once occupied by Count Gabriel de Montgomery (who killed Henri II), set in a pretty little market town just inland of the Mont-St-Michel, has oodles more character than hotels on the mount itself (none of which have parking) or the motels that line the approach to the tourist attraction. It has retained its splendid wooden staircase, Renaissance painted ceilings, wooden panelling and original floors, and also boasts a conservatory and a garden with a well, fountains, statues, tables and chairs and loungers. The rather chintzy décor in the guestrooms only adds to the old-fashioned charm. Families have a choice of a triple with a double and a single bed, quadruples with either a double and two singles or a double and a sofabed, or interconnecting rooms with two double beds or one double and two singles; all have a bath. There's also a plush, old-fashioned dining room open every night except Sunday; it's popular with non-residents for its local fish and *agneau pré-salé* (p. 212) so book ahead. Children don't get their own menu, but the obliging staff tailor dishes to their needs and tastes, and there's a highchair. In the morning it's the setting for good buffet breakfasts (€10/£6.70 or €5/£3.35 for children).

13 rue Couesnon, Pontorson, 10 km (6.2 miles) from Mont-St-Michel on D976 (☎ 02 33 60 00 09; www.hotel-montgomery.com). 32 rooms. Double €55–250 (£37–168), room for four €145 (£97), interconnecting rooms €173–181 (£116–121). Cot €8 (£5.35). Amenities: restaurant; garden; salon/bar. In room: satellite TV, telephone, Internet access, hairdryer, jacuzzi (some).

INEXPENSIVE

Camping Saint Michel ★

VALUE Away from the tourist hordes, in the pretty village of Courtils with its Maison de la Baie and bird observatory overlooking the sandflats and Mont-St-Michel, this is a good-value

three-star site planted with lush palms and colourful plants and decorated with old farm machinery. Its outdoor pool is unflashy but just fine, and there's an animal park to keep little ones amused, with pigs, donkeys and more, plus a playground. You also have access to a games room, table tennis, mountain bike hire, a basic restaurant in high season, grocery, launderette and baby-bathing/changing facilities. If you don't camp, there are mobile homes for up to six, with and without TV and terrace, and more attractive wooden chalets for 2/4, though these don't have bathroom facilities and squeeze a double bed and bunk bed into one bedroom.

The nearby **Auberge des Oiseaux de la Mer** (☎ 02 33 70 95 81) serves galettes, crêpes, grills, including *pré-salé* lamb (p. 223), and a €6 (£4) children's menu.

35 route du Mont-St-Michel, Courtils, 8 km (5 miles) from Mont-St-Michel on D75 (☎ 02 33 70 96 90; www.campingsaintmichel.com). Pitch for car + tent/caravan or motorhome €4–4.50 (£2.70–3), then €3–5 (£2–3.35) per adult, €1.40–2 (£0.94–1.34) per child under 7. Mobile home for 4–6 with TV and terrace €275–590 week (£184–395); chalet for 2/4 €170–380 week (£114–255) (weekend rates available). Amenities: restaurant (July and August); outdoor pool (May to September); play area; games; animal park; bike hire; shop; launderette; baby facilities. Closed October to mid-March.

FAMILY-FRIENDLY DINING

Northern Cotentin Peninsula

MODERATE–EXPENSIVE

Le Panoramique ★★★ On a hilltop in the idyllic Val de Saire east of Cherbourg (p. 199), this is known for its sea views, but the food's not at all bad, and there's family-friendly brasserie service through the day plus inside and outside play areas – who could ask for more? Depending on their age and tastes, children can choose from a €7 (£4.70) *Menu des Bambins* offering steak, sausage, ham, omelette, chicken Cordon Bleu or breaded fish with chips, followed by ice cream or crêpe with sugar, or a more sophisticated (and nutritionally sound) *Menu des P'tits Gastronomes* (€11/£7.40) with homemade ham pâté with chutney, then skate in sorrel sauce with vegetables or local ham on the bone in a creamy sauce with vegetables, and a homemade pastry or ice-cream caramel with whipped cream. From the main *menus* you might choose oysters from nearby St Vaast-la-Hougue, two-fish terrine with lemon butter sauce or scallops with stuffed mushrooms. The seafood is generally from Cherbourg fish market, the vegetables from a local organic farm. Families congregate in the conservatory-style room with views over both the sea and the countryside and the indoor play area.

1 Village de l'Eglise, La Pernelle, 20 km (12½ miles) north-east of Valognes on D902 (✆ 02 33 54 13 79). Menus €13.90–30 (£9.30–20). Open Fri–Wed (daily in July and August) lunch and dinner noon–1.45pm and 7–9pm, brasserie service (crêpes, galettes and mussels) noon–9pm. Highchairs available.

Le Quai des Mers ★★ FIND In a modern conservatory within the old transatlantic terminal that also houses La Cité de la Mer (p. 189), this is a fine setting for quick meals before catching the ferry, or leisurely gourmet lunches or dinners while watching boats go in and out of the bay, admiring *Le Redoutable* (p. 190) and observing the activity in the open kitchen. The chairs resemble those on cruise liners, and there's a terrace where you can bask in the sun. The children's menu (under-10s €7.90/£5.30) is nothing out of the ordinary (steak or breaded fish with chips, ice cream or apple tart, plus a drink), though the ingredients are top notch. Little ones might prefer something from the main menu, which features lots of fabulous seafood – *moules frites*, *choucroute de poissons* (salmon, pollack, haddock and prawns on a bed of cooked cabbage), seafood paella (fish, chicken and chorizo) and more – plus the likes of rib of beef with chips and salad, lamb with green beans and ratatouille, or grilled ham with Camembert sauce and mash. If you have room, American-style brownies, Norman pannacotta (with apple compôte) or rice pudding with chocolate sauce feature amid the desserts. The long lunch opening hours mean that you can come before it gets too busy.

1 allée Prés Menut, Cherbourg (02 33 88 75 60). Main courses €7.90– 26.90 (£5.30–18). Open mid-June to mid-September Sun–Fri 11.45am– 2.45pm and 7.15–10pm, Sat 11.45am–2.45pm and 7.15–10.30pm; rest of year Sun–Tue 11.45am– 2.45pm, Wed–Fri 11.45am–2.45pm and 7.30–9.30pm, Sat 11.45am– 2.45pm and 7.30–10.30pm. Highchairs available.

Le Père Alta ★★ This crêperie knows its stuff so well, it's got its own crêpe-making school (for adults). A convivial, unpretentious place just south of Port-Bail (p. 199), it takes local farm produce and seafood as the basis for its crêpe and galette recipes. Parents may be tempted by one of the famous chestnut-flour galettes or *foie gras* specialities. Children with eyes bigger than their bellies will be intrigued by the galettes inspired by the signs of the zodiac – you get a huge plate with galettes holding a starter, main course and cheese. There are also two children's menus: the *Bambino* for tinies (€6.10/£4.10 but often offered free) and the *P'tit Loup* ('Little Wolf', €9.20/£6.20); the first consists of a ham and cheese galette with homemade chips and an ice cream or lolly, the second of a ham, cheese and egg galette with salad and a portion of Camembert, the same dessert

and a glass of cola. In good weather you can eat on a terrace shaded by parasols, with a fountain (fenced off from wandering children). Inside there's a children's 'relaxation area' where they can read books and play unobtrusive games, and a baby-changing space.

La Rose des Vents, 10 rue Général Leclerc, La Haye-du-Puits, 18 km (11.2 miles) south-east of Barneville-Carteret on D903 (02 33 46 45 57). Main courses €6–12 (£4–8). Highchairs available.

Southern Cotentin Peninsula

Le Moulin de Jean ★★ Foodie parents will be interested to know that this gorgeous restaurant in an old watermill was set up by superstar chef Jean Christophe Novelli (don't worry: standards have remained high despite his departure). Children are more impressed by the adventurousness of it all – you have to walk across two bridges to get in, while inside, the 'wheel room' retains the mechanism that used to turn the mill's three wheels. Your two-or three-course meal, which might be enjoyed by the fireside in winter or on the terrace in summer, accompanied by bird-song, may include marinated tartare of salmon with anchovy mayonnaise and a poached quail's egg or potato roulade with goats' cheese and truffle oil, followed by spinach-stuffed tomato with auberge risotto and parmesan or braised pig's trotter stuffed with black pudding, served with celeriac mash. Desserts include an unmissable caramelised lemon tart with lime sorbet. For the prices, this is exceptional fare. Things are necessarily simpler for children: for €12–20 (£8–13.40), they get superior steak or fish and great mash, then homemade ice cream. There's only one highchair though, so make sure to request it at the time of booking. Service is technically impeccable if a little cool.

La Lande, Cuves, 20 km (12½ miles) east of Avranches on D911 (02 33 48 39 29; www.lemoulindejean. com). Menus €23.50 (£15.75) and €30 (£20). Open daily noon–2.30pm and 7.30–10pm. Highchair available.

MODERATE

Le Phare Granville's harbour front is lined with places to eat; Le Phare's first-floor dining room with its superior views over the fishing port gives it the edge over the opposition, while the seafood, brought in from the fish market just steps away, couldn't be fresher. According to the daily catch, you might feast on lobster from the Iles Chausey (p. 180), monkfish and cod with chive sauce or a cheaper dish of *moules*. Children get a good €8.50 (£5.70) menu featuring tomatoes and carrots *au vinaigrette* or cold meats, then fillet of fish or ham with steamed potatoes, finishing up with fruit salad or ice cream. If it's full, **Le Cabestan** (02 33 61 61 58) just down the quay also serves good seafood, including an under-12s

menu (€7/£4.70), and has a stylish decked terrace for people- and boat-watching.

11 rue du Port, Granville (02 33 50 12 94). Open Tue and Thur–Sun noon–2pm and 7–9.30pm. Main courses €8–16 (£5.35–10.70). Closed mid-December to mid-January. Highchair available.

INEXPENSIVE

Chez François ★ You could walk past this eccentric place for years without realising it's a restaurant – squirreled away inside a low-ceilinged stone house, it doesn't even have any menus posted up outside. Appearances are deceptive, however: you'll invariably find it packed out, and you'll be lucky to get a table without booking. Inside it's a combination of bar/tobacconist (meaning it can get smoky) and grill specialising in meats cooked over the vast fireplace. All produce is seasonal, but typical dishes include potato salad with grilled pig's ear, warm green lentil salad with walnut oil and chitterling sausage, and mackerel *rillettes*. Prices are rock bottom (all starters and desserts are €3.30/£2.20). There's no children's menu, but if you have unsqueamish ones like mine, you might find they enjoy the hearty country fare such as onion sausages, served with homemade chips and green salad, and they will almost certainly go a bundle for the home- made egg custard, the caramel rice made to François's grand- mother's recipe and the curd cheese with homemade jam. An authentic place to warm up after a gusty walk across the bay of the Mont-St-Michel (p. 197), this also has five dirt-cheap guest rooms (€30/£20).

Genêts (near town hall), 8 km (5 miles) west of Avranches on D911 (02 33 70 83 98). Open Fri–Tue noon–2.30pm and 7–9.30pm.

The Mont-St-Michel & Around

For more eating options around the bay, see *Brittany With Your Family*, the companion to this guide.

MODERATE–EXPENSIVE

Chez Mado ★ **FIND** With a groovy 1970s soundtrack in your ears, the sun beating down and the bay of the Mont-St-Michel spread out below you like some fantasy landscape, you could almost believe you are in a film while eating on the terrace of this *bistrot de la mer* on the Mount's ramparts (there's a less interesting

ground-floor room accessed from the main street). Popular even out of season, with tightly packed tables, it offers French bistro classics such as roast chicken with mash plus lots of seafood, good if expensive pasta dishes (the creamy tagliatelle with fresh salmon is recommended) and – best of all – a fabulous leg of *pré-salé* lamb (p. 212) with green beans. Try not to overdo it on the delicious bread given out while you browse the menu. The under-12s menu is great value at €6 (£4) for steak or roast chicken with chips, chocolate mousse or vanilla and strawberry ice cream, followed by a plate of chocolate cookies or Norman butter biscuits; outside busy periods it also features cheese and ham and sugar crêpes. Service is sprightly despite the rather harassed-looking staff.

Grande Rue, Mont-St-Michel (02 33 50 14 08). Main courses €8–28 (£5.35–18.75). Open daily noon–2pm and 7–9pm (July and August noon–9pm). Highchair available.

Sheep grazing near Mont-St-Michel

Melt in the Mouth

Said by some chefs to be the best lamb in the world, the agneau pré-salé that features on so many menus in this area (and sometimes elsewhere) comes from the lambs you will see grazing peacefully on the salt marshes around the bay of the Mont-St-Michel. Their salty flavour and tenderness comes from the 70 or so plants that grow there. The other famous specialities of the area are the **Mère Poulard** omelettes in the hotel-restaurant of the same name on the Mont (☎ *02 33 89 68 68*); if you don't mind the steep prices and nonsense surrounding their preparation (costumed waiters stand in front of a crowd of tourists in the restaurant doorway and beat some of the 1600 eggs used here every day), you'll find them delightfully fluffy. The restaurant also offers a good *Petits Gourmets* menu (€15/£10, under-12s) with a plain omelette, cod *Parmentier* (a kind of fish pie) or farmyard chicken with pan-fried potatoes, then apple tart, little vanilla and chocolate pots or sorbets. And service is 'non-stop' (11.30am–10.30pm).

INEXPENSIVE

For **Auberge des Oiseaux de la Mer** at Courtils, see p. 207.

Les Tartines Bavardes This enchantingly named little tearoom ('The Talkative Sandwiches') is a vibrant, modern space for light and homely daytime fare such as baguettes, paninis, salads, waffles, pastries and ice creams, with lots of variety. With only a handful of tables and a tiny terrace, it's situated by the town hall square in handsome, laid-back little Pontorson by the Breton border. Service can be rather slow, but the food (and the choice of teas and coffees) is worth it.

Another good, if unlikely-looking, option in Pontorson is the **Bar de l'Hôtel de Ville** (25 rue de Tanis, ☎ *02 33 60 01 98*), a very 'down home' bar serving sandwiches and heavier fare such as sausage and chips all day. It's also a handy spot for cheap, but good, cooked breakfasts for those who've overdosed on croissants.

32 rue St-Michel, Pontorson, 10 km (6.2 miles) from Mont-St-Michel on D976 (☎ 02 33 60 67 04). Sandwiches €4–7 (£2.70–4.70). Open Tue–Sat 10am–4.30pm.

Appendix
Useful Terms & Phrases

Resources: Learning French with Children

The following resources are all available on **www.amazon.co.uk**.

First 100 Words in French Sticker Book (Heather Amery)

French is Fun with Serge, the Cheeky Monkey (BBC Active); includes DVD and CD.

Les Portes Tordues/The Twisted Doors: the Scariest Way in the World to Learn French (Kathie Dior); includes audiobook.

Let's Learn French Colouring Book (Anne Françoise Hazan)

Let's Sing and Learn in French (Matt Maxwell)

Muzzy (BBC English); see below.

Snap Cards in French (Jo Litchfield)

It's not essential to speak French when visiting France, but outside Paris – and especially in very rural areas – you will certainly struggle if there is no single member of the family with some degree of proficiency in the language. Certainly, any stay in France will be immeasurably enhanced if you all speak decent French, and children, who will be able to mix with French children and join in French-language activities at museums, farms and so on, will get much more out of their trip abroad. Remember, too, that being seen to be making an effort will predispose you much more to local people.

Children pick up new languages much more easily than adults – at the end of our most recent trip, even my youngest son, not quite two, was happily switching between basic phrases – *bonjour*, *au revoir*, *merci* – in the two languages, depending on who he was talking to. Capitalise on this facility by introducing your children to a fun language-learning programme: one of the most highly reputed is the award-winning BBC course *Muzzy*, which includes DVDs with cartoons, available at **www.bbcshop. com** or **www.muzzyonline.co.uk**. There's nothing to say you can't learn from it too by watching with your children! Alternatively, use the language options available on many DVDs to allow them to watch their existing favourite shows and films in French.

Children love stories, and the best way of interesting them in the sights of Normandy is to tell them the legends and histories surrounding them, many of which I've summarised in this book. Once you're in France, stock up at media stores such as Fnac with French-language story books for your child's age group, and for song and story CDs or cassettes in French – a great way of making long car journeys more productive for all the family. *Le Petit Prince* is a classic; for materials specific to Normandy, see p. 46. See below for more language-learning recommendations.

Lastly, when your child is older, there's no better way of instilling in them a love of the French language and culture than by sending them to stay with a French family – you can arrange this through *www. french-exchange.co.uk*, or ask the French department of your child's school or French friends who may know people with children the same age as your own. For summer residential French courses for children aged 11–19, including sporting activities and workshops, at a well-equipped private school with an indoor pool near Verneuil-sur-Avre in the Eure, see *www.cactuslanguage.com*.

Basic Vocabulary and Greetings

English	French	Pronunciation
Yes/No	**Oui/Non**	wee/nohn
Okay	**D'accord**	*dah*-core
Please	**S'il vous plaît**	seel voo play
Thank you	**Merci**	*mair*-see
You're welcome	**De rien**	duh ree-*ehn*
Hello (daytime)	**Bonjour**	bohn-*jhoor*
Good evening	**Bonsoir**	bohn-*swahr*
Goodbye	**Au revoir**	oruh-*vwahr*
What's your name?	**Comment vous appellez-vous?**	ko-*mahn*-voo-za-pell-ay-*voo*?
My name is	**Je m'appelle**	*jhuh* ma-pell
How are you?	**Comment allez-vous?**	kuh-mahn-tahl-ay-*voo*?
I'm sorry/excuse me	**Pardon**	pahr-*dohn*

Getting Around

English	French	Pronunciation
Do you speak English?	**Parlez-vous anglais?**	par-lay-voo-on-*glay*?
I don't speak French	**Je ne parle pas français**	jhuh ne parl pah fron-*say*
I don't understand	**Je ne comprends pas**	jhuh ne kohm-*prahn* pas
Could you speak more loudly/more slowly?	**Pouvez-vous parler plus fort/plus lentement?**	Poo-*vay* voo par-lay ploo for/ploo lan-te-*ment*?
What is it?	**Qu'est-ce que c'est?**	kess-kuh-*say*?
What time is it?	**Qu'elle heure est-il?**	kel uhr eh-*teel*?
What?	**Quoi?**	kwah?

English	French	Pronunciation
How? or What did you say?	Comment?	ko-*mahn*?
When?	Quand?	kahn?
Where is?	Où est?	oo *eh*?
Who?	Qui?	kee?
Why?	Pourquoi?	poor-*kwah*?
here/there	ici/là	ee-*see*/lah
left/right	à gauche/à droite	a goash/a drwaht
straight ahead	tout droit	too-*drwah*
Fill the tank (of a car), please	Le plein, s'il vous plaît	luh plan, seel-voo-*play*
I want to get off at	Je voudrais descendre à	jhe voo-*dray* day-son drah-ah
airport	l'aéroport	lair-o-*por*
bank	la banque	lah bahnk
beach	la plage	lah plarj
bridge	le pont	luh pohn
bus station	la gare routière	lah *gar* roo-tee-*air*
bus stop	l'arrêt de bus	lah-*ray* duh boohss
broken down (in car)	en panne	ahn *pan*
by car	en voiture	ahn vwa-*toor*
cathedral	la cathédrale	luh ka-tay-*dral*
church	l'église	lay-*gleez*
driver's licence	le permis de conduire	luh per-*mee* duh con-*dweer*
entrance (building or city)	une porte	oon port
exit (building or motorway)	une sortie	oon sor-*tee*
first floor	le premier étage	luh prem-ee-*ehr* ay-*taj*
hospital	l'hôpital	low-pee-*tahl*
lift/elevator	l'ascenseur	lah sahn *seuhr*
luggage storage	la consigne	lah kohn-*seen*-yuh
museum	le musée	luh moo-*zay*
no smoking	défense de fumer	day-*fahns* de fu-may
petrol	du pétrol/de l'essence	duh pay-*trol*/de lay-*sahns*
one-day pass	le ticket journalier	luh tee-*kay* jhoor-nall-ee-*ay*
one-way ticket	l'aller simple	lah-*lay* sam-pluh
police	la police	lah po-*lees*
return ticket	l'aller-retour	lah-*lay* re-*toor*
slow down	ralentir	rah-lahn-*teer*
street	la rue	lah roo

English	French	Pronunciation
underground/Tube/ subway	le Métro	luh *may*-tro
telephone	le téléphone	luh tay-lay-*phone*
ticket	un billet	uh *bee*-yay
toilets	les toilettes/les WC	lay twa-*lets*/les vay-*say*

Shopping

English	French	Pronunciation
How much does it cost?	C'est combien?/Ça coûte combien?	say comb-bee-*ehn*?/sah coot comb-bee-*ehn*?
That's expensive	C'est cher/chère	say share
Do you take credit cards?	Acceptez-vous les cartes de crédit?	aksep-*tay voo* lay kart duh creh-*dee*?
I'd like	Je voudrais	jhe voo-*dray*
I'd like to buy	Je voudrais acheter	jhe voo-*dray* ahsh-*tay*
aspirin	des aspirines/des aspros	deyz ahs-peer-*een*/deyz ahs-*proh*
boots	des bottes	day bot
colouring book	un livre de coloriage	uh lee-vr duh colo-ree-*arj*
gift	un cadeau	uh kah-*doe*
hat	un chapeau	uh shah-*poh*
map of the city	un plan de ville	uh plahn de *veel*
newspaper	un journal	uh zhoor-*nahl*
phonecard	une carte téléphonique/ télécarte	uh cart tay lay-fone-*eek*/ tay-lay cart
postcard	une carte postale	oon cart pos-*tahl*
raincoat	un imperméable	uh am-per-mey-*arbl*
road map	une carte routière	oon cart roo-tee-*air*
shoes	des chaussures	day show-*suhr*
soap	du savon	doo sah-*vohn*
stamp	un timbre poste	uh *tam*-bruh post
sweets	de la confiserie/des bonbons	duh lah kohn-feez-eree/day bon-bon
swimming trunks	un slip de bain	uh sleep duh ban
swimsuit/swimming costume	un maillot de bain	uh *my*-o duh ban
suntan cream/sunscreen	de la crème solaire	duh lah krem sol-*air*
toothpaste	du pâte dentifrice	doo pat den-tee-*frees*
shop	le magasin	luh ma-ga-*zahn*

English	French	Pronunciation
bakery	**la boulangerie**	lah boo-*lahn*-jeh-ree
butcher	**la boucherie**	lah *boosh*-eree
cake shop	**la pâtisserie**	lah pah-tees-eree
dry cleaners	**la blanchisserie**	lah blon-*shi*-ser-ree
fishmonger	**la poissonnerie**	lah pwah-*sohn*-eree
grocery	**l'épicerie**	lay *pees*-eree
launderette	**la laverie automatique**	lah la-vairy auto-mah-*teek*
market	**le marché**	luh mar-*shay*
farmers' market	**le marché fermier**	luh mar-*shay* fair-mee-*ay*
off licence	**le magasin des vins**	luh mah-gah-zahn day *vahn*
supermarket	**le supermarché**	luh sue-per-mar-*shay*
very large supermarket	**le hypermarché**	luh ee-per-mar-*shay*
shopping trolley	**le caddy**	luh cah-*dee*
shopping bag	**un sac/une poche**	uh sack/oon posh
till	**la caisse**	lah kes

Children's Stuff

English	French	Pronunciation
baby-changing	**un table à langer**	uh tahb-le a lahn-*jay*
baby equipment	**matériau de puériculture**	ma-tay-re-o duh pu-ray-ee-cult-*oor*
bottlewarmer	**une chauffe-biberon**	oon showf-bee-ber-*on*
buggy/pushchair	**une poussette**	oon poo-*set*
child seat	**un siège enfant**	uh see-erj on-*fon*
children's Paracetamol	**Paracétamol à dose pédiatrique**	Pa-ray-say-tam-ol a dos pay-day-at-*reek*
dummy	**une sucette**	oon sue-*set*
formula milk (newborn–4 months; 4 months–1 year)	**lait formule** (premier âge; deuxième âge)	lay for-*moole* (pray-mee-ehr *arge;* dur-zi-em *arge*)
follow-on milk	**lait de croissance**	lay de cwa-*zance*
highchair	**une chaise haute**	oon chayz *oht*
nappies	**les couches**	lay coo-sh
playground	**aire de jeux**	air de jurs
seesaw/swing	**une balançoire**	oon bal-on-*swar*
slide	**un toboggan**	uh tob-o-*gan*
sterilising tablets	**comprimés de stérilisation à froid**	com-pree-*may* de stery-lee-za-shon a fwa
wet wipes	**les lingettes**	lay lan-*jets*

In Your Hotel

English	French	Pronunciation
we're staying for . . . days	on reste pour . . . jours	ohn rest poor . . . jhoor
is breakfast included?	petit déjeuner inclus?	peh-*tee* day-jheun-*ay* ahn-*klu*?
are taxes included?	les taxes sont comprises?	lay taks son com-*preez*?
room	une chambre	oon *shom*-bruh
double room	une chambre double	oon *shom*-bruh *doo*-bluh
twin room	une chambre aux lits simples	oon *shom*-bruh o lee s*am*-pluh
triple room	un triple	uh *tree*-pluh
family room	une chambre familiale	oon *shom*-bruh fam-ee-lee-*ahl*
family suite	une suite familiale/ un appartement familial	oon sweet fam-ee-lee-*ahl*/ uh apart-a-ment fam-ee-lee-*ahl*
interconnecting rooms	des chambres communicantes/ un appartement	day shom-bruhs com-oo-ni-*cont*/ uh apart-a-*ment*
extra bed	un lit supplémentaire	uh lee sup-lay-mon-*tair*
cot	un lit bébé	uh lee bay-*bay*
shower	une douche	oon doosh
sink	un lavabo	uh la-va-*bow*
suite	une suite	oon sweet
the key	la clé (la clef)	la clay
balcony	un balcon	uh *bahl*-cohn
bathtub	une baignoire	oon bay-*nwar*
bathroom	une salle de bain	oon sal duh *ban*
shower room	une salle de douche	oon sal duh *doosh*
hot and cold water	l'eau chaude et froide	low showed ay fwad
babysitting	le babysitting/garde d'enfants	luh bay-bay sitting/gard don-*fons*
swimming pool (heated; indoor)	une piscine (chauffée, couverte)	oon pee-*seen* (show-*fay*, coo-*vairt*)

Numbers and Ordinals

English	French	Pronunciation
nought/zero	zéro	*zayr*-oh
one	un	uh
two	deux	duh

English	French	Pronunciation
three	trois	twah
four	quatre	*kaht*-ruh
five	cinq	sank
six	six	seess
seven	sept	set
eight	huit	wheat
nine	neuf	nurf
ten	dix	deess
eleven	onze	ohnz
twelve	douze	dooz
thirteen	treize	trehz
fourteen	quatorze	kah-*torz*
fifteen	quinze	kanz
sixteen	seize	sez
seventeen	dix-sept	deez-*set*
eighteen	dix-huit	deez-*wheat*
nineteen	dix-neuf	deez-*nurf*
twenty	vingt	vahn
thirty	trente	tron-te
forty	quarante	ka-*rahnt*
fifty	cinquante	san-*kahnt*
sixty	soixante	swa-sont
seventy	soixante-dix	swa-sont-deess
eighty	quatre-vingts	kaht-ruh *vahn*
ninety	quatre-vingts-dix	kaht-ruh vahn *deess*
one hundred	cent	sahn
one thousand	mille	meel
first	premier	*preh*-mee-ay
second	deuxième	*duh*-zee-em
third	troisième	*twa*-zee-em
fourth	quatrième	*kaht*-ree-em
fifth	cinquième	*sank*-ee-em
sixth	sixième	*sees*-ee-em
seventh	septième	*set*-ee-em
eighth	huitième	*wheat*-ee-em
ninth	neuvième	*nurv*-ee-em
tenth	dixième	*dees*-ee-em

The Calendar

English	French	Pronunciation
Sunday	dimanche	dee-*monsh*
Monday	lundi	luhn-*dee*
Tuesday	mardi	mahr-*dee*
Wednesday	mercredi	mair-kruh-*dee*
Thursday	jeudi	jheu-*dee*
Friday	vendredi	von-druh-*dee*
Saturday	samedi	sahm-*dee*
yesterday	hier	ee-*air*
today	aujourd'hui	o-jhor-*dwee*
this morning/this afternoon	ce matin/cet après-midi	suh ma-*tan*/set ah-preh mee-*dee*
tonight	ce soir	suh *swahr*
tomorrow	demain	de-*man*
January	janvier	jon-vee-*ay*
February	février	fay-vree-*ay*
March	mars	mars
April	avril	av-*reel*
May	mai	may
June	juin	juh-wan
July	juillet	jo-wee-*yay*
August	août	oot
September	septembre	sept-om-*bruh*
October	octobre	oct-oh-*bruh*
November	novembre	no-vom-*bruh*
December	decembre	day-som-*bruh*

Food/Menu/Cooking Terms

English	French	Pronunciation
I would like	**Je voudrais**	jhe voo-*dray*
to eat	**manger**	mon-*jhay*
Please give me	**Donnez-moi, s'il vous plaît**	do-nay-*mwah,* seel-voo-*play*
a bottle of	**une bouteille de**	oon boo-*tay* duh
a cup of	**une tasse de**	oon tass duh
a glass of	**un verre de**	uh vair duh
breakfast	**du petit-déjeuner**	doo puh-*tee* day-zhuh-*nay*

English	French	Pronunciation
the bill	l'addition/la note	la-dee-see-*ohn*/la noat
dinner	le dîner	luh dee-*nay*
lunch	le déjeuner	luh day-zhuh-*nay*
a knife	un couteau	uh koo-*toe*
a napkin	une serviette	oon sair-vee-*et*
a spoon	une cuillère	oon kwee-*air*
a fork	une fourchette	oon four-*shet*
Cheers!	A votre santé!	ah vo-truh sahn-*tay*!
fixed-price menu	un menu/une formule	uh may-*noo*/oon formool
menu	la carte	la kart
gastronomic tasting menu	menu dégustation	may-*noo* day-gus-ta-see-*on*
menu based on daily market produce	le menu du marché	luh may-*noo* doo mar-*shay*
children's menu	le menu enfant/ menu bambino/ menu Moussaillons	luh may-noo *on*-fon, may-*noo* bam-bee-no/ may-*noo* moo-*sigh*-on
extra plate	une assiette supplémentaire	oon ay-see-et sup-lay-mon-tayr
small portion	une petite portion	oon puh-*teet* por-see-*on*
Waiter!/Waitress!	Monsieur!/Mademoiselle!	muh-*syuh*/mad-mwa-*zel*
wine list	la carte des vins	la kart day *van*
appetiser	une entrée	oon on-*tray*
main course	un plat principal	uh plah pran-see-*pahl*
homemade	maison	may-*zon*
dish of the day	le plat du jour	luh plah doo jhoor
tip included	service compris	ser-*vees* cohm-*pree*
Is the tip/service included?	Le service est compris?	luh ser-*vees* eh com-*pree*?
pancake house	une crêperie	oon *kray*-pay-ree
small informal restaurant	un bistrot	uh *bee*-stro
small restaurant and bar with long hours	une brasserie	oon bra-ser-*ee*

Norman Specialities

English	French	Pronunciation
cream and butter sauce with apple slices, flambéed in Calvados	sauce normande	sows nor-*mond*
fish braised in white wine	poisson à la normande	pwa-son a lah nor-*mond*

English	French	Pronunciation
creamy fish stew from Dieppe	marmite dieppoise	mar-meet dee-ep-*was*
tripe stew with Calvados	tripe à la mode de Caen	treep a lah mode duh kern
saltmarsh lamb	l'agneau pré-salé	lah-nyo pray-salay
buttery, rich soft cheese	Camembert	*cah*-mom-*bare*
rich, full-bodied soft cheese	Pont-l'Evêque	pon lev-*eck*
strong-smelling, spicy soft cheese	Livarot	*lee*-var-row
soft, unripened goats' cheese	Neufchâtel	nerf-sha-tell
rice pudding with cinnamon	la tergoule	lah tare-*gool*
apple pie with flaky pastry	le flan normand	luh flon nor-*mond*
apple baked in pastry	le bourdelot	luh bor-*dul*-o
pear baked in pastry	le douillon	luh *dwee*-yon

The Basics

English	French	Pronunciation
organic	biologique/d'agriculture biologique (or just 'bio')	bee-oh-lodge-*eek*/dag-ree-cull-tyour bee-oh-lodge-*eek*/(bee-oh)
bread	du pain	doo pan
wholemeal bread	du pain complet	doo pan com-*play*
slice	une tranche	oon tron-*sh*
toast	du pain grillé/un toast	doo pan gree-*yay*/uh tost
butter	du beurre	doo buhr
breakfast cereals	des céréales	day say-ray-*al*
sugar	du sucre	doo *sooh*-kruh
honey	du miel	doo mee-*el*
jam	de la confiture	duh lah con-fee-*tur*
cheese	du fromage	doo fro-*mahje*
eggs: boiled	des oeufs à la coque	day zuhf a lah cok
eggs: hardboiled	des oeufs durs	day zuhf door
eggs: fried	des oeufs au plat	day zuhf o plat
eggs: poached	des oeufs pochés	day zuhf posh-*ay*
eggs: scrambled	des oeufs brouillés	day zuhf bwee-*yay*
omelette	une omelette	oon om-uh-*let*

English	French	Pronunciation
pasta	**les pâtes**	lay paht
pizza	**un pizza**	uh peet-*zah*
pizza Margherita (with tomato and cheese, and sometimes ham)	**un pizza margherita**	uh peet-*zah* mar-zhe-reeta
rice	**du riz**	doo ree
dumplings (egg, chicken, veal or fish)	**des quenelles**	day ke-*nelle*
sauerkraut	**de la choucroûte**	duh lah shew-*kroot*

Snacks

English	French	Pronunciation
sandwich (open sandwich)	**un sandwich/une tartine**	uh sohn-*weech*/oon tart-*een*
ham and cheese toastie (with fried egg/with Camembert)	**croque monsieur (croque madame/croque normande)**	crow-kuh muh-*shur* (crow-kuh mah-*dam*/ crow-kuh nor-*mond*)
savoury (buckwheat) pancake	**une galette de blé noir**	oon gal-et duh blay *nwah*
with ham, cheese and egg	**complète**	com-*playt*
pancakes	**les crêpes**	lay krayps
wheatflour pancakes	**les crêpes de froment**	lay krayps duh fro-*mon*
buttery bread made with eggs	**du brioche**	doo bree-*osh*
crisps	**les chips**	lay *sheeps*
nuts/walnuts	**les noix**	lay nwa
almonds	**les amandes**	lay a-*mond*
cashews	**les noix de cajou**	lay nwah duh ca-*yoo*
chestnuts	**les marrons, les châtaignes**	lay mah-*rohn*, lay shah-*tay*-nyuh
hazelnuts	**les noisettes**	lay nwah-*zet*
peanuts	**les arachides, les cacahouètes**	lay ah-rah-sheed, lay kah-kah-*wayt*
coconut	**le noix de coco**	luh nwah duh ko-ko
chocolate	**du chocolat**	doo shok-o-*lah*
ice lolly/ice cream	**une glace**	oon glass
lollipop	**une sucette**	oon sue-*set*
salted-butter caramels	**des caramels au buerre salé**	day cara-mel o buhr sa-*lay*

Starters and Side Dishes

English	French	Pronunciation
chips	des pommes frites	day pohm *freet*
garnish/side vegetables	la garniture	lah gar-nee-*tur*
snails	des escargots	dayz ess-car-*goh*
coarse pork (or mackerel)	pâte des rillettes	pat day ree-*yett*
potted meat/pâté	une terrine/du pâté	oon *tai*-reen/doo pah-*tay*
clear broth	du consommé	doo kon-*somay*
onion soup (with bread and cheese)	de la soupe à l'oignon	duh lah soop ah low-*nyon*
vegetable soup	du potage (de légumes)	doo poh-taj duh lay-*guhm*
creamy soup	du velouté	doo veh-loo-*tay*
creamy soup with seafood	de la bisque	duh lah beesk
seafood stew	de la bouillabaisse	duh lah boo-ee-yah-*bayz*
leek and potato soup	du vichyssoise	doo vee-shee-*swahz*
rich consommé with meat and veg	une petite marmite	oon puh-teet mahr-*meet*

Meat

English	French	Pronunciation
meat	la viande	lah vee-*ond*
poultry	les volailles	lay vol-*eye*
game	le gibier	luh *gee*-bee-ay
ham	du jambon	doo jhom-*bon*
pale sliced ham	du jambon blanc	doo jhom-*bon* blonk
smoked ham	de la poitrine fumée	duh la pwa-treen foo-*may*
chicken	du poulet	doo *poo*-lay
duck (meaty Rouen breed)	du canard (Rouennais)	doo can-*ahr* (roo-en-ay)
goose	de l'oie	duh l'wah
pheasant	du faisan	doo fay-*zan*
pigeon	du pigeon	doo pee-*zyon*
turkey	de la dinde	duh lah dahnd
quail	de la caille	duh lah kay-ee
lamb	de l'agneau	duh lah-*nyo*
rabbit	du lapin	doo *lah*-pan
sirloin	de l'aloyau	duh lahl-why-*yo*
steak	du bifteck	doo beef-*tek*

English	French	Pronunciation
hamburger patty/ child's steak	du steak haché	doo tek a-*shay*
veal	du veau	doo voh
gizzards (ducks' innards)	les gésiers	lay *jey*-zee-ay
chitterling (tripe) sausage	de l'andouille	duh lon-*dwee*
black pudding (blood sausage)	le boudin noir	luh boo-dan *nwah*
frogs' legs	des cuisses de grenouilles	day cweess duh gre-*noo*-wee-yuh
goose liver	du foie gras	doo fwah *grah*
chicken stew with mushrooms and wine	du coq au vin	doo cock o van
beef stew	du pot au feu	doo poht o *fuh*
meat stew with red wine, onions and garlic	daube	dohb

Fish

English	French	Pronunciation
fish (freshwater)	du poisson de rivière/d'eau douce	doo pwah-*sson* duh ree-vee-*aire*/d'o *dooss*
fish (saltwater)	du poisson de mer	doo pwah-*sson* duh *mehr*
seafood	les fruits de mer	lay fwee duh *mehr*
shellfish	les coquillages	lay cok-ee-*arj*
crustaceans (crabs, lobsters, shrimps etc)	les crustacés	lay kruhz-ta-*say*
catch of the day	le poisson du jour	luh pwah-*sson* duh *jhur*
breaded/cooked in breadcrumbs	pané	pah-*nay*
anchovies	les anchois	lay an-*shwa*
clams	les palourdes	lay pah-loord
cockles	des coques	day cok
dog cockles	des amandes	day zah-*mond*
cod	du cabillaud/de la morue	doo cab-ee-*yo*/duh lah mo-*ru*
crab	de la crabe	duh lah crab
hermit crab	un tourteau	uh toor-*toe*
spider crab	de l'araignée de mer	duh la-ray-nay duh mehr
herring	du hareng	doo ahr-*rahn*
lobster	du homard	doo oh-*mahr*
mackerel	du maquereau	doo ma-ker-row

English	French	Pronunciation
monkfish	de la lotte	duh lah lot
mussels (grown on posts)	des moules (au bouchot)	day moohl (o boo-show)
mussels in white wine with shallots and herbs	des moules marinières	day moohl mar-ee-nee-*air*
oysters	des huîtres	days *wee*-truhs
European oysters	des huîtres plates	days *wee*-truhs plat
Pacific oysters	des huîtres creuses	days *wee*-truhs crurz
pollack	du lieu (lieu jaune)	doo lee-uh (lee-uh jhown)
prawns	les gambas	lay gahm-bah
red mullet	du rouget	doo roo-jhay
sardines	des sardines	day sar-*deen*
scallops	des coquilles St-Jacques/ des noix de St-Jacque	day cock-*eel* san-jack/day nwah duh san-jack
bay Atlantic sea scallops	des pétoncles	day pet-*onk*-l
scampi/large prawns	des langoustines	day lohn-gus-*teen*
sea bass	du loup de mer/du bar	doo loo duh mehr/doo bar
sea bream	du dorade	doo dor-ard
shrimp/small prawns	des crevettes	day kreh-*vet*
skate wing	un aile de raie	uh ay duh ray
smoked salmon	du saumon fumé	doo sow-*mohn* foo-*may*
swordfish	de l'espadon	duh *lez*-padon
tuna	du thon	doo lohn
turbot	du turbot	doo ter-bow
trout	de la truite	duh lah tru-*eet*
whelks	des bulots	day boo-*low*
winkles	des bigorneaux	day bee-gohr-*no*
seafood with sauerkraut	de la choucrôûte de mer	duh lah shew-*kroot* duh mehr

Fruits

English	French	Pronunciation
fruit	les fruits	lay frwee
citrus fruit	les agrumes	layz ag-*room*
berries	les fruits rouges	lay frwee rooj
apples	les pommes	lay pohm
apricot	les abricots	layz *ah*-bree-koh
bananas	les bananes	lay bah-*nahn*
blackberries	les mûres	lay myur

English	French	Pronunciation
blueberries	**les myrtilles**	lay mehr-tee
cherries	**les cérises/les griottes**	lay say-*rees*/lay gree-*yot*
dates	**les dattes**	lay daht
figs	**les figues**	lay feeg
gooseberries	**les groseilles**	lay grow-*say*
grapefruit	**un pamplemousse**	uh pahm-*pluh*-moose
grapes	**les raisins**	lay ray-*zan*
lemon/lime	**du citron/du citron vert**	doo see-*tron*/doo see-tron *vaire*
melon	**du melon**	doo meh-*lohn*
oranges	**les oranges**	layz or-*on*-je
peach	**une pêche**	oon pesh
pears	**les poires**	lay pwar
pineapple	**de l'ananas**	duh lah-na-*nas*
plums	**les prunes**	lay prewn
pomegranate	**une grenade**	oon greh-*nad*
prunes	**les pruneaux**	lay prew-*noh*
raspberries	**des framboises**	day fwahm-*bwah*z
strawberries	**des fraises**	day *frez*
watermelon	**une pastèque**	oon pas-*tek*

Vegetables

English	French	Pronunciation
vegetables	**les légumes**	lay lay-*guhm*
artichoke	**de l'artichaud**	duh larh-tee-*show*
asparagus	**des asperges**	day as-*sperj*
aubergine	**de l'aubergine**	duh loh-ber-*jheen*
avocado pear	**de l'avocat**	duh lah-voh-*kah*
beetroot	**de la betterave**	duh lah beht-*rahv*
broccoli	**du brocoli**	doo broh-koh-*lee*
cabbage	**du choux**	doo *shoe*
carrots	**les carottes**	lay *cah*-rot
cauliflower	**du chou-fleur**	doo *shoo*-flur
celery	**du céleri**	doo say-leh-*ree*
courgettes	**des courgettes**	day coor-*jet*
endive	**de la scarole**	duh lah scah-*roll*

English	French	Pronunciation
fennel	du fenouil	doo feh-nou-*eel*
garlic	de l'ail	duh lie
garlic cloves	des gousses d'ail	day goose dye
green beans	des haricots verts	dayz *ahr-ee-coh vaire*
leeks	des poireaux	day pwah-*row*
mushrooms	des champignons	day sham-pin-*yon*
morel mushrooms	des morilles	day moh-*ree*
onion	les oignons	layz on-*nyohn*
peas	des petits pois	day puh-tee *pwah*
peppers (green, red, yellow)	les poivrons (verts, rouges, jaunes)	lay pwah-*vrohn* (vehr, rooj, jhown)
potatoes	des pommes de terre	day pohm duh *tehr*
baked potatoes	des pommes de terre au four	day pohm duh *tehr* o foor
mashed potatoes	des pommes de terre en purée	day pohm duh *tehr* ohn *poo*-ray
potatoes au gratin	des pommes de terre dauphinois	day pohm duh *tehr* doh-feen-*wah*
shallots	des échalotes	dayz ay-sha-*lot*
sorrel	de l'oseille	duh lo-say-ya
spinach	des épinards	dayz ay-pin-*ar*
sweetcorn	du maïs	doo may-*eez*
truffles	des truffes	day truhf
turnips	des navets	day nah-*vay*
assortment of vegetables	un méli mélo de légumes	uh may-lee may-lo duh lay-*guhm*
diced mixed vegetables	une macédoine de légumes	oon mah-say-dwahn duh lay-*guhm*
steamed vegetables	des légumes à vapeur	day lay-*guhm* a vah-*purr*
boiled vegetables	des légumes bouillis	day lay-*guhm* buw-*yee*
raw vegetables	des légumes crus	day lay-*guhm* crew
raw vegetable sticks	crudités	crew-dee-*tay*

Salads

English	French	Pronunciation
green salad	une salade verte	oon sah-lahd *vairt*
main-course salad	une salade composée	oon sah-lahd com-po-*say*

English	French	Pronunciation
lettuce	**de la laitue, de la salade**	duh lah lay-*too*, duh lah sah-*lahd*
lettuce leaves	**des feuilles de salade**	day fuh-eey duh sah-*lahd*
watercress	**du cresson**	doo creh-sohn
tomatoes	**des tomates**	day to-*maht*
cucumber	**du concombre**	doo kohn-*kohm*-br
radish	**des radis**	day rah-*dee*
spring onions	**les ciboules**	lay see-*bool*
salad dressing	**la sauce de salade/la vinaigrette**	lah sows duh sa-*lahd*/lah veen-ay-*gret*

Herbs

English	French	Pronunciation
herbs	**les herbs**	layz airb
basil	**le basilic**	luh bah-zee-*leek*
bay leaf	**la feuille de laurier**	lah fuh-eey duh loh-*ree*-ay
chive	**la ciboulette**	lah see-boo-*leht*
dill	**l'aneth**	lah-net
lavender	**la lavande**	lah la-vond
mint	**la menthe**	lah mont
oregano	**l'origan**	loh-ree-gahn
parsley	**le persil**	luh per-*seel*
rosemary	**le romarin**	luh row-ma-*ran*
sage	**la sauge**	lah sowj
tarragon	**l'estragon**	les tra-gohn
thyme	**le thym**	luh teehm

Spices and Condiments

English	French	Pronunciation
salt	**du sel**	doo sel
salted	**salé**	sal-ay
pepper	**du poivre**	doo *pwah*-vruh
rock salt	**le gros sel**	luh grow sel
vinegar	**du vinaigre**	doo vin-*ay*-gruh
capers	**les câpres**	lay *cay*-pr
mayonnaise	**de la mayonnaise**	duh lah mayo-nez

English	French	Pronunciation
garlic mayonnaise	de l'aïoli	duh lah-ee-oh-lee
spicy garlic mayonnaise served with fish soup	de la rouille	duh lah rwee
ketchup	du ketchup	doo ket-sup
mustard	de la moutarde	duh lah moo-*tard*
curry	le curry	luh kuh-*ree*
cardamom	la cardamome	lah car-da-mum
cinnamon	la cannelle	lah ka-*nel*
coriander	la coriandre	lah ko-ree-*on*-dr
clove	le clou de girofle	luh clue duh jhee-*ro*-fle
cumin	le cumin	luh koo-man
ginger	le gingembre	luh jeen-jom-br
nutmeg	la noix de muscade	lah nwah duh moos-cad
pimento	le piment	luh pee-mon
saffron	le safran	luh sah-frahn

Cooking Methods

English	French	Pronunciation
fish, meat, vegetables or fruit simmered in a reduction of their own fat or juices	un confit	uh khon-*feeh*
baked	cuit au four	kwee o foohr
boiled	bouilli	boo-ee-*yee*
cooked over a wood fire	cuit au feu de bois	kwee o fuh doo *bwoi*
cooked in parchment paper	en papillotte	on pah-pee-*yott*
cooked on a skewer	en brochette	on bro-*shet*
cooked in alcohol set alight	flambé	*flom*-bay
cooked with spinach	florentine	floh-ron-*teen*
deep fried	frit	free
grilled	grillé	gree-*yay*
marinaded	mariné	*ma*-ree-nay
medium (cooked, i.e. steak)	à point	ah-*pwahn*
pan-fried	à la poêle	a lah *pwel*
poached	poché	po-*shay*

English	French	Pronunciation
Provençal-style (cooked with tomatoes, onions, olives, herbs, perhaps anchovies)	**Provençale**	proh-von-*sahl*
puff pastry shell	**vol-au-vent**	vhol-o-*vhon*
rare (cooked, i.e. steak)	**saignant**	say-*nyohn*
roast	**rôti**	row-*tee*
simmered	**mijoté**	mee-jo-*tay*
steamed	**à la vapeur**	ah la va-*puhr*
sautéed	**sauté**	so-*tay*
stuffed	**farci**	far-*see*
very rare (cooking, i.e. steak)	**bleu**	bluh
well done (cooking, i.e. steak)	**bien cuit**	byahn *kwee*

Sauces

English	French	Pronunciation
sweet and sour	**sauce aigre-douce**	sows aygr doos
butter and egg with shallots, tarragon and wine	**sauce béarnaise**	sows bare-*neyz*
white with milk, butter and flour	**sauce béchamel**	sows beh-sha-*mel*
creamy white wine and egg	**sauce blanquette**	sows blon-*ket*
white wine with vegetables	**sauce à la bonne femme**	sows ah lah bon fam
wild mushroom	**sauce forestière**	sows foh-rehs-tee-*air*
egg yolk, butter and lemon/vinegar	**sauce hollandaise**	sows o-lon-*dez*
vegetable	**sauce jardinière**	sows jahr-dee-nee-*air*
butter with parsley and lemon juice	**sauce maître d'hôtel**	sows may-tr do-*tel*
butter, cream and parsley	**meunière**	*muhr*-nee-ayr
white with cheese	**sauce mornay**	sows mohr-*nay*
mayonnaise with mustard	**sauce rémoulade**	sows ray-moo-*lahd*
creamy béchamel and fish/chicken stock	**sauce velouté**	sows veh-loo-*tay*
wine and grapes	**sauce véronique**	sows vay-ron-*eek*
butter and egg yolk	**sauce hollandaise**	sows o-lon-*dez*

Drink

English	French	Pronunciation
water	**de l'eau**	duh *lo*
drinking water	**de l'eau potable**	duh lo pot-*ah*-bluh
spring water	**de l'eau de source**	duh lo de sors
still mineral water	**de l'eau minérale plat/sans gaz**	duh lo min-ay-*ral* pla/son gahz
sparkling mineral water	**de l'eau minérale gazeuse/ pétillante**	duh lo min-ay-*ral* gahz-*uhze*/pay-tee-*ont*
milk	**du lait**	doo lay
apple juice	**du jus de pomme**	doo joo de pohm
orange juice	**du jus d'orange**	doo joo d'or-*on*-jhe
pear juice	**du jus de poire**	doo joo duh pwar
lemon juice	**un citron pressé**	uh see-*trohn* preh-*say*
fruit cordial with water	**un sirop (à l'eau)**	uh see-*ro* (al-o)
fizzy drink	**du soda**	doo so-*dah*
cider	**du cidre**	doo *see*-druh
cider in a traditional porcelain cup	**du cidre en bolée**	doo *see*-druh on bollay
pear cider	**du poiré**	doo pwa-*ray*
apple brandy	**du pommeau/Calvados**	doo pom-*o*/doo Cal-va-*doh*
shot of Calvados between courses of a meal	**un trou normand**	uh troo nor-*mond*
beer	**de la bière**	duh lah bee-*aire*
red wine	**du vin rouge**	doo vhan *rooj*
white wine	**du vin blanc**	doo vhan *blonk*
carafe	**un pichet**	uh pee-*shay*
white wine with blackcurrant liqueur	**un kir**	uh keer
champagne with blackcurrant liqueur	**un kir royale**	uh keer roy-*al*
cider with blackcurrant liqueur	**un kir normand**	uh keer nor-*mond*
coffee (black)	**un café noir**	uh ka-fay *nwahr*
coffee (with cream)	**un café crème**	uh ka-fay *krem*
coffee (with milk)	**un café au lait**	uh ka-fay o *lay*
coffee (decaf)	**un café décaféiné (slang: un déca)**	un ka-fay day-kah-fay-*nay* (uh *day*-kah)
coffee (espresso)	**un café espresso (un express)**	uh ka-fay e-*sprehss-o* (uh ek-*sprehss*)
tea	**du thé**	doo tay

English	French	Pronunciation
herbal tea	une tisane	oon tee-*zahn*
hot chocolate	un chocolat chaud	uh shok-o-laht *show*

Desserts

English	French	Pronunciation
dessert	le dessert	luh deh-*sehr*
fruit salad	une salade de fruit/ une macédoine de fruits	oon sah-lahd duh *fwee*/oon mah-*say*-dwan duh fwee
ice cream	de la glace	duh lah *glass*
vanilla	...à la vanille	a lah vah-*nee*
strawberry	...à la fraise	a lah frez
chocolate	...au chocolat	o shok-o-*lah*
mint	...à la menthe	a lah mont
pistachio	...à la pistache	a lah pis-*tash*
ice-cream cone	un cornet	uh kohr-*nay*
scoop	une boule	oon bool
ice-cream sundae	une coupe glaceé	oon coop glah-*say*
multi-flavoured ice-cream dessert	une bombe	oon bohmb
yoghurt	du yaourt/yogourt	doo yow-*urt*/yog-urt
creamy white cheese	le fromage blanc	luh fro-*mahj* blonk
sour thick cream	la crème fraîche	lah krem *fresh*
whipped cream with sugar	la crème Chantilly	lah krem shon-*tee*
waffles	les gaufres	lay gowfr
pastries	des pâtisseries	day pah-tee-ser-*ree*
cake	du gâteau	doo *gha*-tow
sponge cake filled with pudding	une charlotte	oon shahr-*lot*
stewed fruit	de la compôte	duh lah com-*poht*
chocolate mousse	de la mousse au chocolat	duh lah moos o shok-o-*lah*
half-cooked chocolate cake	du fondant au chocolat	duh fon-don o shok-o-*lah*
thick custard dessert with caramelised topping	de la crème brûlée	duh lah krem bruh-*lay*
egg custard with caramelised topping	une crème caramel	oon krem kah-rah-*mehl*
caramelised upside-down apple pie	une tarte Tatin	oon tart tah-*tan*

English	French	Pronunciation
tart	**une tarte**	oon tart
doughnuts	**des beignets**	day beh-*nyay*
cream puffs with chocolate sauce	**des profiteroles**	day proh-fee-ter-ohl
meringues in custard sauce	**des oeufs à la neige**	dayz uhf ah lah *nezh*
battered fruit, especially cherries	**du clafoutis**	doo kla-foo-*tee*
poached pears with vanilla ice cream and chocolate sauce	**des poires Hélène**	day pwahr ay-lehn
baked Alaska	**une omelette norvégienne**	oon om-let nohr-*vay*-jhee-en
Bavarian cream (cream dessert with custard)	**une bavaroise**	oon bah-vahr-*wahz*

Family Travel

Travelling as a family can be fun, exciting and create memories to savour, but a bit of preparation will go a long way in forging a smooth journey and holiday. There are plenty of sites providing parents with essential holiday information and even sites popping up for youngsters, too. From what to pack and coping with flights to childcare and accessories, the sites below will help give you a headstart.

www.babygoes2.com: An innovative guide for parents travelling with babies and children with independent recommendations.

www.all4kidsuk.com: Links to tour companies offering family-friendly holidays.

www.youngtravellersclub.co.uk: Currently in its early days, this is a site for children themselves, which deserves to succeed.

www.deabirkett.com: The website of *Guardian* journalist Dea Birkett, who specialises in travelling with children. It includes a very useful Travelling with Kids Forum.

www.babycentre.co.uk: The travel section throws up some interesting articles on family holidays.

www.mumsnet.com: Set up by a journalist, TV producer and radio producer. Product reviews, interviews and planning help.

www.travellingwithchildren.co.uk: Comprehensive site with lots of handy tips for travelling parents.

www.travelforkids.com: An American site that has some good information on different countries with 'what not to leave at home'-type tips.

www.familytravelforum.com: Lots of useful stuff on family travel in general.

www.travelwithyourkids.com:
Easy to navigate with advice you feel comes from real experience of things having gone wrong!

www.thefamilytravelfiles.com:
Heavily American, but with a section on Europe.

www.family-travel.co.uk:
Independent advice on travelling with children. Lots of sound general advice.

Responsible Tourism

Although one could argue any holiday including a flight can't be truly 'green', tourism can contribute positively to the environment and communities UK visitors travel to if investment is used wisely. Firstly, by offsetting carbon emissions from your flight, you can lessen the negative environmental impact of your journey. Secondly, by embracing responsible tourism practises you can choose forward-looking companies who care about the resorts and countries we visit, preserving them for the future by working alongside local people. Below are a number of sustainable tourism initiatives and associations to help you plan a family trip and leave as small a 'footprint' as possible on the places you visit.

www.responsibletravel.com: A great source of sustainable travel ideas run by a spokesperson for responsible tourism in the travel industry.

www.tourismconcern.org.uk:
Working to reduce social and environmental problems connected to tourism and find ways of improving tourism so that local benefits are increased.

www.climatecare.org.uk: Helping UK holidaymakers offset their carbon emissions through flying by funding sustainable energy projects

www.thetravelfoundation.org.uk:
Produces excellent material on how to care for the places we visit on holiday. There is also a special guide for children aged 7–10 and parents incorporating 'Hatch the Hatchling Hawksbill' with a play and puzzle book. Highly recommended.

www.abta.com: The Association of British Travel Agents (ABTA) acts as a focal point for the UK travel industry and is one of the leading groups spearheading responsible tourism.

www.aito.co.uk: The Association of Independent Tour Operators (AITO) is a group of interesting specialist operators leading the field in making holidays sustainable.

Index

See also Accommodations and Restaurant indexes, below.

Accommodations

Restaurants

Notes

Frommer's®

with your family
TRAVEL GUIDES

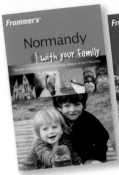

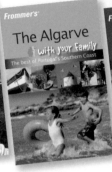

Frommer's
Normandy With Your Family
ISBN 10: 0470319518
ISBN 13: 9780470319512
£12.99 ▪ $18.99

Frommer's
Brittany With Your Family
ISBN 10: 0470055251
ISBN 13: 9780470055250
£12.99 ▪ $18.99

Frommer's
The Algarve With Your Family
ISBN 10: 047005526X
ISBN 13: 9780470055267
£12.99 ▪ $18.99

Frommer's
Croatia With Your Family
ISBN 10: 0470055308
ISBN 13: 9780470055304
£12.99 ▪ $18.99

Frommer's
Mediterranean Spain With Your Family
ISBN 10: 0470055286
ISBN 13: 9780470055281
£12.99 ▪ $18.99

Frommer's
Northern Italy With Your Family
ISBN 10: 0470055278
ISBN 13: 9780470055274
£12.99 ▪ $18.99

Frommer's
The Balearics With Your Family
ISBN 10: 0470055294
ISBN 13: 9780470055298
£12.99 ▪ $18.99

Available from all good bookshops

Frommer's®
A Branded Imprint of ⑱**WILEY**